England - France - Belgium - Germany

PATTON'S ILL-FATED RAID

BY

HARRY A. THOMPSON
WW II POW

Edited by Karin K. Ramsay

Historical Resources Press
Corinth / Denton, Texas 76210
November 11, 2002

Battle of the Bulge - Remagen - Rhineland - Ruhr Pocket

Library of Congress Control Number: 2002106470

Printed in the United States of America

ISBN 0-9642511-1-6

November 11, 2002
First Edition

All inquiries for volume purchases of this book should be addressed to Historical Resources Press, 2104 Post Oak Court, Corinth / Denton, Texas 76210-1900. Telephone inquires may be made by calling
940.321.1066.

This book is dedicated to my wife, Virginia,

And to my brother, Franklin, and his wife, Helen,

for their continued support.

———————————

I would also like to dedicate this book to

my father and mother,

And to Virginia's father, mother and brother, Jack Wiley,

all who have passed on.

I truly believe that the love and prayers of my family

in some way did help bring me back home.

99th Infantry Division Map
"Route of the Battle Babies"

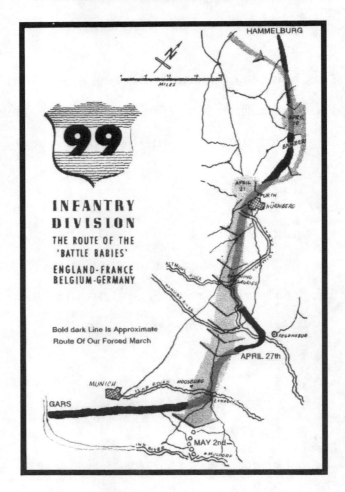

Our Forced March as Prisoners of War
Captured During the Battle of the Bulge

Bold line marked by Harry Thompson on copy of Original Map copied from

99th Division BATTLE BABIES by Maj. Gen. Walter E. Lauer

with permission of General Lauer's Daughter

granted "any member of the 99th Division".

Warrant Officer
Harry A. Thompson

Portrait was taken in a photography studio in Natchez, Mississippi
February 24, 1943, the day after appointment as
Warrant Officer, junior grade.
August 1943 Harry was promoted to

Chief Warrant Officer.

AFFIDAVIT

To Whom It May Concern:

     I hereby certify that the events and happenings described in this book are absolutely true to the best of my recollections. It has been over fifty years, but it seems like yesterday that this ordeal took place, and to this day I shudder to think that all this could happen to me. I will always remember each day, and I have kept notes of the time I served in the U. S. Army. This manuscript has been rewritten several times since the end of World War II.

This statement signed and notarized on the _29th_ day of _April_ , _2002_

Harry Thompson

STATE OF TEXAS
COUNTY OF HUNT

Subscribed and sworn before me, this _29th_ day of _April, 2002_

by Harry Thompson.

Notary Public

Acknowledgments

This, my true story, would never have been written without the encouragement and support of those who lived my story with me and without the love and prayers of my family.

James Park's affidavit gives much credence to the validity of this book. James and I were drafted about the same time, took basic training together and transferred to Fort Ord California together. We were both assigned to the 57th Field Artillery Battalion of the 7th Infantry Division on June 6, 1941 – in the later part of October 1942, while on Desert Maneuvers, we were transferred to the 924th Field Artillery Battalion of the 99th Infantry Division on or about November 25, 1942. On February 23, 1943 we were both appointed Warrant Officers. Park was a Battalion Supply Officer and I was Battalion Personnel Officer. We remained with the 924th Field Artillery Battalion and served over seas together. On December 17, 1944, while we were both assigned to quarters in the small town of Büllingen, Belgium, the German Wafen SS 6th and 15th Panzer Armies broke through the American Lines during the Ardennes Offensive (better known as the Battle of the Bulge) and we were both captured. Somehow, we continued to remain together as POWs. I am grateful for James Park and for his help on this book.

Chaplain Mark Moore, a First Lieutenant, a former member of the 106th Infantry Division, was also a POW in Hammelburg at the same time as I was. As a result of Patton's ill-fated raid on Hammelburg (where Patton's son-in-law was also a POW), all POWs were to be evacuated from camp and begin a forced march further into Germany. Chaplain Moore and I were together in the same group that walked 241 miles through Bavaria before our liberation May 2, 1945. I am grateful for Chaplain Moore and his affidavit attesting to our experiences on the forced march and bombing which gives further proof of the authenticity of my book.

Roger V. Foehringer, also a member of 924 Field artillery and captured at the same time as I was, helped furnish several important details such as the recipe for War Bread, which you will find is not my favorite food or my favorite memory! Somehow he managed to "work as a POW in a German bakery". I thank him for sharing the recipe, his memories and experiences of Heeresbäckerei 1945.

After writing in longhand, page after page for days and days, weeks and years, I finally was fortunate that John Paul Roundtree put my story on computer, furnishing me with printed copies whereby I could "add in" as I remembered. I consider John Paul Roundtree a very good friend who helped me ever so much.

I then turned to my preacher, Lewis Smith, a former college history teacher, currently a history teacher at Greenville Christian School, Greenville, Texas and my incredible friend. His patient and persistent questioning reawakened my memories and experiences and helped me recall important details and organize them into more of a book form. I cannot thank him enough. Lisa Wilson, a schoolteacher, then took the computer disk and made copy after copy, checking my spelling, shortening sentences until I thought the book was ready for print. I turned the book over to Historical Resources Press. I did not know at the time, but both Karin and Jack Ramsay, owners of Historical Resources Press, are real professionals. Both have qualifications beyond the standard techniques of Library Science, and both have a rare intuitiveness, agile minds and the ability to write, having books of their own published and in bookstores and libraries.

I am grateful to Thom Cashman of Wright Type Company for the cover design and for using his great talent and special care to capture and preserve as keepsakes for my family and friends the papers pictures, letters, telegrams, dog tags and mementos I have treasured over the years.

Virginia, my darling wife, has been through every stage of this book. While I was overseas she was on state side, waiting, wondering, hoping, praying. She was one of the first to listen and among the first to encourage me to write a book so our family could understand what we had been through.

Without the enthusiastic and able assistance of all these people, *Patton's Ill-Fated Raid* could never have been written. I know so many veterans who have kept their war memories to themselves, never shared with anyone. Until I began writing this book, I too was living with those memories popping into my thoughts many times during each day and often during long nights of agony. I am grateful that my military buddies, my wife and family and several others, over a long and sometime agonizing time, helped me to write my view of America during wartime. Writing this has put meaning to my memories and taken away some of the agony of sleepless nights. My hope is that other Veterans and other POWs will share their stories and that together we can record what it is for America to be at war, what it is to serve in the Armed Forces of the United States of America and, after service during wartime, what it means to salute the flag as well as why we, as Veterans, sometimes have a tear or two when we see a patriotic ceremony or parade.

"This type of account of American POWs is rather rare among the World War II literature. Thompson's book, *Patton's Ill-fated Raid* should appeal to a wide audience, military historians, veterans and general public interest in WWII. I know this will be a useful tool to our understanding of the many sacrifices of our men and women who served in World War II."

  Jim Conrad, PhD., Texas A&M University Archivist and Instructor of History

"Dear Harry:
 Here is your manuscript back. It tells a harrowing, gripping story. The best account of Kriegie Life I've read. A copy is on the way to Will Cavanagh with my recommendation for the book. I intend to put a second copy in a loose-leaf folder with the War Room 'Kriegie' Display. I hope you don't mind. .. It will go into the 99th Archives in Carlisle Barracks Under your name."

Dick Byers, 99th IDA Archives CMTE.

"Harry Thompson's memoirs put the reader right alongside World War II prisoners of war. 'We' are captured during the Battle of the Bulge, march 241 miles across Germany through bitter cold, eating bread made from sawdust, beets and straw and stealing whatever else is available. .. Thompson says he holds no bitterness about his POW experiences, but wants people, particularly the young who know little about that era, to understand how precious our freedoms are."

Carol Ferguson, Feature Writer, Greenville (Texas) Herald Banner

"I have read Harry Thompson's account of his capture and imprisonment by the Nazis in the Battle of the Bulge during WWII. It was so good that I intend to read this book again. His narration of the terrible circumstances he endured made it seem as if I was also there. .. The American people owe so much to so many for our current freedom. .. I highly recommend this book be published and read by anyone interested in WWII. It was fantastic."

Jimmy Felty, Principal
Wolfe City School

"A gripping – not say harrowing – narrative.   … genuinely exciting; the story is well told.   … An account of life as a prisoner of the Germans during the collapse of the Third Reich is almost in a category by itself; most POW literature deals with escapes – this one deals with simple endurance, marked by no small measure of heroism. Likewise the period it concerns is of extraordinary interest. We have here an eyewitness account, from an American standpoint."

William Murchison, Dallas Morning News Senior Columnist
MA, Modern U.S. History, Stanford University

CONTENTS

INTRODUCTION

This is a true story of an American prisoner of Germany in World War II. It is my true story. I lived it.

Many American POWs may have had more horrible experiences than I while others had less traumatic. I was not beaten or locked in a cage. I did live through being shot at and bombed; being pushed, slapped around and lined up for execution; being forced to walk over 240 miles in a weakened condition with no food supply while suffering starvation and dysentery; being locked in railroad boxcars in subzero weather, packed in so tightly we had to take turns just to sit down. Our boxcars had shell holes allowing snow and ice to accumulate to a depth of four to six inches inside. We were so cold we had to keep running in place for days just to keep from freezing. During this time we went for thirteen solid days with nothing other than snow to eat. I was liberated, recaptured, choosing to return to the POW camp when vicious enemy shelling and small arms fire seemed a worse fate than being inside my POW camp.

The fiftieth anniversary of the Battle of the Bulge has passed. World War II seems ancient history to my grandchildren as much as the Civil War seemed to me when I was growing up. This narrative is for my family as much as for the public, a memoir of a horrible time, the likes of which I hope they will never have to live.

Please note that this story is absolutely true to the best of my memory and knowledge. I have consulted my own letters and writings as well as other documents to make sure that my recollections are accurate. My story is a story I do not believe has been often told. I tell it here in behalf of all who lived it: my family, close friends, total strangers, and best and most important of all, Americans.

I was a warrant officer in an artillery Battalion, caught in one of the greatest engagements in the history of warfare. Hitler's last gamble of World War II, an attempt to drive a wedge between the American and British armies and capture the Allies' main supply port at Antwerp, Belgium, has become known to history as the Battle of the Bulge. This main drive went through what is known as the North shoulder of the Bulge and was stopped at Elsenborn Ridge in one of the bloodiest battles of the war, a battle in which inexperienced American soldiers distinguished themselves with remarkable bravery. It was on the second day of the Battle of the Bulge that I was captured.

As a prisoner of war, I was caught in what has been called "General Patton's greatest mistake of the war". Patton sent a task force of approximately 307 American soldiers and 53 vehicles, including Sherman tanks, on what turned out to be a suicide mission, 80 miles behind the enemy front, to liberate Hammelburg, the German POW camp for American officers where I was being held, AND to rescue his son-in-law, Colonel John Waters, who had been captured at Kasserine Pass in North Africa in 1942. The task force was completely destroyed and countless American officers were killed and wounded in the battle around the camp. Shortly after this, along with many other officer POW's from Hammelburg, I was caught in the horrible Allied bombing raid on Nuremberg that killed many American officers. I survived the American air raid on Nuremberg in which dropping bombs hit not only Nuremberg but American POWs and, according to what I heard at Camp Lucky Strike, resulted in the casualties of 24 officers killed and 105 wounded, the death toll rising to 35 the next day. Only four German guards were killed while nearly all left in our column of POWs struggled, holding one another up as they became "walking wounded".

Perhaps I write this book to answer my own questions which continue to haunt me even after all these years: Were the 99th and 2nd Infantry Divisions to be sacrificed in the Battle of the Bulge so that the Germans could be lured into a trap? Did it seem like a small sacrifice to lose twenty or thirty thousand American troops to kill or capture some 250,000 Germans? There is some proof that Allied Supreme Headquarters knew of the massive German buildup. To this day I wonder if we were the bait used to trap the German Army in the Ardennes in December of 1944.

I can hardly remember what happened last week but I can vividly recall all the daily happenings that occurred over fifty years ago while in the United States Army, especially while I was a prisoner of war in Germany. The humiliation of being forced to relieve myself in front of women and children, and begging or stealing anything to eat is still very real to me, as is wondering if I would see tomorrow and what tomorrow would bring. Would the German troops carry out Hitler's orders to kill all prisoners? Would today be my last? Would tomorrow?

Thanks to the good Lord, Hitler's orders did not happen to me and I am here to relate my story, **Patton's Ill-fated Raid.**

Harry Thompson

Harry A. Thompson, 2002 A.D.

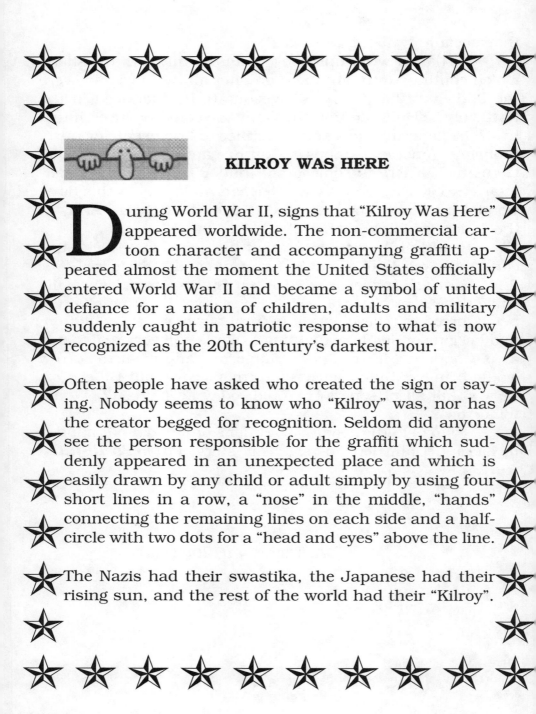

KILROY WAS HERE

During World War II, signs that "Kilroy Was Here" appeared worldwide. The non-commercial cartoon character and accompanying graffiti appeared almost the moment the United States officially entered World War II and became a symbol of united defiance for a nation of children, adults and military suddenly caught in patriotic response to what is now recognized as the 20th Century's darkest hour.

Often people have asked who created the sign or saying. Nobody seems to know who "Kilroy" was, nor has the creator begged for recognition. Seldom did anyone see the person responsible for the graffiti which suddenly appeared in an unexpected place and which is easily drawn by any child or adult simply by using four short lines in a row, a "nose" in the middle, "hands" connecting the remaining lines on each side and a half-circle with two dots for a "head and eyes" above the line.

The Nazis had their swastika, the Japanese had their rising sun, and the rest of the world had their "Kilroy".

Harry A. Thompson

This picture was taken shortly before I entered the military.

Who Am I?

Time has gone by, yet there has not been a day since my discharge from the Army that I do not think of something that happened while I was a prisoner of war. As I write this, my story, America is at war again. Unbelievable! They say this is different. I don't know. When are the results of war different?

My story takes place during the last stages of WWII and is not about heroes or heroic action, but is about fighting, trying to survive and somehow hold on, waiting for the American Army to liberate me, liberate me from terror beyond my wildest imagination.

The story of Harry Thompson at war is a little different from some of the stories of war you have heard. I had a pistol but that was taken. The Germans took my gun from me December 17, 1944, the morning of the second day of the Battle of the Bulge. I remained in the hands of the Germans virtually until VE Day, five months later.

My story is not about battles and landings; it is about survival, about hunger, exhaustion, and fear I never could quite let go.

Was Harry Thompson a red, white and blue hero? Not in my mind. In POW camp we did not think about heroes. We

1

thought about staying alive – just lasting long enough for our buddies to rescue us. Our buddies were pounding on Germany's gates. We were inside those gates. The harder they pounded, the more we inside the POW camp liked it even when we knew that their pounding probably would lead to more physical danger and suffering for us.

Who am I? Where did I come from? How did I get into this story?

Henry A. Thompson and Audrey Hathaway Thompson (my parents) and my three-and-a-half year-old brother (Franklin Thompson, born October 10, 1911) welcomed me into the family in Dallas, Texas May 5, 1914. Franklin and I were most fortunate to have had such wonderful parents. They were very lenient as long as we brothers behaved but did know how to correct us when we got sassy or misbehaved. I really believe children appreciate getting corrected when they do a wrong. My parents always taught me to know right from wrong; to never, never associate with wrong crowds; to always be respectful to the girls. I always, to this present day, have tried to abide by these rules.

I had all childhood diseases and was so very fortunate not get the dreaded Polio disease that crippled so many children in those days.

I can think of no sport, with the exception of basketball, that I did not like. I was on the soccer and baseball teams in grammar school. I loved baseball and played on the twilight team at the park in the afternoons. Franklin and I learned to play tennis and played in the local parks from daylight to dark. We loved playing tennis. Franklin played on Forest Avenue High School Tennis Team. When I went to high school, I was on the tennis team only a short time because I also tried to play football and, on the first day of football practice, I broke my wrist. I was too small to play football.

Our family always enjoyed doing things together. Mother and Dad liked to take us fishing, attend the Texas League ball games or just go driving. They were always so considerate of

Franklin and me. I learned to drive at age ten because in 1924 there was very little traffic and no law against a child driving.

I started delivering papers for Dallas Morning News in the morning and the Dallas Times Herald in the evenings. I did have two good paper routes I delivered from my bicycle. The bad part was trying to collect fifteen cents weekly for the papers. People would not come to their doors. I pestered them so much that I was finally paid.

At age twelve, from my paper money, I bought an old Model T Ford. It surely was hard to keep that old Model T running. I quit delivering papers and went to work for Clarence Saunders Grocery, then Helpy Selfy, Safeway and finally, A&P. I had an afternoon job after school and on Saturdays.

My old Model T would not run half the time, so I sold it and rode my bicycle everywhere, even going to downtown Dallas, about three miles from home, and to White Rock Lake, six or seven miles from home. In those days my parents felt I was safe. We never heard of evil people molesting children.

When I was eight, we moved next door to the Goldstein family. Their son Arthur and I became very close friends even to this present day. Once we found an old horse walking down the street. We took the horse home and rode that old nag bareback. We never could understand why he kept running into everything until a couple of days later when we learned the horse belonged to an old man. His wife told us that she had hoped her husband would never find the old horse, for it was blind and she was afraid for her husband to use him on a wagon while he collected junk.

I always had a dog. I had a German Shepherd that gave birth to eleven puppies. What a time I had trying to give away all those puppies. Mother made me get rid of mamma dog because she was so mean.

A new Jewish synagogue opened a block from us and had an open house with free ice cream and cake. Arthur Goldstein and I naturally went for the ice cream and cake. We had a big laugh. The Rabbi thought I was the Jew and had brought a Gentile friend.

After I sold the old Model T, I bought a very good 1925 Model T touring car at a bargain for twenty-five dollars from the money I saved from working at the grocery store. I thought that I was a real big shot driving my own car to school as a freshman in high school.

I joined ROTC. In those days there was always a big parade in downtown Dallas on Memorial Day, Fourth of July and Armistice Day. All Dallas High School ROTCs participated and the high school girls went through the crowd selling poppies to benefit the Veterans.

In 1931, at the height of the Depression, Dad lost his job with Texas & Pacific Railroad after being with them in the telegraph department for fifteen years. That hit us really hard. I think everyone else was in the same situation. I did not have money for gasoline for my car, so I used kerosene. Kerosene was only five cents per gallon. My car would run well on kerosene as long as it was started on gasoline. I would pour a little gas in the carburetor to get it started, then let it run on kerosene. I left a white smoke screen behind, but went anywhere I wanted to go.

As a junior in high school, I quit school after A&P Grocery gave me full time work as a checker. (Later I went to night school and finished high school.) I sold my Model T Ford for the same price I had paid so that the money could help pay some bills and buy some groceries for our family.

In 1934, a very big break came my way. A customer at the grocery store with whom I had become friends asked me if I wanted an office boy job with Sims Oil Company in downtown Dallas. I was hired and worked in the supply room and as an office boy. In 1935, all employees of Sims Oil Company were advised that the company was selling out to Tidewater Oil and Gas in Oklahoma. I started looking for another job.

A week or so later, the President of Sims Oil called me to his office and asked if I had found a job. I told him no and he asked where I had applied. I gave him a list of fifteen places I had tried with no results. When he saw Continental Oil Field Supply Company, he picked up the phone and called the Vice President of Continental. I had a job with Continental starting the following Monday. I started as an office boy and helped in the mailroom for fifty-two dollars per month. Later, since I had learned to type at night school, I was promoted to the billing department. Then I was promoted to the purchasing department, where I had a pretty good job and many new friends. I was making one hundred twenty-five dollars per month. That was really a pretty good salary at that time. I really enjoyed working there and became a member of their softball and bowling teams.

Our softball team won Dallas City Championship. I played second base and left field. If I do say so, I was a good softball player. During the game, I usually was good for a single or a double but during the play-off for championship I accidentally hit a homerun.

Dad had been called back to work part time for T&P Railroad, so the effect of the depression was easing up. In 1937, I purchased a new Pontiac. (At last I had my own new car!) Insurance for my car was purchased wholesale through Continental. Can you believe it— full coverage for twenty-five dollars per year!

I had dates with many girls. (I never went out with any girl with whom I worked and never went steady until I met my wife.) Big Band music was my favorite. At one time or another most Big Bands came to Dallas or Fort Worth. I believe we danced to all of them.

In 1936 my brother obtained a position with the newly established Social Security Administration and moved to Baltimore, Maryland. I was glad I could stay in Dallas where the weather was warm. I have always liked warm weather. It allowed me to stay busy with baseball, tennis and other activities. I always dreaded the coming of colder weather that kept me inside, for I did love outdoor sports.

I remember, back in 1932, articles began appearing on

the front page of newspapers about Japan fighting China and around 1937 there was unpleasant news of Hitler in Europe. Hitler's raving speeches occupied too much radio time, interrupting my music by the Big Bands. From what I could understand from the radio and newsreels, big trouble was brewing in Europe. I never paid much attention to the news until Germany invaded Poland. Charles Lindberg had already come home and warned America of German air power and what a great army they had. Why everyone turned on Charles Lindberg I will never understand. I think it was uncalled for when the City of Dallas changed Lindberg Avenue (a busy street) to Skillman Avenue. News of the war in Europe was now making headlines and every time we went to the movies, the Pathe News always showed pictures of the war.

In 1939 I went to Baltimore to see Franklin and his new bride whom I really liked. They, a couple of their friends and I went to the New York World Fair. When we got to New York, we rented a real nice suite at a hotel. Can you imagine only twelve dollars and fifty cents per night for a large suite, two bedrooms and a large living room, plenty of room for all! We had a wonderful time. Helen's girl friend, Grace, and I decided to ride the Life Saver — a very tall tower in which we were to be pulled to the top in a parachute and, upon reaching the top, the parachute was supposed to unsnap and let us float down, but it malfunctioned and did not unsnap. We were left hanging at the top for about an hour until the ride was repaired. We had a good chance to see all of the fair ground from above. I have heard that this tower was taken over by the Army for paratroop training during WWII. We had a wonderful time before we went back to Baltimore. I had a good time with them but was ready to return home and go back to work.

In 1940 I purchased another new car, another Pontiac. I had only 900 miles on the speedometer when I had a very bad wreck. It made the front page of The Dallas Morning News. I was coming home alone after a date. A car was coming on the wrong side of the road, straight for me. I stopped my car, got in the middle of the seat and grabbed both doors. The left front door was ripped off and about half the left side of the car was gone. The other car went over an embankment and landed in a pond, completely submerged. It was so dark I could not see who was driving. I told her I would run for help. I do not know how she got out of the car and was sitting on top. After the police came and finally got her off the roof of her car, she was sent to the hospital. She did not know whether or not her child was in the car. I waited until 6 A.M. for wrecker crews to pull the car out of the water. Fortunately, no one else was in the car. The police said they could not prove that she was drunk because of the amount of head injuries she had, but she definitely reeked with the smell of alcohol.

About this time President Roosevelt started to lend and lease to England our World War I mothballed destroyers and other supplies. U.S. ships carrying supplies to England and Russia were being sunk, but Washington kept saying we were going to stay out of the war. Since the U.S. government had neglected our military, we would be hurting in case of war. President Roosevelt had the foresight to start drafting civilians into the Armed Forces. Shortly afterward, all young men were ordered to register for the draft. In early October 1940 the first draft number was drawn. I checked the newspaper daily for my number. It was finally drawn and I was ordered to report to the main post office in Dallas for a physical. I was then sworn in to the U.S. Army on March 5, 1941. I was told to board a train with other draftees headed for Fort Sill, Oklahoma.

HEADQUARTERS
FIELD ARTILLERY REPLACEMENT CENTER

Fort Sill, Oklahoma

March 30, 1941   PWB/as

To Each Selective Service Trainee Of The Field
  Artillery Replacement Center, Fort Sill, Oklahoma:

Since an individual greeting is impossible, I hope each of
you will accept this letter as a personal message.

You are about to become a soldier - a service which means
hard work and at times personal discomfort; a service whose
only reward is the satisfaction of duty well performed and
the knowledge of your contribution to the security of our
country and its institutions.

Already you have made a sacrifice in leaving your home and
work, whether humble or luxurious, whether from the field or
the bench, the laboratory or the desk. You are experiencing
a complete and abrupt change of life and environment. Not
only have you new tasks to perform, but you must adjust
yourselves to a new way of life. Your adjustment to army
life will require a real effort on your part. You will find
that your comfort and health and the comfort and health of
your comrades will require sacrifice on your part and com-
pliance with many orders and regulations that at first may
seem unnecessary. You will soon discover why they are
necessary.

Many of you will have problems that may worry you—problems
both personal or connected with your army work. It is just
as much the duty of the officers and non-commissioned officers to help you solve those problems as it is to train you.
Do not nurse your difficulties and grievances to yourself.
Go to your chief of section, to your battery commander with
your problems. If they cannot help you, there is still your

battalion commander and regimental commander and I stand
ready to help whenever other help proves inadequate.

Your Battery area is to be your home for the next three
months. There will be many visitors - relatives and friends
to see you. You want them to see a neat and orderly camp.
To accomplish this we all must work together. Remember that
when you throw trash on the ground some one has to pick it
up. By remembering that and reminding your comrades of it,
you will help to improve the neatness of the camp.

You have been sent here to get your first military training.
You will be here for twelve (12) weeks. Then you will go to
some Field Artillery Battalion or Regiment. Many will go to
National Guard regiments, others to newly organized units.

We will try to place you in positions that best fit your
experience and ability as far as possible. If any man feels
that he has experience and ability to better serve in some
other position, he may apply to his Battery Commander for
reclassification. As far as there are positions available,
it is advantageous to have you perform duties for which you
are best fitted.

You are now in the Field Artillery. As a Field Artilleryman
with over thirty years service, I want to congratulate you.
It is a branch with a proud heritage. I hope that each one
of you will prove to be worthy of wearing the uniform of the
Field Artillery in the Army of the United States.

                    Sincerely,

                    Phillip W Booker

                    Phillip W. Booker
                 Colonel Field Artillery
                       Executive

Note: This fragile and brittle paper, given Harry after being drafted and upon his
arrival at Fort Sill, Oklahoma in 1941, has been re-typed for readability. The signature of Phillip W. Booker, Colonel Field Artillery Executive, has been scanned.

March 1941

S	M	T	W	T	F	S
						1
2	3	4	5	6	7	8
9	10	11	12	13	14	15
16	17	18	19	20	21	22
23	24	25	26	27	28	29
30	31					

I Received A Form Letter From President Roosevelt
March 5, 1941

Never in my wildest dreams would I have imagined what the future held for me when on one day in October of 1940, I signed up for the draft into the military service of the United States, as millions of other young men had done at that time. I, like most of them, was looking forward to being drafted into the military and doing my little bit for our wonderful country. I did not really want to enlist, for that meant having to serve three long years in the army (a draftee only had to serve for one year). At the time, I had a good job with the Continental Oil Field Supply Company in Dallas, Texas, and I did not want to be away for more than a year. I had so many friends, and looking back, that was the most enjoyable position I ever had. The day before leaving for the Army, the entire office pitched in and gave me the very best portable radio available at the time. I kept it all the way to Europe. My immediate boss, Mr. McGinnis, for whom I cared so much, lost his son on Iwo Jima.

During the latter half of February 1941, I received a form letter from President Roosevelt, congratulating me on being selected to serve a year in the United States Army and to report for duty at Fort Sill, Oklahoma on March 5, 1941. It was the only lottery I ever won. The pay for new recruits at that time was twenty-one dollars a month for three months, followed by a raise to thirty-six dollars a month. After buying PX coupons, paying for laundry, and buying theater coupons, we actually received about seven dollars cash each month. We had two old Army sergeants who, on each payday, would cut playing cards. Highest card would get the other sergeant's complete month's pay. The winner went to town and lived it up. The loser stayed in camp for the month. It did not make much difference since all his clothes and meals were furnished - just no trips to town for a month.

10

After receiving draft notice, I had to report to Army Head-quarters at the U.S. Post Office in Dallas. I, along with many others, was sworn in and given a brief inspection, which consisted of doctors checking for venereal disease, checking our eyes and ears, then having us bend over and spread our buttock's cheeks apart. I do not guess military training has ever been easy. When I arrived at Fort Sill, we were quartered at the Tent City of the fort. Elements of the activated 45th Infantry Division, Oklahoma National Guard who had been quartered there had just been transferred to some other camp. Shortly after being assigned to our quarters all of us were lined up and taken to the main part of the fort. First we were given shots for tetanus, typhoid, and several other diseases - both arms and both cheeks were pretty sore when they got through with us, which made for some uncomfortable sleeping. Then we were taken to supply headquarters where we were issued uniforms, shoes, etc. When we got to where the shoes were issued, one of the recruits was arguing because they could not find shoes to fit him - they told him when he bought shoes as a civilian that no store carried size 13 double E, so why should the army have them? He agreed and shut up. After basic training was over he still had not received his shoes and stayed at Fort Sill until they came in.

After receiving our full uniforms, we found that the caps were about the only thing that fit, and we frequently had to do a little horse-trading to get that to come out right. The old cliché about uniforms coming in two sizes, too large and too small, was certainly true in our case. We were a motley-looking bunch of raw recruits, and it was a couple of weeks before we finally were fitted properly. We did not really have anybody to impress at first anyway - we were confined to camp for the first two weeks in case we might have measles or some other communicable disease.

Our training was pretty trying for us - none of us were used to such rigid regulations. First they taught us how to march. I had no trouble with drilling, since I had been in ROTC, but some of the men just could not keep in step. One such recruit was my barracks buddy, Harry Schwartz, who was also from Dallas and a very good friend of mine. He was a nice fellow but just could not coordinate himself. He tried and tried, but just could not keep in step with the rest of us. After we all (supposedly) had learned to march, we were issued rifles and had to learn the manual of arms and how to march carrying the rifles. Harry did his best to learn, but once, while we were drilling, he whacked me good on the top of the head with his rifle barrel (he did a left flank while the rest of us did a right). It raised a big nasty knot on my head which never would go down - the doctor had to cut it out a year later.

We were inspected almost daily - the bunks had to be made just right. The inspector would drop a dime on the bed, if the dime did not bounce and the bed was not made to Army specifications, we would be chewed out, made to redo bed and punished by doing extra K. P. duties like picking up cigarette butts or doing latrine duty or by not getting a weekend pass. Uniforms had to be neat; the belt buckles polished to shine like a mirror, and the shoes had to be shined. One of our sergeants showed us how he shined one pair of shoes, which he never wore but used for inspections only. After ordinary polishing and shining, a dried bone was vigorously rubbed in, then more polish. After four or five polishes, the shoes shone like a mirror. That was too much trouble for me.

In the middle of the tent we had a wood stove shaped like a cone with a smoke stack going out through the middle of the roof. One day we heard a small explosion a couple of tents down from us. One of the men who had never used a wood stove before could not get it to light, so he poured some cigarette lighter fluid in and threw a match in, causing the stove to jump about three feet in the air. We got there right after the accident - the lucky recruit was not hurt but when I looked up I had to laugh. There were so many small holes burned in the tent roof that it looked like a starry summer sky!

Once we went on a field exercise and pitched pup tents. During the night there was a hard rain. We ran for higher ground and the river rose over our campsite and washed all our tents and gear away, so we had to return to camp without finishing our field objective. I pulled my usual KP and latrine duty. For me, KP was usually washing dishes and large cooking utensils and mopping the floors; latrine duty consisted of keeping the latrines and toilets clean, and keeping the boilers that produced hot water properly regulated. One guy from our tent, whose name I cannot recall, was latrine orderly. He forgot to check the boiler pressure and when our Commanding Officer went in to inspect, the steam pressure was so high that it had backed up and was blowing steam out of all the commodes. We had to turn the boiler off and open all the faucets to relieve the pressure. It was so strong that for a few minutes steam was coming out of all the faucets, cold and hot, plus the toilets. We were lucky the boiler did not blow, but when the CO walked away we noticed he was laughing. Most of us were too; the steam coming out of all those toilets looked pretty silly.

Another friend, Private James Pounds, also from Dallas, was a reporter for the Dallas Times Herald before being drafted. Shortly before basic training was finished, orders came through, transferring him to Marine Officer candidate school. He rose to the rank of Lt. Colonel of the Marines and after the war was Commanding Officer of Marine Reserves in Dallas.

Basic training went pretty smoothly, overall - the usual marches, drills, etc. We got to fire howitzers later on - the big 105 mm howitzers were not available, so we trained with the 75mm's instead. We could stand beside the howitzers and watch shells going to target. Our last part of training was going through gas training - that meant going into a tent, then putting on our gas masks. Then the gas was released. We walked around a while and could not feel a thing. Then we were told to take off the masks and go outside. Wow, we could not get out fast enough. That gas burned and took our breath away. It took about ten minutes after leaving the tent to be able to breathe without gagging. The three months passed by pretty quickly, then we were transferred. Some of us went to the 69th Infantry Division and some to the 7th Infantry Division. I was assigned as cadre to the newly formed 7th Infantry Division, along with enough men to form all the artillery battalions of the 7th Division.

13

June 1941

S	M	T	W	T	F	S
1	2	3	4	5	6	7
8	9	10	11	12	13	14
15	16	17	18	19	20	21
22	23	24	25	26	27	28
29	30					

Soldiers, Sailors, Marines And Dogs Stay Off The Lawn
June 3, 1941

We boarded a train from Fort Sill for California on June 3, 1941, arriving at Fort Ord, California on June 6. In route, the trip was very good and I think enjoyed by all. The train stopped several times at points of interest - one being at the bottom of the Royal Gorge in Colorado. We had dining and Pullman cars. The sleeping accommodations were very good. They did take us first class. We were wearing our summer uniforms when we arrived. While it was pretty hot in the afternoon, as soon as the sun went down it turned pretty cold. We desperately started digging through our barracks bags for our field jackets - none of us realized that sunny California got so cold after dark!

I was assigned to the 57th Field Artillery Battalion of the 7th Infantry Division. I realize that this terminology is highly unfamiliar to those who have never served, so let me try to quickly and simply explain what a Field Artillery Battalion is and what it does. An Infantry Division during World War Two had Headquarters, medics, ordnance, engineers, divisional artillery and three infantry regiments. The Division Artillery had three battalions of 105 mm howitzers and one battalion of 155 mm howitzers. Each 105 mm howitzer battalion was part of one of the three infantry regiments, furnishing forward observers to work with the regiment and call down artillery fire where needed. The 155 mm battalion was used to provide supporting fire wherever it might be needed for the division. Each Field Artillery Battalion consisted of three firing batteries, Alpha, Bravo, and Charlie; plus a Service Battery and Headquarters Battery. Each firing battery had four 105 mm howitzers plus its own forward observers, while the headquarters battery served as a fire control center, C-D, G-1, G-2, message center, communication and personnel center. The Service battery was mainly for supply purposes but, most importantly, it served as the ammunition supply. That's a basic breakdown of the kind of unit in which I now found myself serving.

Shortly after we arrived, the entire division was assembled at Fort Ord parade grounds for a parade of the entire division honoring the 7th Division Commanding General who was leaving. (I heard that the general's name was General Joseph Stilwell.) Our camp was located in the East Garrison of Fort Ord - on a steep hill formerly occupied by the Civilian Conservation Corps who had cut into a hill and laid out concrete slabs all up and down the hill as spaces for tents. When we arrived there was a tent, along with poles and stakes, lying folded up next to each slab, and all personnel had to work together to erect their tent. At the bottom of the hill was the latrine, a very large outdoor privy with no running water except in the lavatory. The Battalion Headquarters and mess hall were located together on top of the hill. All the personnel, most of us were draftees, seemed to get along real well. We went through the usual training until we were moved to our new quarters in the main garrison of the fort, in the latter half of November 1941.

Many events happened while at East Garrison. One sad memory was about Corporal Joe Riddle of Sherman, Texas. Joe, three others and I played penny ante poker until around one A.M. The next morning Joe was sick and reported to the

15

doctor. He was immediately taken to the hospital and by noon he was dead, diagnosis was spinal meningitis. What a tragedy! Joe was such a good soldier and a good friend. Fort Ord has had many cases of spinal meningitis and I often wonder if the cause was those outdoor latrines used by thousands of soldiers for many years. Fort Ord is an old fort and many outdoor latrines were used for soldiers. After Corporal Riddle died, armed guards were posted around our battalion with orders to shoot anyone entering or leaving until quarantine was removed.

While at East Garrison, we watched the filming of an army picture featuring Wallace Berry as an old cavalry soldier. A short walk took us to an area where we could look at the Salinas Valley where the Ferry Seed Company grew flowers for seed. All the flowers were in bloom - What a beautiful sight! Flowers were so bright it was hard to look at them.

In C battery the Mess sergeant was a regular Army man and almost illiterate. While stationed at a previous camp a year or so earlier, he married a prostitute and brought her to Salinas, California when he was transferred to Fort Ord. I think many men visited his wife while he was on duty. Once on a weekend pass, he found his cousin in bed with his wife. He came back to camp and got his 45-caliber pistol. Our First Sergeant Dodson (an old army soldier back to W.W.I and a very humorous old man) asked the sergeant where he was going with that pistol. The sergeant said, "I am going to kill my cousin. I caught him in bed with my wife." First Sergeant Dodson humorously said, "What's wrong with him in bed with your wife? He is your cousin is he not? She is just keeping it in the family, is she not?" The sergeant said, "That's right! I never thought of that." He put his gun up and went to visit his wife and cousin. That is a true story. I heard the conversation between First Sergeant Dodson and the sergeant.

My friend, Harry Schwartz, never did learn how to drill or even learn how to fire a rifle while at Fort Ord. He was finally transferred out. I never saw him again. I made one trip to Salinas. Signs were on many lawns reading "Soldiers, Sailors,

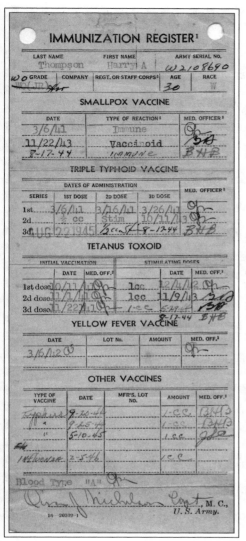

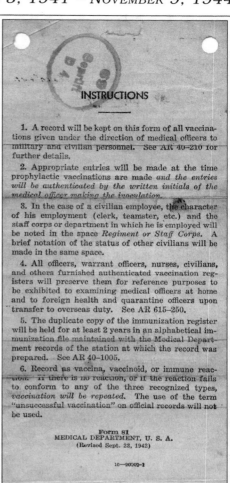

Form 81
MEDICAL DEPARTMENT,
U.S.A.
(Revised Sept. 23, 1942)

Reverse side of Form 81
MEDICAL DEPARTMENT, U.S.A.
(Revised Sept. 23, 1942)

"We also received a new series of shots, many of them the same that we had already gotten at Fort Sill. I suspect many army doctors of having a fetish about needles."—Comment by Harry Thompson

INSTRUCTIONS TYPED NEXT PAGE

INSTRUCTIONS

1. A record will be kept on this form of all vaccinations given under the direction of medical officers to military and civilian personnel. ...

2. Appropriate entries will be made at the time prophylactic vaccinations are made and the entries will be authenticated by the written initials of the medical officer making the inoculation.

3. In the case of a civilian employee, the character of his employment (clerk, teamster, etc.) and the staff corps or department in which he is employed will be noted in the space Regiment or Staff Corps. A brief notation the status of other civilians will be made in the same space.

4. All officers, warrant officers, nurses, civilians, and others furnished authenticated vaccination registers will preserve them for reference purposes to be exhibited to examining medical officers at home and to foreign health and quarantine officers upon transfer to overseas duty. ..

5. The duplicate copy of the immunization register will be held for at least 2 years in an alphabetical immunization file maintained with the Medical Department records of the station at which the record was prepared. ..

6. Record as vaccina, vaccinoid, or immune reaction. If there is no reaction, or if the reaction fails to conform to any of the three recognized types, vaccination will be repeated. The use of the term "unsuccessful vaccination" on official records will not be used.

Marines, and dogs stay off lawn!" I thought, "To hell with that town." I left and never went back. After that, many others and I spent our money in Monterey, California. Monterey was a more beautiful city anyway.

In September of 1941, I received my first full physical from the Army. Previous exams had mainly been ear and throat checkups. We also received a new series of shots, many of them the same that we had already gotten at Fort Sill. (I suspect many army doctors of having a fetish about needles.) That same month I was promoted to Corporal. Imagine that! Corporal - a raise in pay. My monthly check rose to the huge sum of fifty-four dollars a month.

Before moving to our new quarters, Division Headquarters sent word to our commanding officer that some of our men could volunteer or be selected to fill vacancies in an artillery battalion assigned to Philippine Island. That did sound exciting and, if we had been transferred, it would have been a little too exciting. There was the usual way of picking: most selected were men the CO did not like. Then they picked the army way: "you, you and you".

November 1941						
S	M	T	W	T	F	S
						1
2	3	4	5	6	7	8
9	10	11	12	13	14	15
16	17	18	19	20	21	22
23	24	25	26	27	28	29
30						

A Confusing, Honking, Screaming Mess
November 28, 1941

Nearly every Saturday night, Sergeant T. R. Clifton, Private Young and I went to the Post Theater. As well as I can remember, admission was ten cents. Private Young stayed with the 7th Infantry Division and was killed in action in the Pacific area of the war. Mess Sergeant Clifton was sent home after sustaining shrapnel injuries and a leg broken during the Battle of The Bulge.

On November 28, we finally moved into our nice, new two-story barracks. They were great accommodations - it seemed as if we had just settled in when the disaster of December 7, 1941 struck the U. S. fleet at Pearl Harbor. Before that, I had never even heard of Pearl Harbor. It is difficult for

19

anyone who was not there to realize the panic that struck the entire nation in the days after that sneak attack. The country braced for an invasion of the West Coast at any moment, and modern historians who dismiss the possibility that Japan ever could have invaded the United States simply were not there to taste the raw fear felt by all of us.

That same night, under cover of darkness, we evacuated the whole Fort. Each road leading out of the base was lined with vehicles with their blackout lights on, and it was a confusing, honking, screaming mess. We wound up deployed along the coast among the scrub oak trees - since an invasion was expected at anytime, we stayed there under small scrub oak trees for two or three days. We were then moved to the parking lot of San Jose State College football stadium. The parking lot was unpaved. It started raining, leaving mud and water two to three inches deep. Water was up to our sleeping bags and we slept one night in water. They moved us to the gym where we slept on the floor or in seats of the gym. The floor was hard and our sleeping bags were wet, so I slept in the seats. It was better than sleeping in water. When we were fed fried chicken or steak, we were lined up on the sidewalk along side of a busy street. When we were fed stew (It was called slum.), we ate in rear of the college.

At the college, when we pulled guard duty, there were four posts, one on each side of the college. On a rainy night, one guard was caught drinking coffee, while some girl held his rifle and an umbrella over him while he enjoyed his coffee. I do not remember any punishment for this, but I think all the G. I.'s in California heard about it. San Jose was a very nice city and our stay was very pleasant.

After about a week, we were moved to Crissy Field, located in San Francisco next to the Golden Gate Bridge. At that time we were all issued live ammunition - everyone had shells in their pockets, ready to load up and fire at the first sign of an invading Japanese soldier. We were slated to go to Angel Island and then be shipped overseas. While at Crissy Field, the

57th FA Battalion pulled guard duty on the wharves at San Francisco. Several of our soldiers were killed while on night watch there. The assailants were never found, which surely did not ease our minds.

The barracks at Crissy Field were very good. I was in the main building, a large two story building. One afternoon, Sergeant Adrian Troop, a couple of other soldiers and I were playing penny ante poker. We were enjoying music from my portable radio when a special announcement came in, stating the Japanese had bombed the Golden Gate Bridge. We were next to the bridge, but we dropped money and cards and ran to the window. A silly radio announcement! It was a false alarm!

On December 24, 1941 we had an alert to go to McClelland Air Force Base at Sacramento where the higher authorities thought an air raid was a possibility. Our battalion pulled out and embarked on what turned out to be the fastest convoy ride I ever rode. As soon as we reached the airfield we set up our artillery in an anti-aircraft configuration in case of dive-bombers. Then extra troops were deployed into Sacramento to guard courthouses, telephone buildings, auto and rail bridges and so on. I was Corporal of guard and, as soon as we got to the air base, was assigned to guard both ends of a Railroad Bridge as well as an automobile bridge over the river. One of the guards, Private Ryan (always in trouble), said he heard a noise and hollered, "Halt!" three times. They did not stop, so he started shooting. I said, "Ah hell!" I got my flashlight to check. He had killed a cow. The raid did not come off, of course, but we stayed at the airfield for several days just in case. At that point in time, anything seemed possible.

We ate at the Air Corps mess hall that night, and the food was excellent, certainly better than standard G. I. fare. We were told to eat all that we wanted, but eat all we took. That went for all meals. The next day we had Christmas dinner, which was also delicious, but all of us got a bad case of "the runs" from it. I guess Air Corps food was too rich for our blood. At 2 A.M. the next morning I woke up in a hurry to get to the latrine. To my dismay, I found it to be full, with a line of groaning soldiers clean out the door. Most of us could not wait and dropped our drawers where we were. The first sergeant fell down in his own mess trying to unbuckle his pants, then laughed and said, "Oh well, I could not have made it to the latrine anyway." Some poor guys did not even manage to get out of their sleeping bags - what a mess!! Everyone spent the next day on cleanup duty, understandably enough.

After leaving this airbase, we arrived back at Crissy Field. This time we were sent to airplane hangers. The kitchen was outside next to the bay. While eating, we had a hard time keeping the sea gulls out of our meals. They would fly right down while we were eating and help themselves. They could not be run off. We hollered and batted at them; they just kept coming.

We were carrying all the ammo we could carry. Our pockets and field jackets were full of ammo. They must have expected trouble. Every once in a while we could hear an accidental firing of guns. Our BAR (Browning Automatic Rifle) Man was reduced in rank and the BAR job was given to another soldier. He was in the back of a truck trying to find out how the gun worked. He accidentally fired the gun and the bed of the truck ended up full of holes. Fortunately, he was not hurt.

We were to be sent to Angel Island. At that time it was a Port of Embarkment for overseas but Japanese submarines were supposedly in the area, so plans were changed and we started patrolling the coast. We had a brief stay at Camp McQuaid, just outside of Watsonville, California which I remember because they had a large highway sign: "Artichoke Capitol of the World". I wonder if that sign is still there. While stationed at Camp McQuaid, we had an outbreak of crabs or lice (better known in the army as motorized dandruff). I was lucky that I was spared. Evidently some of the army six men wooden huts were infected.

From Camp McQuaid, we drove in a convoy to San Luis Obispo, which I thought was one of the better camps in California. I never was much of a drinker but, once while at San Luis Obispo, I got so homesick that I went to town to a bar on a pass. I had only one drink, but that was the first and only time that I ever considered going AWOL. I shrugged that thought off and went back to camp. Unless you have experienced it, a person really cannot know the feeling of being homesick. It has made more than one soldier go AWOL.

We were to be given two weeks furlough to go home. I had sent money home to be saved for furlough. Mother sent money to me through Western Union but they never sent it to camp. When the time came to receive furlough we had to show that we had money for transportation. I borrowed money to show my Commanding Officer to get furlough then returned the money to the lender. I left for Dallas with two or three dollars. I got lucky catching rides, for I made about as good time as I would have by train. At that time, civilians considered it a patriotic duty to share rides, especially with the military. After furlough was up, I returned to camp and all homesickness was gone. It seemed like, after that, I started enjoying the army. I was thinking about maybe staying in after the war.

April 1942						
S	M	T	W	T	F	S
			1	2	3	4
5	6	7	8	9	10	11
12	13	14	15	16	17	18
19	20	21	22	23	24	25
26	27	28	29	30		

Stop Sleeping On Top Of The Trucks
Late April, 1942

The patrol up and down the California coast continued. Our patrol perimeter extended from Eureka to the North and terminated at San Luis Obispo to the South. We prepared for desert maneuvers in the latter part of April 1942. We went down to Antelope Valley, which was like an oven. This hot desert was full of (I guess) sage bushes. The pale skinned northern boys did not handle heat too well. I was a little more accustomed to hot weather but this was still uncomfortable. The kitchen stove turned over and caught those bushes on fire. About one hundred of us took our G. I. fatigue jackets off to fight the flames. It took a lot of hard work from all of us to extinguish the fire.

PATTON'S, ILL FATED RAID

From Antelope Valley we moved on in to the Mojave Desert proper, just outside of Needles, California, where our division started on desert maneuvers. At the start of desert maneuvers, I was appointed Sergeant and performed messenger duties. Once, out in the desert, I was sent to the rear to deliver a message to the division artillery headquarters. On the way, an umpire drove up and declared me dead. On the way to the rear, I was again declared dead. They had not seen my black armband.

The 7th was a very good division and I was proud to be a part of it. The 57th FA Battalion was a crack unit with a fine complement of outstanding officers. Most of them had been with the battalion since its activation and later acquitted themselves very well in combat.

During desert maneuvers, we frequently received passes to go into the town of Needles, California. I always went to the Harvey House (an old motel chain located along the railroad) and rented a bathtub for fifty cents. Many of the men would go to the bars and buy beer while on their passes and, as everyone knows, a restroom becomes a necessity after a few beers. However, there were none available in Needles - all restrooms were locked while the soldiers were in town. Since there was no place to go, one sergeant got angry and relieved himself in the middle of Main Street. He was arrested, but the Commanding Officer of the Seventh Division came, had him released without punishment, and told the town officials that if the restrooms were not opened to the soldiers, he would put the whole town off limits. They did not want to lose our business so, from that day forward, the restrooms of Needles were open to the men in uniform.

Bathing facilities were made available. Showers were taken by numbers because of long lines waiting to bathe. You had so many seconds to get wet and soap down, then just a few seconds to rinse, then get out so the next group could do the same procedure. One night, my buddy, Sergeant Adrian Troop, and I got up around 2 A.M. and sneaked into the show-

24

ers. The only soap I had was the smelly orange colored Lifebuoy soap. We turned the water on and got wet. We then started soaping down good. We were feeling so proud of ourselves. We turned the facet on to rinse off and there was no more water. We had drained the pipes. I smelled like Lifebuoy soap until I could get another shower or a pass into Needles.

Desert maneuvers must also have been training for survival. One week we were given sardines and canned fruit juices. Another week we were given canned chicken and fruit juices. We also had cold chili. Everyone got so sick and tired of hot canned fruit juices that they would not drink them. I will bet there are about two truck loads of juices buried somewhere in Mojave Desert. Once, for water, we were allotted a half canteen of water to drink and half a helmet of water to bathe and wash clothes.

Before starting on desert maneuvers, we were given yellow fever shots in our buttocks. It looked as if those needles were two to three inches long. It turned out that the shots were defective and caused reactions in a large number of the troops. All during the maneuvers, there were about ten percent of the troops in and out of the hospital. It affected them like yellow jaundice. Eyes and skin had a slight discoloration. I was lucky to have no reaction, but some of the men had reactions for years. There were several soldiers who died in the desert due to perforation of the lungs (so they say) caused by sand and dust.

Once we were issued breathing masks before we drove off in a convoy for a mock battle. We drove for miles through sand that was like powder. We perspired so heavily that the powder was caked on our faces so you could not tell where the masks were. The maneuvers were supposedly against General Patton's tanks. I was in a jeep when those tanks broke through. It was frightening with those big tanks passing only a few feet from our jeep. It felt like no protection at all. To tell the truth, it scared the hell out of me.

The desert was full of sidewinders (rattlesnakes). One

25

afternoon, just as we were preparing to go to bed, a medic truck stopped and asked if we minded if they made camp next to us. We were glad to have the company. They killed eight rattlesnakes before going to bed. Everyone knew to give a good shake out to sleeping bags before using them. Rattlesnakes liked going inside sleeping bags. We started sleeping on top of the trucks' tarps to avoid snakes. Headquarters thought the trucks looked so ugly with all the tarps sunk in that orders were given to stop sleeping on the top of the trucks.

Once Sergeant T. R. Clifton called me aside and said he had enough dough to make a few hot cakes. I followed him to the kitchen only to find that mice were in all the batter. No hot cakes!

Latrines were dug in the sand about twelve to fifteen feet long and three to four feet deep. Sometimes, with all the various diets, there was a rush to the latrines. You always wanted to get an end position, for sometimes, there were four or five men using it at the same time. It was not too good scenery, looking at the backsides of soldiers straddling the ditch. Also we had to be very, very careful for those sand ditches easily caved in. I have seen several men getting out of a caved in latrine - including myself.

In September of 1942 I was promoted to Technical Sergeant. In the latter half of October, I was selected as Cadre and transferred October 31, 1942 to the 924th Field Artillery Battalion of the 99th Infantry Division to help train new recruits for the newly formed division at Camp Van Dorn, Mississippi (better known as Tar Paper City), located just outside of Centreville.

I left desert maneuvers with no transportation provided. I got a ride to the highway. Then, with three dollars in my pocket, I started hitchhiking to Dallas. There were so few cars that catching a ride was very difficult at times. It took about three days before I reached Dallas. Mother and Dad could not get over my very dark brown complexion from being in the desert for so long. Mother told me, she would wash my underwear and I told her they were all washed before I left the desert. She laughed at my washing, for all the underwear looked like sand. When I left home for Mississippi all my undies were again white. I stayed at home two or three days before I arrived at Camp Van Dorn around November 25th.

November 1942

S	M	T	W	T	F	S
1	2	3	4	5	6	7
8	9	10	11	12	13	14
15	16	17	18	19	20	21
22	23	24	25	26	27	28
29	30					

In The Middle of Nowhere
November 25, 1942

When enlisted cadre and newly appointed officers arrived at Camp Van Dorn, Mississippi, we found only a Tar Paper City built in a huge open field of red clay in the middle of nowhere. Everyone in the battalion had to pitch in to build walkways over the muddy ditches so we could get to the road. Second Lieutenant Don Spittler got the roughest assignment. Our Division Artillery Commander, General Seibert, saw Lt. Spittler working and asked him if he could build a mess hall. What else could Spittler do but say yes he could build a mess hall if he had a crew and material. He was given a crew, but the material had to be confiscated some way or other throughout the camp - in other words stealing it. Military Police, trying to find the stolen materials, kept checking the building, knowing that the supplies were coming from some place but could not prove it. Poor old Captain Pyatt had to try to explain where they obtained the supplies. Whatever he said evidently worked, so the mess hall was completed to General Seibert's satisfaction.

When racial troubles broke out in our camp, which I understood were happening in all the army camps in America, we were all confined to our area. The camp Military Police took control and, as far as I know, no racial troubles happened at Camp Van Dorn. I once went to Centreville, Mississippi, the only town near the camp, but found nothing to do, so I returned to camp. The town consisted of three or four stores and a few houses, about all, as far as I could tell.

At every headquarters where I was stationed, there was

a huge map of the world. We used to stand around and look at all the territory that the Japanese had captured in the Pacific - nearly all the islands, Korea, and a lot of China. Then we looked at all of Europe that had been captured by Hitler, and wondered how on earth the United States would ever manage to take all of that territory back - what an awesome task!

All the men were raw recruits, just out of city life. We had to give them basic training. Some of the men were illiterate and could not even sign their own names. On the payroll, they had to mark an "X". Some had never worn socks and became belligerent when they were made to wear socks. Inspections were made several times a day to make sure socks were being worn. One illiterate man, I will never forget his name. On his record, his middle initial was "O". I received word from Army headquarters that this man was not suppose to have middle initial. I called him to the office and told him that the middle initial he was using was not on his birth records. He grinned and proudly said that his recruiter gave him a middle name - Oscar. He was smiling and proud of his new name. Well, after about six months and a couple of inches of correspondence, I was so proud that he and his records were finally transferred.

Another incident happened. Two new recruits came by and said that they were assigned to 371st F. A. Battalion of the 99th Division but that they were lost and could not find it. I took them to the street and pointed to where they were to report, then called 371st F. A. I told them the recruits were on the way. About an hour later, I received a call from the 371st. They asked where were the recruits. I told them what I had done and they should be there by then. Six months later, the 371st called and said that the men had been found and sent back. The men said that they got tired of looking for the place to report and decided to just go back home.

Some of the recruits tried everything to get discharged. A couple kept wetting the bed. Some would get up at night and pretend they were walking in their sleep. We transferred them to the hospital for evaluation since we had no way to know.

In February 1943, I was appointed Warrant Officer, junior grade, and the following August I was promoted to Chief Warrant Officer. I was battalion personnel officer - solely responsible to the Battalion Commander only and under his direct authority. The new 99th Division consisted of all new recruits, mainly from Pennsylvania, West Virginia, Ohio, Illinois, and Indiana.

While at Camp Van Dorn, I finally got to where I liked Army life. I had decided that I would make a career in the

GENERAL ORDERS FOR SENTINELS ON POST:

My General Orders are:

1. To take charge of this post and all Government property in view.
2. To walk my post in a military manner, keeping always on the alert and observing everything that takes place within sight or hearing.
3. To report all violations of orders I am instructed to enforce.
4. To repeat all calls from posts more distant from the guardhouse than my own.
5. To quit my post only when properly relieved.
6. To receive, obey, and pass on to the sentinel who relieves me, all orders from the commanding officer, officer of the day, and officers and noncommissioned officers of the guard only.
7. To talk to no one except in line of duty.
8. To give the alarm in case of fire or disorder.
9. To call the corporal of the guard in any case not covered by instructions.
10. To salute all officers and all colors and standards not cased.
11. To be especially watchful at night and, during the time for challenging, to challenge all persons on or near my post and allow no one to pass without proper authority.

F. A. S., Fort Sill, Okla., (3-21-41—4000) 22994

"GENERAL ORDERS FOR SENTINELS ON POST"
POCKET CARD HARRY THOMPSON CARRIED (and saved as a souvenir)

Army. I tried to get a permanent position in grade promotions but at that time the Army was not transferring anyone to the regular Army. I had every intention of re-enlisting once the war was over.

I once decided to take an examination for Adjutant General Department. I passed, and word came to the battalion. My C. O., Colonel Clarke, asked me if I was transferring. I told him no way. I was happy where I was. I just wanted to see if I could pass the exam.

The funniest thing that happened at Camp Van Dorn was when Captain Frank Bell had been teaching the recruits how to pull guard duty - he spent quite some time telling them to challenge any stranger by calling out, "Halt! Who's there?" When they answered, proper procedure was to tell them to advance and be recognized. After he thought they had it down right, he picked the largest man in the group, gave him a club, and put him on guard at the motor pool. Late that night Captain Bell, as officer of the day, went by to check the motor pool. The guard called out "Halt, who is there?" The captain answered and the guard did not say anything. Bell asked what was the matter. Had the guy forgotten what to say? The guard raised his club and said, "Yes, sir, and you better not move till I remember it!". We all got a good laugh when Bell told us about it.

Camp Van Dorn was in the middle of nowhere. It was forty miles to Natchez, Mississippi, forty miles to McComb, Mississippi, and eighty miles to Baton Rouge, Louisiana. One of the most embarrassing things in my life happened at Natchez, Mississippi. I borrowed another soldier's car and drove to Natchez on a weekend pass. Sunday afternoon before I left for camp the gasoline gauge showed empty. Of course I did not have any gas coupons, so I went to a service station and told the station attendant I had no coupons but needed gas to get back to camp. After a lot of begging, he finally agreed to let me have five gallons. As he was filling the tank and had put only two gallons in, to my embarrassment, the tank ran over. I had no idea that the fuel gauge was broken.

30

In April 1943, General Walter Lauer was assigned as commander of the 99th Infantry Division. I would realize later, he was the best thing that ever happened to the 99th Infantry Division.

The usual basic training was accomplished and after several months of combat training, the division started on Louisiana Maneuvers in May of 1943, lasting until November of that year. The maneuvers started with two or three weeks training in Mississippi, where the red clay, after a heavy rain, was terrible. All the vehicles were covered with mud. Once, I had to go to Division Headquarters and, on the way back, my jeep driver and I became lost in the woods. After several hours of driving in circles, I saw a jeep approaching and flagged it down - I froze in mid-sentence asking directions when I realized that it was General Lauer, our Division commander. He said, "What is the matter, son, are you lost?" After I sheepishly admitted I was, he gave us directions back to our battery. I had not recognized his jeep because the mud on the front covered up the stars!

Chiggers (or red bugs) were also terrible while we were on maneuvers - one officer, Captain Pyatt (later killed during the Battle of the Bulge), had such bad chigger bites he had to be admitted to the hospital for a week. I always liked Captain Pyatt. He would never go on pass into town. He saved every penny. He said that after the war there was a wonderful girl waiting for him and they were going to get married. He said that his savings from his Army pay was $1500.

I think one of the most stupid officers we had was the commanding officer of Service Battery. He was rank happy and no one liked him. When we left for maneuvers, his wife somehow followed and spent each night with him in his pup tent. We would move, winding around in the woods with none of us knowing where we were, but when we stopped for night there his wife was. How she found our positions is beyond me. One day when we made camp, he called everyone in Service Battery together. I did not have anything to do, so I listened to his speech. His actual words were, "I am the smartest man to graduate from the University of Pennsylvania and I don't want any-one to doubt any decision I make." I just had to laugh. I heard some of his men say, "I'll kill that son-of-a-bitch if we ever go into combat together." Most of the men just laughed. That night he was immediately transferred. I do not know anyone who saw him go. Good riddance.

We also had to sleep with mosquito netting every night because the mosquitoes were awful. If I had to choose between desert and Louisiana maneuvers, I think that I would prefer the desert - both had their share of heat and snakes, but in the desert you marched on sand instead of mud and it actu-ally got cool at night and no mosquitos! In Louisiana, we had heat night and day, and the humidity was so high that our clothes were always soaking wet by nine in the morning.

We had to camouflage all vehicles by placing branches from pine trees or shrubs over them. Some of the small jeep trailers were camouflaged so well we lost them. We probably replaced them by finding vehicles lost on other maneuvers. The pine trees and many shrubs were so large and thick; it was understandable why vehicles were lost.

I saw a jeep stuck only twice and both times I was a passenger. Once, while driving through the woods, we got stuck on top of a log. The rear wheels would not touch the ground for traction. The other time, my driver drove us into a large hole. The rear wheels were straight up in the air.

One time, while we were on maneuvers, a tank column passed. It had to cross a bridge over a deep ravine. The driver did not turn just right and the tank fell off the bridge, landing on top of the tank commander who was standing on the tank, killing him. On maneuvers, it is not unusual for men to be killed or wounded.

The razorbacks (wild pigs) snorted around us all night every night while we slept - they were so bad that the trash pits from the mess hall had to be dug five or six feet deep to keep the hogs from getting in and scattering trash all over the place. One morning, 1st Lieutenant John Tompkins, came to the kitchen for a cup of coffee. He fell in the sump. We all had a big laugh and teased him for days.

We had a Battalion Medical Officer for whom I felt sorry. He was a little too old for a combat outfit and, before he had been called to active duty, he had been (according to him) a very successful pediatrician back home in Ohio. It had taken him years to build such a successful practice. The only trouble was he took to drinking to drown his troubles. When he could find no place to buy liquor, he would drink his medical supply of alcohol. Before maneuvers were over he was transferred. I never heard of him afterward. His replacement was Dr. Bernard Burbank, a young, very efficient doctor, liked by everyone.

One night a cold front moved in and we woke up with ice everywhere. Orders came down that all jeep windshields would be laid down. What a time for such orders to be received. I was in a jeep, feeling so sorry for myself, cold and wrapped up in my overcoat. I thought I was freezing. We came upon a bridge, which was barricaded, and a Military Police would not permit us to cross because it was simulated that the bridge was blown up. We had to detour to another bridge. I looked down in the river, and there were those poor combat engineers in waist deep water, building another bridge. After that I did not feel quite so cold. Another time, at another bridge that the Army said was not strong enough for our jeeps and trucks, we all started laughing, a large logging truck, loaded with logs, drove right over the bridge. No problem! We still were not allowed to use the bridge.

On one occasion, I escorted a prisoner to Camp Polk. Before I got to Leesville, Louisiana, near Camp Polk (and off-limits to military personnel at the time), I ran into my cousin, Captain Ralph Layne. Imagine, in the middle of nowhere, running into my own cousin. I still wish I had been able to stop and have coffee with him instead of the prisoner I was escorting.

During maneuvers, we lost many of our forward observ-

May-November 1943 Louisiana Maneuvers
Back Row: Sgt. Hartley, Cpl. Howell, Cpl. Bertram, Cpl. Ernest Clore. Middle: Cpt. Manny Mazer, Cpl. Jiles Lunsford. Front Row: Tech Sgt. Leibrock, CWO Harry Thompson, Cpl. Charles Dissinger, Cpl. Minert.

Maj. Gen. C.G. Lauer: "I talked to every unit in the 99ᵗʰ division".

Photograph as found on page 164 BATTLE BABIES, The story of The 99ᵗʰ Infantry Division in World War II, By Maj. Gen. Walter E. Lauer, courtesy Gen. Lauer's family.

CAMP VAN DORN, MISS.

Both service clubs burned down before Christmas. The camp was isolated and the men were not happy. The 63rd Division took over from the 99th when it went to the Louisiana maneuvers.

U.S. Army Photo. *as found on page 93* BATTLE BABIES, The story of The 99th Infantry Division in World War II, *By Maj. Gen. Walter E. Lauer, courtesy Gen. Lauer's family.*

"This Division was to gain for itself, on the field of battle, the sobriquet ' BATTLE BABIES.' "

"99TH 's FIRST YEAR EVENTFUL Raw Recruits of 12 Months Ago Now Field-Hardened Soldiers*"*

"The past year of the Checkerboard Division's existence has seen it develop through its various stages of training into an aggressive, fast-moving, hard-fighting outfit of soldiers which has won many commendations for its achievements."

"We completed our maneuver training and we're rated an 'Excellent' Division, 'Ready for Combat' on this our First Anniversary—The 15th of November 1943."

Publication permission courtesy of General Lauer's Family for Photographs and Quotes from General Lauer's Chapter IV, "Retrospect", including article published in The Checkerboard, *official newspaper of the 99th Infantry Division.*

Major General W. E. Lauer, C.G.

ers who were transferred to various other units destined for combat before we were fully trained and ready - many of them made the D-Day landings on June 6, 1944. Of those I remember, Lt. Harold Panich, Kansas City, Kansas, made D-Day landing (I think on Utah Beach, though I am not sure) and, a few days later while in the hedgerow, his right hand received a lot of damage. He spent a couple of years in the hospital. In 1969 I saw him and he was showing me how he could write again. A Lt. Hergenrather was sent to Italy, where he was badly injured. I do not know where Lt. Gus Mayer, Lt. Snellingburg, and others were transferred.

In Louisiana, my face broke out all over with small bumps (blisters) - the doc thought it was impetigo and began treating it as such - it did not get any better and was spread all over my face and neck by the time we got to Camp Maxey. I was put in the hospital and my face was painted with Genson Violet (a deep purple salve). All the guys and nurses took to calling me "Bluebeard," but, after a week or so, the doctors decided that it was not impetigo but some kind of chemical poisoning and treated it with sulfa drugs and an ultraviolet lamp and it healed almost immediately. I never figured out how I got it, and no one else in my division ever did as far as I know. After completing all these maneuvers, the 99th was rated an excellent division, ready for combat at the end of their first year.

November 1943						
S	M	T	W	T	F	S
	1	2	3	4	5	6
7	8	9	10	11	12	13
14	15	16	17	18	19	20
21	22	23	24	25	26	27
28	29	30				

The Best Move I Ever Made
November 1943

Truck convoy then moved us to Camp Maxey, just north of Paris, Texas. This delighted me no end, as my home was in nearby Dallas. What a great surprise! Camp Maxey, Texas was a beautiful camp. The buildings were painted white with green roofs. There were paved streets and grass around all the buildings. Everything was so clean. I had been in many Army camps and this, by far, was the prettiest of all, if you can call an Army camp pretty. Also, to set if off, I later found that the citizens of

Paris, Texas were the nicest to soldiers of any camp I had ever been in.

One of our officers, Lieutenant Claude Giraud, a field artillery observer, with whom I had gone to Natchez, Mississippi and to Baton Rouge, Louisiana, told everyone about his uncle, General Giraud of France. General Giraud came to the U. S. for a visit and the Army thought it would be nice for Lieutenant Giraud to visit his uncle in Washington D. C. An F. B. I. investigation was made and they found that Lieutenant Claude Giraud was no more kin to General Giraud than I was. I never saw him after that, and no one knew where he went.

Many things happen at an Army camp. We had a Pvt. (Name withheld) who was homesick and homesickness got to where it was interfering with his duties. He was given furlough to go home but, when he returned, I guess he could not control himself, for he slashed both his wrists and bled profusely. One of his buddies ran to my office and told me. I ran and got the medical officer who doctored him and then transported him to the hospital. They saved his life and put him in a padded cell until other doctors could evaluate him. Somehow, while in the cell, he removed his bandages and hung himself. He was pronounced dead. The whole battery was shocked by his death, for he was well liked. I was ordered to witness his autopsy. He was sent home for burial. Homesickness is an awful feeling and has caused many a serviceperson to do things that he or she knows better, such as going AWOL.

On base, there was an enlisted men's and an officer's club, which were open each evening for entertainment. On Saturday each club had a band for dancing. On one occasion, I brought my future wife, Virginia, whom I met in a grocery store in Dallas in January 1944, for an evening of entertainment. There were five or six other officers at our table, and girls were kept busy dancing. We all had a great time.

In our battalion, we had a Dr. Burbank who was also a very gifted saxophone and piano player. Lt. Shamblin, a guitar player, played with Bob Wills band before entering the service.

37

Virginia's brother, Jack and his wife, Helen, Virginia Wiley and Harry Thompson are pictured on a date at LouAnn's.

Harry says, "I could nurse a bottle of beer all night".

Lt. Balmert played the drums for bandleader Charlie Spivak, and our Lt. Chaplain (I think his name was Musgrove) sang and played piano. Once in a while, they got together and put on a show for us. All were very good.

While at Camp Maxey, I joined the Masonic Lodge. Dr. Burbank was also a Mason and helped me through all degrees. I remember only one man in our battalion who received a dishonorable discharge for stealing from another soldier.

I kind of missed maneuvers for, when on maneuvers, no charge was made for officers' meals, but in camp, we had separate mess halls and had to pay monthly for meals, whether we ate at officers' mess hall or not. The charge was minimal. The cooks always knew what I wanted for breakfast - three hotcakes and two eggs.

I still had the portable radio that I was given when leaving Continental Supply Company. I could not find the large battery required, but the radiomen always kept me supplied by wiring "D" batteries together to equal the strength of large battery. I do not know what I would have done without that radio.

Several times we were taken in groups of two or three, two or three miles from camp, and then given a compass. We had to go east or west to a designated spot and then retrieve a note to another spot. We kept on until the notes led us directly to our battery. That proved to be very good training.

Once some of the officers came in the barracks and had what looked like putty. They played catch with it and then threw it against the wall. I was getting out of there when they told me it was dynamite. They laughed and told me it would not go off without a cap. I still cringed every time they threw it against the wall.

In camp there were many German and Italian POW's who did not have too much to do. They picked up cigarette butts, and that is about all I ever saw them do. They all were from the German and Italian Africa Corps.

Some time around June 1944, the 395th Infantry Regiment and the 924th Field Artillery were sent just south of Abilene, Texas with some armored division on a special mock battle maneuver. Theoretically, according to the umpires, we won the battle against a whole division. While there, we were each issued a life size silhouette, which we erected where we were standing. We left, and that area was shelled with live ammunition. We returned later and all silhouettes were knocked down. Shrapnel had demolished my silhouette. While looking around, someone yelled, "Hit the dirt!" We fell down just as the engineers exploded a live 155mm artillery shell. A piece of shrapnel (a sharp jagged piece of steel) weighing at least a couple of pounds hit, no more than ten feet from me. I was lucky. I still have the piece of shrapnel, which I picked up and kept as a souvenir.

In July 1944 orders came to start building crates for

overseas shipment. The government knew exactly what each divisional unit, large or small, needed for overseas. Instructions were given to build each crate strong enough for an elephant to stand on. Everywhere we looked, someone was building crates. In going to divisional headquarters, it seemed so strange, seeing everyone doing the same thing. However, with a divisional strength of 14,500 men, a lot of crates were needed. Rumors had it that we were headed for Europe.

At Camp Maxey, all work was dedicated to the final preparation for combat. Morale was high, and I was very proud to be a member of the 99th Infantry Division. During my stay at Camp Maxey, I was able to visit home often. On January 12, 1944, while running to the grocery store for my folks, I met Virginia, the girl I would marry. That night we went to the movies, or the picture show, as we called them back then. I was fortunate to be stationed so close to home. I could come in and see my folks (and Virginia) nearly every weekend. Money was tight, but we could usually afford the movies and an occasional night of dancing. On a couple of occasions Virginia came to camp and we danced at the Officer's club.

We were married September 12, 1944 two days before my departure for an overseas staging area. This was the best move I ever made. We have been blessed with a loving daughter and three granddaughters. We have been married for over fifty-eight years and I love her more and more as time goes by.

September 13, the day after Virginia and I married, our family went back to camp with me. All our equipment had already been transported ahead of the battalion. I drove them around camp and, nearly everywhere we drove, we saw men with their barrack bags waiting for transportation to the train. It is a shame that about ten percent of these men never made it back home, for the 99th Division suffered heavy casualties. My family was just awed by the number of men they saw in the 99th Division. They said it was such a sad sight.

I boarded the train for Camp Miles Standish September 14, 1944

Virginia's Story

- As written Dec. 5ᵗʰ, 2001

"I met Harry in an A. & P. Grocery Store.

" My mother worked part time in Grocery Produce of the A. & P. She began working January 1944 when the grocery store manager, badly needing workers, asked her to help. She, like many women, considered filling in to help on the home front her patriotic duty.

"I came home from work and went next door to the store to see her. While there, I saw Harry. I told my friend Estelle at the coffee counter, 'I saw a cute soldier' and I pointed him out to her. She said, 'That is Harry Thompson; he is not married. He is shopping for his mother and they live on the street in back of the store.'

"I told Mother, 'See that nice looking soldier over there? His name is Harry and I want him." Mother said out loud, "Harry, she wants you." I nearly died! We eyed each other over shelves of canned goods and looked away when we caught each other looking.

"The next day, Estelle told me Harry wanted to meet me.

So that evening, she introduced us. He went over to Produce where Mother was working and I introduced him to Mother. Then we went over to our apartment where I introduced him to my Dad.

"We talked for about an hour, and he asked me for a date for the next night.

"We dated for nine months, then, on September 11, 1944, I told him goodbye, as he was to go overseas on September 12. We said we wanted to be married when he returned.

"He called me at work on the 12ᵗʰ and said he was coming in that afternoon. Sure enough, he came in and we went for a drive. I asked him where we were going and he said we were going to get married. We drove to Rockwall, Texas, got the Justice of Peace out of bed, and she married us. Our family and I took him back to Camp Maxie the next day. We saw all the boys with their bags packed and having a last beer. It was so sad and, when I had to tell him bye, it was the hardest thing I have ever done."

Virginia.

The Secret 99ᵗʰ
September 14, 1944

On September 14, my Battalion boarded a train for Camp Miles Standish, Massachusetts, the designated staging area for the port of embarkation at Boston, Massachusetts. As anyone in the Army knows, troop movement during wartime is a very hush-hush affair. I never could figure out how the soldiers' wives knew where we were going. They usually were accurately informing their husbands and also telling them when they would be leaving. Transporting the 99th Division took many long troop trains to move the entire division. Some took the most northern route through the U. S. Some went through the middle of the country and several others took the southern route through Louisiana, Mississippi, and Georgia and then along the Eastern coast to Camp Miles Standish, Massachusetts. We took the southern route. The train ride was rather uneventful, but an enjoyable trip. I spent a good bit of my time in the enlisted men's coaches. They were stacked up in bunk beds like a bunch of sardines, but I heard few complaints (come to think of it, all through training and overseas I heard very few gripes and complaints.) Several times I walked back to the caboose and chatted with the brakeman. During the whole trip, I was the only casualty - I got a cinder in my eye and a doctor at Camp Miles Standish had to remove it.

When the train pulled into Camp Miles Standish, huge steel gates, at least twenty feet high, opened for the train, then closed once we were inside. All of us had to get off and a high-ranking officer told us that the 99th was now a secret division. Secret? Good one! Everyone knew the 99th was at Camp Miles Standish. All 99th insignia and patches were removed, and we were direly warned to tell no one the name of our division. Then everyone was issued a pass to go to Boston.

A couple of weeks later, we were ready to leave for overseas. The Mess Sergeant from B Battery went AWOL to avoid going overseas. I am sure that, time and again, he regretted that stupid decision the rest of his life. As far as I know, he was the only one in our division to disgrace himself.

We boarded a train for Boston, our port of embarkation. We were told we could not even raise the shades on our window, and to talk to no one for this movement was secret. Then at the first town we came to, there was a huge crowd, a band playing "Over There," and pretty girls running up and down inside our cars. We had the shades in the train up, and the girls were blowing kisses (which we enthusiastically returned) and holding up big banners that said "Good Luck 99th." I never could figure out what the brass meant by "Secret"! By the time we reached the port of embarkation, needless to say, all the window shades were still up.

On September 29, 1944 we boarded the SS Exchequer, an English merchant Marine ship, for Europe. The powers that be decided we were still a secret division and gave orders for us to stay below deck until we were out to sea, then we could come up. When it was dark, our ship left Boston Harbor, all alone. The next morning, after we had assembled and begun sailing east, I took a stroll on deck. I had never before in all my life seen so many ships. We were on the bottom line of ships - as far as I would see, to the right and all the way to the bottom line, I saw nothing but ships: light carriers, sub chasers, destroyers, cargo ships loaded with airplanes, troop ships - a huge flotilla of American arms, troops, and supplies. Wow! Where did all the ships come from? To me, the personnel in charge of supplies were the real heroes of the war - they managed to deliver the supplies all over the world in a timely manner, making them available when needed. Just think - clothing, shoes, guns, tanks, and trucks, parts for repairs and replacement, even Bibles - What a gigantic task! Just providing doctors and medical supplies - to every corner of the earth was more than I could imagine. I have heard it said that it takes four supply personnel to support one fighting soldier in the field, and even though the combat soldiers grumbled about the "Supply pukes," we would have been in sorry shape without them.

The trip overseas was uneventful except for one notable occasion. A U.S. Navy submarine chaser supposedly located a submarine and was dropping depth charges about 1000 yards from our ship. We had our life jackets on, expecting the worst at any moment. The depth charges were sending huge sprays of water into the air. Our ship continued on course and, as far as the eye could see, the sub chaser had not moved from the spot where the submarine was supposedly located.

Our bunks were just below deck at the front of the ship. In rough water, the ship would rise thirty to forty feet, and then fall back. We had to take a deep breath and hold on. When the front of the ship fell back, it made a large crashing sound as if it was breaking up. I could never understand what kept the ship from breaking in half. Of course the ships were made to withstand rough seas.

Bathing on the ship was quite an ordeal. I took my regular soap to shower. Soap would not lather. We had to use special salt-water soap. After I got used to that soap, showers aboard ship felt pretty good.

I think the sickest men on the entire trip were Sergeant Carl Leibrock, Sergeant Burrell Hartley, Corporal Charles Dissinger, and Corporal Ernest Clore. Hartley would sit on the deck, propped up against the bulkhead, and spend the entire day nibbling on one Saltine cracker. The ship was from the British merchant marine, and I do not think they were as clean as the American ships. Whenever we opened the hatch, the stench was so bad we would gag on it. Other than the odor, however, the ship was fairly nice.

I do not know why, but I never got seasick. At times, I felt a little queasy, but a deep inhale of fresh air took care of that. When I went to the mess hall, I had no trouble eating anything they served, even liver and onions. Once the British cooks for the enlisted personnel, were going to cook chicken without removing the entrails before cooking. Our Mess officers raised such a fuss that the British cooks were made to remove the entrails before cooking.

I did have time to catch up on all my letter writing. On deck, I could not help but watch the baby aircraft carrier in front of us. I tried to figure how the airplane could be retrieved after its launching. A catapult made launching possible.

October 1944						
S	M	T	W	T	F	S
1	2	3	4	5	6	7
8	9	10	11	12	13	14
15	16	17	18	19	20	21
22	23	24	25	26	27	28
29	30	31				

The Ruins of War
October 10, 1944

On October 10, 1944, the ship anchored in the Firth of Clyde, a beautiful Scottish bay that was surrounded by high, emerald-green hills - Beautiful! Before debarking, we watched the ship's crew unload a cargo of mail contained in large canvas bags, which were hoisted over the side and dropped into small boats. We debarked by climbing down a rope ladder into a small motorboat. Once we were all ashore, we boarded a train at Gourock, Scotland to be taken to the southern part of England. En route, the train stopped briefly at the huge London rail station where the Salvation Army served us crumpets and coffee. Crumpets are a kind of biscuit with meat inside, and very tasty. We later arrived at Weymouth, England, a beautiful coastal town overlooking the English Channel on the southeastern side of England. All along the way from Scotland we looked for damage from the Luftwaffe's bombing raids on England, but saw very little - I think the English cleaned up the bomb damage very quickly. I did not get a chance to see any damage in London, and Weymouth was almost completely spared - I only saw one home that was damaged. I received several passes to go into town and found the people there very hospitable and courteous to the soldiers - more so, in fact, than some California towns which I have mentioned before. Salinas, for example, had signs posted on many lawns saying, "Soldiers, Sailors, Marines and Dogs Keep Off the Grass." Those signs made all of us angry - most of us at Fort Ord had been drafted into this mess, and we felt Salinas should have been placed off limits until those signs were removed.

While at Weymouth, I naturally went to the pub and tried a stein of warm or room temperature beer. Beer, much less warm beer, is really not to my liking, though. A couple of sips of that beer was all I could swallow. Beer in America is six percent alcohol. In Europe, beer contains twelve percent alcohol. I went to eat in the town hotel, a very old and prominent historic building. Signs were posted throughout the building noting the different English noblemen and kings who had stayed there at one time or another. I also visited a very old Masonic Lodge, where I had to show my Masonic card, with current membership, to a caretaker and prove myself to be a Mason before I was allowed to enter, even though the lodge was empty. Beautiful red velvet drapes hung throughout the lodge and original suits of armor, worn by knights attending the lodge in the Middle Ages, lined hall walls. I was told that the armor was hung in the exact location the knights hung their armor centuries ago while attending the meetings. The old suits of armor were priceless. There was a Worshipful Master's chair, prominently displayed, with a date of 1400 A.D. The lodge was truly beautiful. The caretaker told me that, back in the olden days before 1700, a man had to be a knight or better before he was even eligible to join the lodge. Knight or better? What is higher than a knight? King?

I also made several trips to our division headquarters, located in an old castle at Dorsetshire, several miles west of Weymouth. I walked around the castle and thought I could make out where the moat used to be. I walked up several flights of stone stairs, but most of the castle was roped off and I did not get to see too much of it. I wondered if the present owners were living in the roped off area. Living in that old castle would be very uncomfortable by today's standards - everything is drab stone and damp and cold inside.

Driving on the wrong side of the road was another unusual experience, especially with my steering wheel on the left side of the jeep and the English cars traveling on the left side of the road. I had to constantly remind myself which side of the road to drive, and invariably, if my mind wandered, I would catch myself on the right side of the road which was the wrong side. I had fun and did not hit anything, as there was not any traffic and I pretty much had the road to myself.

After our short stay at Weymouth, the battalion moved to Southampton, a major channel port in Southern England. A huge crowd of dignitaries came to see us off. Even the Red

Cross, since there was a lot of publicity, gave us a donut and a cup of coffee. We boarded a U. S. Navy LST to cross the English Channel at Southampton on or about November 2nd. The huge ramp was lowered, and we actually drove our jeeps and trucks on board the ship. I was surprised at the size of the LST and could not get over how many trucks the ship could accommodate, with plenty of room left over for the howitzers! After boarding, it still took several days for us to actually get across the Channel. I was bunked in a cabin with a Navy lieutenant and we became good friends. In one of our conversations, he commented that he could not obtain a watch but that the ship had plenty of other surplus items. I traded him my GI watch for a fur-lined Navy parka. That was the best trade I ever made - in the damp, cold weather I now had the warmest coat I had ever owned, and I was immediately reissued a new watch to boot! While en route, we were furnished a new set of impregnated clothing, which we had to put on before debarking. The clothes felt as if they had been dipped in wax and were very uncomfortable, but in case of gas attack they would repel any airborne gas - Miserable!

When we finally made it across, I was amazed at how close the LST pulled to the shore. They lowered the huge ramp again and we drove right off the ship and onto the beach. We landed at Le Havre, France, a port at the mouth of the Seine River. Part of the port had just been reopened; the rest was still blocked by sunken ships of all kinds, German and Vichy French. Mines were still in the water and, I understood that a mine struck one LST carrying 99th troops - no one was killed but the ship was beached away from the designated docking area. There were huge concrete gun emplacements, which the Germans had built in the harbor that had sustained heavy bombardment from the Air Corps and Navy warships.

The ruins of war were noticeable wherever you looked. What a mess! There were many half sunken ships blocking the harbor. Huge concrete gun emplacements, 8 to 10 feet thick, were toppled over like a child's building blocks. Other gun emplacements, visible at a distance on the high cliffs overlooking the port, had also been demolished. The town of Le Havre itself had sustained heavy aerial bombardment for several months prior to our arrival, and some sections of it were still in shambles. A short distance from the shore, there was what appeared to be a luxury resort hotel that was severely damaged by bombs and naval bombardment. It must have been a very popular beach for the French people.

As we drove off in a convoy we were told that our destination was Aubel, Belgium, some 285 miles to the North. We passed through Normandy, Amiens, Picardy, Flanders and many other French towns and provinces. In every French town we passed, the children came running out, begging us, not for food, but for chocolate and cigarettes. I even offered them food but they did not want it. I had plenty of cigarettes but did not give them any. Cigarettes and chocolate must have been a hot item on the black market. After we left France, I never saw another child begging. On the trip I think everyone started shedding their impregnated uniforms - they were too uncomfortable to wear, and lay discarded alongside the road all the way from France to Belgium along with gas masks that had been issued to us.

The first Belgian town of any size that we entered was Leige, where we saw our first buzz bomb. All through this trip, we passed battlefields littered with numerous disabled trucks, tanks, and other military vehicles, battle-scarred and rusting. They all had Nazi markings.

Aubel was a small town north of Verviers, Belgium. The 99th Infantry Division assembled at Aubel and became a unit of the Fifth Corps of the First Army, under the command of General Courtney Hodges. We relieved the Ninth Infantry Division on November 9, 1944. We now saw many more buzz bombs flying overhead. The buzz bomb was a small rocket, shaped like an airplane, which sounded a little as if an outboard motor was in the sky and delivered a payload of 2000 pounds of TNT. In the distance, we could hear the rumbling of heavy artillery fire. We wondered what might be ahead for us.

November 1944

S	M	T	W	T	F	S
			1	2	3	4
5	6	7	8	9	10	11
12	13	14	15	16	17	18
19	20	21	22	23	24	25
26	27	28	29	30		

Black Clouds of War
November 11, 1944

Drawing near to a combat zone is an eerie feeling - the excitement and adventure to which we all had been looking forward since our first day of training, coupled with the knowledge that many of us might never return. We were a little afraid that the war might be over before we had the chance to participate. Late on the night of November 11, 1944, in the distance where a battle was raging, the sky was bright from the constant artillery barrages. The next day it was very cold and, as the day dragged on, it clouded up and started to rain then, in the night, the rain turned to snow. Snow accumulated up to a foot in depth.

I had my first lesson in sleeping in the field in Europe while near Aubel - we had our pup tents set up (two men to a tent) with our sleeping bags on the ground and a Coleman lantern inside to keep the tent warm. I was comfy, if one can call sleeping in a pup tent in an open field comfy. I was, until orders came through late in the afternoon to take down and load the tents and our lanterns but to hold on to our sleeping bags. After the truck left, new orders came in telling us to stay where we were for the night. Those orders seemed stupid. Why couldn't we keep the tent and lantern? What good are tents and lanterns that probably stayed in the back of some truck all night?

It was misting rain and cold, so I obtained a truck tarp, folded it over, and put my sleeping bag inside. I took my clothes off, got in the sleeping bag and pulled the tarp over me. Around 4 a.m. I realized I could not breathe and frantically started kicking my way out of my sleeping bag. When I finally wriggled out I realized why I could not breathe - it had snowed about a foot and I was being smothered by the weight of the snow. There I was, standing in the snow with nothing on but my shorts and undershirt. It was so cold that I thought for sure I would freeze before getting dressed. After fumbling around in the cold for some time, which seemed like forever, I found my clothes and put them on, then ran in place to keep warm until the mess kitchen opened and I could get some hot coffee. I slept in my clothes while I was in the field after that!

That day we moved to Camp Elsenborn, a former Belgian Army camp a short distance from the town of Elsenborn, where we stayed for several days.

The Army camp shower house was elaborate - decorated tile through out and very roomy - somewhat different from buildings in the surrounding area. The Army barracks were roomy and very good except there were outdoor latrines, which in the cold weather were not the most enjoyable. They kind of reminded me of East Garrison of Fort Ord. On the campgrounds there were remnants of a German fighter plane that had been shot down. There was not much to see but curiosity got the best of me.

The first one scheduled to go on early patrol the next day was a second lieutenant that was bunked next to me. He was a forward observer for Artillery whose duty it was to call for artillery fire in case the patrol ran into trouble or sighted a good target. He was so worried and scared that he prayed half the night. I cannot say that I blame him for we had no idea

51

(other than maneuvers) what patrol was like. There was a chance that he might be shot or killed. You never know what will happen in war. The next day, after he got back, he was so relieved. I suppose the first time is always the worst.

Several times I drove to division headquarters. What a layout! Headquarters was located in (I don't remember where) a large beautiful brick castle (so they said). There was no tower and the castle was only two stories high. I turned in all reports that had been requested and then I reported back to my Commanding Officer, Lt. Col. Logan Clarke.

Snow and ice were an ongoing problem, especially for driving. While at Elsenborn, we were told to dig foxholes and be in them at a certain time, since there was to be a large air raid to the East of us and a bomb accidentally might be dropped from the planes passing overhead. Never at any time during the war did I see as many planes at once as I did during that raid. There were so many bombers going over us that they almost looked like huge black clouds of war. Their destination was unknown to us and fortunately there were no "accidental explosions" from premature bomb droppings. They did not pass over Camp Elsenborn on their way back. The rumors were that the planes bombed Cologne.

On Thanksgiving Day we had to move to the outskirts of Elsenborn. Our field kitchen was located in a stone building with a cement stairway going to the basement. The basement looked like it previously may have been a bomb shelter. It had thick cement walls.

The Mess Sergeant, Paul Matlock, had been issued all the ingredients for a turkey dinner with all the trimmings (Supply was something else. Most all the troops all over the world, where possible, received the same thing.) The meal was delicious with the exception of the potatoes. They tasted like rubber. Cooks had been issued dehydrated little squares of potatoes with no instructions on how to cook them. They were supposed to be soaked overnight but the cooks did not know this. Just as we had finished eating, someone hollered for us to look. A buzz bomb looked like it was coming right at us. We dove down those cement stairs. The self-steering aerial bomb used by Germany just barely missed us and exploded in a tree about five or six hundred yards away.

My brother Franklin wrote me a letter the day after Thanksgiving but I did not receive it until after the war. I still have it today:

> "Dear Harry,
> Thanksgiving was yesterday and of course we thought of you - wondering how you were and whether you were able to keep warm and what sort of special meal you had for that special day. . . . I am so thankful that you are still O.K. physically and haven't suffered any of the physical horrors of war and I trust that we can all be together again in the not too distant future, celebrating our return to civilian life - but I personally am not in favor of reverting back to a civilian form of life until the Germans and Japs are crushed. From your last letter I draw the conclusion that you are very, very close to the heavy fighting. All hell no doubt will break loose on the Germans before long . . ."

Little did I realize at the time how right he was, except when "all hell broke loose", it broke on us, not the Germans! Later on I was grateful that Franklin was spared the ordeal I went through. In the letter he had also offered to send me cigarettes or anything else I was having a hard time getting, and told me that his wife Helen had lost a cousin, who was killed on November 3rd during the fighting in Hurtgen Forest near Aaken, Germany, which was a few miles North of our area. Cigarettes. An Army truck issued us several packs of cigarettes a day at no charge and those in my group who did not smoke gave me their cigarettes. I had at least five or six cartons on hand and was smoking about four packs a day. I

53

always smoked a lot when nervous, and I was nervous!

From Elsenborn we were moved to Bütgenbach. The snow, slush, and ice were so bad that engineers, spaced at regular intervals all along both sides of the road en route, were shoveling sand and gravel under the tires of the vehicles. There was a railroad bridge that had been completely demolished. I know those poor men from the engineering battalions must have been freezing from shoveling while standing in all of that snow and ice in near or below zero temperatures. My thoughts went back to Louisiana maneuvers, remembering how those combat engineers were standing waist deep in cold water. I just do not think the combat engineers are given the credit they deserved. They definitely deserve it. To my thinking, they have one of the worst jobs in the Army.

"On the Rhine between Koblenz and the Dutch frontier – some 125 miles – lay 21 bridges, prime targets for the Allied air force but vital for the 'Watcht em Rhein' build-up. Düsseldorf-Neuss railway bridge was demolished as the Germans retreated."

(The above quotation and the two photographs of the bridge and their cutlines are reprinted here by permission and are found on page 101 of *Battle of the Bulge Then And Now* by Jean Paul Pallud With Credits to *After the Battle* magazine 1984, Battle of Britain Prints International Limited, London, England, Publishers.)

The above picture is how the bridge looked when I was

"A striking comparison of the railway bridge near Berg, passed by; the men of the 26th Regiment when they moved up to Bütgenbach on December 17. (US Army)"

there. The first time we went through, the road was covered with snow and ice, combat engineers clearing the way. The book, *Battle of the Bulge Then and Now* from which these pictures are copied, states that the bridge is "near Berg". All I knew at the time was that the bridge was near Bütgenbach.

We stayed one day and a night at Bütgenbach in the basement of a church. At least the building was very warm. I had no idea as to the religion. We then moved to Malmedy around December 9, 1944. Our kitchens usually had hot coffee and, let me tell you, you have never really experienced hot coffee until you've had to drink it out of a metal canteen or cup - there is no way to keep it from burning your lips! No sugar or cream was available and I got so sick of black, scalding hot coffee that I made a vow never again to do without cream or sugar when I got back home! I have kept this vow.

It was extremely cold and the snow was deep.

This country was just beautiful as you can see in a postcard given to me by the lady in whose house we stayed!

The trees were so laden with snow that their limbs touched the ground.

55

(Picture postcard, no printing on card other than picture, courtesy of the lady in whose house I stayed in Elsenborn.)

If it had not been so cold I might have enjoyed the scenery more; I had rather be in a warmer climate and look at pictures of beautiful scenery of snow! Being from Texas, I never was used to seeing lots of snow and was amazed at the size of the snowflakes, which were as big as silver dollars and just floated gently down from the sky. Snowflakes were coming down so thick and fast you could not see for more than a few yards. Along with two other officers, I was assigned upstairs to a large, two-story brick home in downtown Malmedy, where we stayed for two days. The residents of the house lived downstairs. The residents in the house would talk to us but we had no idea what they were saying. All I knew to do was to smile back like I understood.

We got to take a bath in real hot water that was heated by a wood-burning heater. The people downstairs were kind enough to prepare baths for the three of us. Little did I realize that this bath would be my last bath until May 8, 1945! My gosh, that is five months! We slept on the thickest feather down mattress I had ever seen. The mattress was so thick that when I lay down in the middle, I sank until both sides rose up higher than my head. Now, for two brief days, that was real life! We did live it up while we could.

People of Elsenborn were gracious and welcomed us. When our Army needed a place for us to stay, people of Elsenborn left and stayed with family or friends so we could have the houses we needed. The lady of the house where we stayed gave me two postcards, one of the trees of Elsenborn in

This treasured postcard, also given to me by my hostess, shows a house typical of the one in which we stayed.

the snow and one of her house. It may have been her house, though with our language barrier, I cannot be sure.

We were then moved to Büllingen where I was assigned to the Service Battery Command Post for quarters, which were also located in a large two-story brick home. I slept in a back room upstairs. Shortly after we arrived I had to drive either to Verviers or Leige on some errand or other for Colonel Clarke, my CO. When we stopped at HQ (Headquarters) we were inter-rogated and had to show ID and give the password of the day. There I saw a detail of troops unloading a truck full of frozen corpses. I do not know if they were American or German, but their stiff bodies and contorted expressions left a nasty im-pression in my mind. Little did I know I would see many such bodies in the days ahead.

Every night just after dark, a single engine German plane flew over. We never could see the plane. We called him "Bed Check Charlie". We could tell it was a German plane because it was a single engine plane and the sound of the motor was somewhat different than ours. It must have been like our Ar-tillery Observer planes.

One morning, I caught a large red rooster and put him in the attic of the Command Post. I went to see Sergeant Paul Matlock. I told him about the rooster. Soon we were going to have chicken and dumplings. I wonder what happened to that rooster when we began receiving all that artillery fire, first from the Germans then from the American artillery fire. (Both Ameri-cans and the English often despairingly called the Germans "Krauts". The Germans called American POWs "Kriege" when referring to more than one and "Krieg" when referring to only one of us. They also were heard to call us "Ame" which some of us thought meant "lover" though the *Ramdom House Dictio-nary* says "Ame" is the first syllable of the German word "Amerika".). Maybe the Krauts ate my rooster.

While at Büllingen we spent time doing routine duties and I made several trips to our artillery's forward CP to report to my commanding officer, Lieutenant Colonel Logan Clarke, of the 924th Field Artillery Battalion. On my first trip there, my driver Private Hutton saw a plane flying right at us - we stopped the jeep and dove into a snow bank, but it was not a plane after all - it was a V-1 buzz bomb flying no more than fifty or sixty feet off the ground. It must have just been launched - we had mistaken it for a German pursuit plane coming after us. We stopped the jeep and dived into a snow bank, trying to avoid being strafed. We both felt a little silly for our mistaken identification. (Little did I realize that, four days later, Private Hutton would be killed. He was found, frozen stiff, the later part of January 1945 and I heard he was shot December 17 while running through the woods trying to escape. Pvt. Hutton was a nice young man, very nice looking, and he was either eighteen or nineteen years old. He was from Philadelphia, Pennsylvania. He never mentioned his mother and said that his grandmother raised him.).

Each of our artillery battalions was located somewhere near the Siegfried Line, the main system of fortifications along the German - Belgian border. We drove for several miles. Various artillery units, positioned up and down the road, were shooting harassing fire. Several rounds were fired as we drove by. Every night our front line troops were shooting at buzz bombs, which we understood to be aimed at Antwerp, Belgium, our principle supply port. Tracer bullets from their machine guns looked like lines of sparks from a large fire. Sometimes the V-1's were hit by American fire and exploded in our area, causing some damage.

On December 14 I made a trip to each of the firing batteries. I arrived at A Battery at noon, just in time for lunch - I asked Captain Donald Spittler where on earth the good steaks came from - He laughed and said they had killed a cow and had plenty of fresh meat. If they had been caught killing a cow, everyone in A Battery had agreed to pitch in and pay for it. I would have liked to eat with them every day. Captain Spittler and I had been good friends. Both of us had joined the 99th Division at the same time. He was a fine officer who came up from the ranks. We still keep in touch with one another.

December 15 - Today the Salvation Army truck came into our area, two girls were serving free donuts and coffee - Hope they got out of this area before the 17th. The Salvation Army, as far as I know, never got publicity for giving free coffee and donuts to the troops. We never saw a Red Cross truck come into the area. If they did, they would probably want to charge us a dime. (During the war, a dime to me was a lot of money.)

59

We were about to be caught up and swept away in one of the most furious battles of the Second World War. Hitler's last great gamble of the war was a carefully planned attempt to drive a wedge between the American and British Armies and seize the main Allied supply port at Antwerp, Belgium, then drive the British into the sea in a bloody repeat of Dunkirk. The main drive, to cut through our area, which later came to be known as the "North shoulder of the Bulge," ground to only a halt at Elsenborn Ridge in one of the bloodiest confrontations of the entire war. Unbeknownst to us, the 99th lay squarely in the path of Hitler's advancing legions.

December 1944

S	M	T	W	T	F	S
					1	2
3	4	5	6	7	8	9
10	11	12	13	14	15	16
17	18	19	20	21	22	23
24	25	26	27	28	29	30
31						

No Way To Escape
December 15, 1944

Around 7 p.m. the evening of December 15 a First Lieutenant came to the Service Battery Command Post and asked for information as to the location of Headquarters Battery and all firing batteries. The service battery commander, a Captain whose name I will not mention, gave him all the information he requested and also showed him the exact locations of all the batteries on an overlay map. Everyone in the CP at the time tried to get the Captain to identify the lieutenant by password, I.D., or something, but he would not listen to anyone, just saying that the man was O.K. Here we were, right near the front lines, and this stupid officer was not even checking ID's! In the rear, ten miles away, you could not get from one place to another without being challenged and thoroughly checked out. He later admitted he did not even know the lieutenant. All I can say is that the captain was just plain stupid and hardheaded. We found out later that each of our firing batteries and the headquarters battery had been accurately surveyed, and each battery of our battalion came under extremely heavy artillery fire on the morning of December 17, 1944. I have a feeling that the German dressed as a U.S. First Lieutenant had a big laugh over how easily he got all the information on the entire 924th F. A. Battalion! (I imagine he was a member of the Skorzenzy brigade, an elite unit of English speaking German Commandos under the command of the famous SS officer assigned to infiltrate the American lines before the battle began.)

A footnote appears on page 42 of *99ᵗʰ Division Battle Babies* by Maj. Gen. Walter E. Lauer, which his daughter's family has so graciously given me permission to quote:

> *"Wire communications had been shot out and radio was the sole means of transmitting messages. The C.O. 924ᵗʰ F.A. Bn. (Lieut. Col. Logan Clarke, U.S.A.) writes: 'The Germans had captured plenty of American equipment and we received a call at the fire direction center that night, directing me and my battery commanders to meet Gen. Black, the division artillery commander, at a certain set of coordinates. When checked these turned out to be well out in the West Wall. This came through in perfect English. We cursed the sender in voluble English and meager German! Later on I thought, 'Jesus! Suppose that had been Gen. Black?' We lost in that operation of the 16ᵗʰ-17ᵗʰ Dec. three 105 howitzers, ninety men and officers and 40 vehicles.' "*

During the morning of December 16 we were ordered to dig foxholes since there might be enemy paratroops in the area. Enemy in the area? The brass had to be kidding. Later we were grateful for those orders, for the foxholes we dug saved a lot of lives during the initial tank attack the next day. Headquarters had not been kidding. A few paratroops with rifles and machine guns are one hellava lot to worry about!

Later that night, about 7 p.m., an American antitank unit came rushing through our area, heading north. The column was in such a hurry that when one of their armored antitank vehicles broke down right in front of our Service Battery Command Post, the crew jumped out and immediately boarded another vehicle without bothering even to see what had broken. The crew left behind all guns and ammunition. All crew acted like they were scared to death. As the column passed by, the men shouted that the Krauts were right on their asses and for us to get the hell out of this sector. We immediately radioed the information to our headquarters but were told not to move from our position and again, there was "nothing to worry about". So we stayed where we were and bedded down for the night around twelve or one o'clock. I never have felt that the order to stay in our sector should in any way be a reflection on our Battalion Commander because he received and obeyed orders the same as we did and did not know why the antitank unit fled through our area. I later learned that this fleeing antitank unit was supposed to help support and protect the southern flank of the 99th Division, which was spread out for about fifteen or twenty miles up and down the Siegfried Line.

After the war, I heard that the antitank group Commanding Officer was relieved of command for leaving the combat area and leaving us exposed without protection. I also learned that the 6th and the 15th Waffen S.S. Panzer Armies formed the spearhead for Hitler's offensive destined for Antwerp, Belgium, the main supply port for the Allies. This supports my opinion that the reason the Germans were able to break through Lines of the 106th Infantry Division and come through our area so fast was because the antitank unit which had retreated through the 99th Division area the night before left little or no resistance. The Germans came into our area and were stopped. At that point, exactly where the 99th and 2nd Infantry Divisions were stationed, at what became known as the "Elsenborn Ridge" or "North Shoulder of the Bulge", their main thrust was completely stopped. In my opinion, the battle on Elsenborn Ridge proved to be more important than some of the battles that took place in the South. The 6th and 15th Panzer Armies had been given the main role in the German Break-through, code-named "Wacht am Rhein" and the 99th and 2nd Divisions were able to completely stop the German drive cold. It was one of the major turning points of the War!

This should be no reflection on the ability of the 106th Infantry Division because they received the first surprise blow of the Bulge. They were surrounded. They fought bravely and, after running out of ammunition, their only alternative was to surrender.

Nothing was happening, so I tried to get a little sleep. I was in a room on the second floor of the house where the service battery CP was located. I thought I would never go to sleep that night as I lay on my cot wondering what was happening. Those antitank vehicles came from the direction of Honsfeld, a small village a couple of miles south of our position. In fact, that area was supposedly well manned - it was supposed to be a rest area for our division. In fact, actress Marlene Dietrich was supposed to come entertain our division on the morning of the 16th, but she was whisked off to the rear as soon as she arrived, further proof, to my mind, that the brass knew the Germans were up to something.

I finally did get to sleep. It seemed I dozed for only a few moments when all hell broke loose. At 5:30 a.m. an intense German artillery barrage opened up on the town of Büllingen. I had undressed before going to bed, thinking I would be O.K. indoors, and now I hopped around in confusion, trying to get dressed in the dark and find my socks and boots - I nearly put my pants on backwards! After a short eternity I got on all my clothes, in some semblance of order, only to be knocked down by the explosion of an artillery shell right in the room next to mine! If I had not had such a hard time getting dressed when the shell hit I would have been in that front room, where the stairs were! Now there was a huge gaping hole in the front wall, big enough to drive a Sherman tank through. Our liquor ration, issued the day before, had been stored in the room that was hit, and now the place smelled like a distillery! (The liquor ration, which consisted of one quart each of bourbon, scotch, sherry, champagne, cognac, and wine, was issued to officers only. I, as an officer who did not drink much, ordered everything they had and let the men under me have it. The colonel saw my list once and said, "Damn, Thompson, you sure drink a lot!" Then he grinned and winked - he knew what I was

63

doing with it!)

The artillery barrage let up shortly thereafter, so I went to the mess kitchen, about a block away, for a cup of coffee and a chat with Mess Sergeant Paul Matlock, a longtime friend of mine. He had also been transferred from the 7th Infantry Division about the same time as I had. We talked for some time about the early morning barrage, but none of his crew was hurt and, as far as we could find out from others, there were few injuries to anyone in the battery. The damage to the town was considerable. The weather was bitterly cold and the hot coffee tasted really good. After an hour or so, I refilled my canteen cup and went back out into the snow and cold towards my quarters. On the way, the artillery started up again, this time with "screaming Meamies," shells that make a loud shrieking sound. They were falling all around, so I fell to the ground to keep from being hit by flying shrapnel. It sounded as if each shell was going to land on top of me. Screaming meamies are meant to disrupt morale and, at the same time, tie the enemy down. They darn sure will tie you down. I will have to give the Germans credit for they did a very good job of scaring the hell out of me.

Suddenly the artillery stopped and German Tiger tanks came lumbering into town. With machine guns on the tanks, SS soldiers standing up in the tanks were firing at anyone in the street and at windows of houses. I tried to run to my quarters but the machine gun fire from an approaching tank prevented me from entering so I ran down a side street just north of my building. I have no idea how to explain how scared I was. I could hear the whining of bullets and the thud of them hitting the brick house. The machine gun kept firing after me, so I ran to the far side of another house where another approaching tank from a parallel street also began firing. I ran to the other side of the house, where a third tank opened up on me. I guess I ran around that house five or six times, ducking machine gun fire all the way, until I dove beneath a two-and-a-half ton truck and jeep that were parked bumper to bumper, both truck and jeep burning fiercely. I lay under those trucks, afraid they would blow up at any minute, scared, cold and shaking like a leaf in a hailstorm. What an eerie feeling. Here I was, under the truck, in plain view of the enemy, the truck and the jeep burning fiercely. I just knew that either the truck or the jeep was going to explode at any time. I knew that usually there are extra gas tanks strapped to Army vehicles.

I looked out from under the truck and saw a Kraut in a black uniform - an SS officer - standing up in a tiger tank and firing a burp gun directly at me. (A burp gun is a machine gun that fires so fast it sounds like a burp. I was told it was the fastest firing gun of the war.) How he missed me I do not know. The Lord was surely watching over and protecting me that day. I could feel and hear the bullets whizzing by and hitting next to me. Snow and dirt were flying up and hitting me in the face. I tried to fire back at him with my forty-five pistol, but I had used up all my shells firing at the black uniformed Germans on pursuing tanks. To this day, I do not know if I hit anyone or not but at least I got the satisfaction of shooting back. I really doubt if I hit any of the Krauts because they were small moving targets standing on tank tops and I was firing on the run, not daring to stop lest I be hit by their machine guns. Those were the only shots I fired at the enemy in combat during all of World War Two.

Every time I had passed the front of the house I had desperately tried the door only to find it locked. As I lay beneath the burning trucks, with burp gun bullets whizzing around me, a buddy unlocked the door from the inside and I half crawled, half ran inside, gasping for breath. Once inside, I went down to the cellar where I found nine other GI's. The only names I can remember of men who were there are Corporal Charles Dissinger of Lebanon, Pennsylvania and Corporal Ernest Clore of Louisville, Kentucky (both now deceased). Part of the cellar had been used to store coal, and the entire room was only about eight by twelve feet. I ran to an upstairs bedroom to get a look around and search for a way out. From

65

there I saw many tanks and troops surrounding our position. There was no way for us to escape, so I went back to the cellar with the others and hoped that we would not be discovered until nightfall. Then, maybe, just maybe, we could sneak out the back door and make our way to American lines.

December 1944						
S	M	T	W	T	F	S
					1	2
3	4	5	6	7	8	9
10	11	12	13	14	15	16
17	18	19	20	21	22	23
24	25	26	27	28	29	30
31						

Standing in the Snow In Their Skivvies
December 17, 1944

From a small window in the cellar we stood and watched the street outside. We could see many tanks, troops, and military vehicles passing by, all bearing the black cross of the Wehrmacht. One of the tanks had an American soldier on the front of it. He had been put there by the Krauts to serve as a human shield in retaliation for knocking out a German tank by using the only bazooka that had been issued to our Service Battery. We could see he was scared to death as the tank, with him as target, rattled down the road. We immediately began discarding any and all personal items we had in our possession that might be German: watches, money and even such personal items as my Masonic membership card. I had a new Masonic ring and I threw it as far away as I could. My dad had given me a new dagger just before I left for overseas duty. I prized that weapon and I had both sides so sharp that I could have shaved with it. I jammed the blade between two bricks in the wall and snapped it in half - I wonder if the tip is still buried in that cellar wall. We had been instructed before going overseas to destroy or discard any personal items if we thought that capture was imminent. Before running into the house, I had thrown into the snow a new gold pocket watch (either German or Belgian make), as far as I could throw it. Scuttlebutt had it that if you were caught with any German items on you, the Krauts would assume you had been stealing from their dead and shoot you on the spot. I was not taking any chances.

We were trying to decide where would be the best place to hide until night and what might be our best escape route. We all agreed on staying put till dark. The town was filled with soldiers and there was no way to escape. German tanks and infantry were moving so fast that we knew we must already be two or three miles behind enemy lines. There was no way out and the cellar seemed as good a hiding place as any. I found myself thinking of home, and I knew my wife and family would be worried about me for they had a good idea where I was located from my letters giving hints as to my location.

Around 11 a.m. one of the men heard footsteps coming towards us from the hall. Suddenly I heard, "Raus! Raus!" I was so scared, wondering what was going to happen to us. We walked out towards the Germans, hesitantly, with our hands raised. I noticed that one of them was holding a potato masher grenade in his hand, ready to toss it down into the coal cellar if we did not come out as commanded. We were then marched outside to the back of the house and the ten of us were lined up against the brick wall. I thought, " My God, they are going to kill us all." All I could think of was my wife and family, whom I loved so much. Who would have dreamed that my life would end like this, so far away from home? Is this really happening to me? My legs were shaking - there is no way to describe just how scared I was, and there was absolutely nothing I could do about it. I could hear the other men and they seemed just as scared as I was. These goons are crazy, I thought. They are actually going to shoot us. I might have expected this kind of treatment from the Japanese, but not the Germans - I had always thought they were more civilized than that! I thought the Geneva Convention agreements were made to prevent massacres.

The soldiers now moved about twenty-five feet in front of us, rifles raised and ready to fire. Suddenly a German officer came running up, motioning them to stop. We heaved a

67

"SS-Obersturmbannführer Jochen Peiper, commander of SS-Panzer-Regiment 1, photographed in the autumn of 1944."

(Photograph reprinted here by permission, Battle of the Bulge, Then And Now *by Jean Paul Pallud With Credits to* After The Battle *magazine 1984, Battle of Britain Prints International Limited, London, England, Publishers, p. 43.)*

huge sigh of relief. He talked to his comrades for several minutes and evidently instructed them to move us to the road where other American prisoners were already lined up. I later found out that these soldiers were under the command of SS Colonel Jochen Peiper, a hard core supporter of Hitler. They were the same ones who, later in the day, massacred all those American soldiers just outside of Malmédy.

Luckily, I happened to be on the front row - I did not really want to be conspicuous, but it's a good thing I was there because I could see my sergeant, Sgt. Burrel Hartley, hiding in a foxhole. The Germans were clearing out all the American GI's, shooting all men still in foxholes. I hollered at Hartley to raise his hands and get out of the foxhole if he did not want to

The house still standing on the left with the big hole in the front was the house where I slept and the house that was hit while I was trying to get dressed. The house in shambles on the right is the house where I was captured. It was demolished shortly after I was captured.

(This photograph is reprinted here by permission of Battle of the Bulge Then And Now by Jean Paul Pallud
With Credits to After the Battle magazine 1984, Battle of Britain Prints International Limited, London, England, Publishers, p. 140.)

get shot, and he complied. As we lined up, without any provocation, a Kraut hit one of our men in the chin with a rifle butt. Why?

The first thing they made us do was discard our steel helmets. They allowed us to keep the wool helmet liner caps, which we needed in the bitter cold. As we proceeded to walk, we noticed that the Krauts were playing around with the captured jeeps, driving up and down the street, blowing the horns like they were little children who had never heard a horn before. We passed the house where I had slept the night before and I saw where that artillery shell exploded. The whole front room of the second floor had been demolished - I was glad I had slept in the back room!

Suddenly everyone looked up as our captors opened fire on artillery observation planes trying to escape - fortunately they got away to safety. After that, the guards stopped our column and some other Germans, apparently SS troops, started shoving us around, making certain GI's remove some of their clothing. Apparently, the uniforms were needed to complete the outfitting of special German SS troops who were to infiltrate our lines and create havoc and confusion while wearing American uniforms. That must have been the reason they did not shoot us. Thank God they wanted uniforms! Although they mostly took overshoes and overcoats, they even took some men's pants away and left them standing in the snow in their skivvies. They did not take anything from me but I sure felt sorry for those men who had to march in the bitter cold without shirts and pants. We walked past our mess hall, where earlier I had shared coffee with Sergeant Matlock. I hoped he was all right. The temperature felt like it was at least zero - hell, I was raised in the South and never got used to this kind of weather.

A footnote appears on page 36 of *99ᵗʰ Division Battle Babies* by Maj. Gen. Walter E. Lauer. His daughter's family has graciously given me permission to quote:

"Lieut. Col Logan Clarke, U.S.A., the C.O., 924ᵗʰ F.A. Bn., writes: 'My service battery commander came into my C.P. at about 7:30 A.M. to see if there was anything we needed. His battery of sixty-nine men-battalion motor maintenance section, personnel section, ammunition train, etc.- was set up in Büllingen. We talked things over and he returned to his battery rather hurriedly at about 8:15, for at about 8:00 A.M. someone brought in a rumor that a tank-destroyer unit near Büllingen had been overrun by German tanks. (Completely incredible, we thought.) About 9 A.M. I received a radio from him, now in Büllingen, that a number of German tanks were in the town, etc. I told him to get out and go to Elsenborn. They did not make it. Almost all were captured along with six forward observers who were there for a rest. One officer and six men, ammunition handlers, escaped. One of these men was credited with killing two German tank commanders and three other Germans. These six came back to Elsenborn about the 19ᵗʰ

Dec., completely shell-shocked. We had T.O.T.d Büllingen time after time with seven to ten battalions of artillery. How they lived through it is a wonder. Those captured we picked up again in Moosburg in April."

(Photographs p. 71-p. 75 of captured POWs. Pictures of Dietrich, Peiper and Nuremburg trial and cutlines are reprinted by permission Battle of the Bulge Then And Now *by Jean Paul Pallud with credits to* After the Battle *magazine 1984, Battle of Britain Prints International Limited, London, England, Publishers, p. 136.)*

This picture is marked: "Their somewhat anxious glances are contrasted by the satisfaction on the face of the Walther-armed paratrouper."

I am behind Captain Cobb (indicated by an arrow). Captain Cobb (in front of me), Sgt. Leibrock, Cpl. Clore, Sgt. Hartley and several others were looking up, as was one of the guards. Though we, as prisoners, were "somewhat anxious", actually we were looking up, watching our liaison planes escape.These two photographs show my group just after we were captured. Actually, this line was behind our group. It was one line, not two as the pictures make it appear, and it was my luck to be near the front of column.

"Into the bag. Casually led by a member of 3. Fallschirm-Jäger-Division, these eighty or so 'Checkerboard' GIs were captured at Honsfeld (sic)."

The *Then and Now* Book was wrong; these pictures were taken in Büllingen, not Honsfeld. I recognize both guards. It is still a strange sensation to see myself in pictures like these, pictures made by the Germans, pictures of an "early conquest of Pieper".

"Note:" I, would would also change the last line of Col. Clarke's footnote to read "SOME captured we picked up again in Moosburg in April"! As you know, I remained a POW in the hands of the Germans.

December 1944

S	M	T	W	T	F	S
					1	2
3	4	5	6	7	8	9
10	11	12	13	14	15	16
17	18	19	20	21	22	23
24	25	26	27	28	29	30
31						

Spared For Our Uniforms
December 17, 1944

German military was every bit as brutal as I had heard. Hitler had evidently done a good job of training brutality into his soldiers - all the troops around us seemed to be well-trained and hardened soldiers. They were the elite of Hitler's army - Waffen SS troops. At the time, I could not tell if they were Wehrmacht or SS, but I do not think any of them had ever heard of the Geneva Convention. If they had they could have cared less. (Later on I found out that the 99th had been hit,

"Josef 'Sepp' Dietrich together with Generalfeldmarschall von Rundstedt at the beginning of 1944, when Dietrich held the rank of SS-Obergruppenführer and was commander of the I. SS-Panzerkorps. By December he had been promoted to SS-Oberstgruppenfüher and was in command of 6. Panzer-Armee. (Bundesarchiv)"

73

full force, by the German 15th and 6th Waffen SS Panzer Armies. The SS Panzergruppe led by SS Colonel Joachim Peiper on December 16 and in the early dark hours of December 17 massacred many American troops who had surrendered at Honsfeld; in the dawning hours of December 17 broke through our sector in Bülligen to capture us; and in the hours after our

"Joachim Peiper, one of the 'stars' of the trial, was interrogated on June 19." "Just like the corpses at Malmédy, each defendant suffered the ignominy of being numbered."

capture continued to kill those outside Malmédy. Why they spared us I do not know, unless it was for our uniforms.)

At home, the German prisoners had been treated very well - I had seen many Africa Corps veterans being held at Camp Maxey. They had nice clean barracks and ate the same food (or better) that we did. What a contrast to what lay ahead for me! German officers held in Camp Maxey did not have to

"In all 74 defendants were brought to trial. The concentration camp at Dachau, just north-west of Munich, provided ready made accommodation for prisoners of war in the American Zone of Occupation, and its former use was no doubt considered ironic justice for the SS who were to be its new inmates. The trial was held in Building 230 of the original SS camp alongside the compound under the auspices of the Third Army. (US Army)"

"The trial lasted exactly two months – from May 16 to July 16. These pictures were taken on the first day as the controversial proceedings got under way. L-R front: Dietrich, Krämer, Priess, and Peiper. Second row: Coblenz, Fischer, Gruhle, Hennecke and Junker. Third row: Knittel, his number 31 half hidden by Fischer, Kühn and Münkemer."

do any work and all the other prisoners did odd jobs such as cleaning the area, picking up any cigarette butts or mowing the grass. I could see no work performed by Germans that I would call "hard work". It was rumored that an SS officer in camp had killed one of his fellow POWs for not participating in escape plans.

Opinion as a POW:

It is a disgrace and a dishonor to the families of murdered men and sets an ugly precedent for any of America's future wars, when the American government does not hold anyone responsible for the treatment of her POW's. Those men responsible for the massacres at Malmédy and Honsfeld should have been publicly hanged. Eventually, an unknown gunman shot Peiper outside his home in Eastern France on July 14, 1976. I hope that the shooter was someone seeking justice for murdered POW's. Unfortunately, today, I see murderers here in the U. S. subjected to the lightest of token punishments for the most brutal of crimes - air-conditioned prisons with TV and conjugal visits! No wonder we have a serious crime problem!

I am still resentful that those responsible for the massacre of those American POW's at Malmédy and Honsfeld, namely the SS Obergruppenführer Josef 'Sepp' Dietrich who commanded the 6th Waffen SS Panzer Army and Col. Joachim Peiper, along with other SS officers in the group, all were sentenced to death at Nuremberg and set free a few years later.

I knew that the road we were walking on led to Honsfeld, not more than two or three miles to the South. The road was jammed with tanks, trucks, and soldiers. Some of the vehicles were horse drawn kitchen wagons. Germany was still using horses to draw various Army vehicles, a lot different from our kitchen trucks that were well equipped. We had walked only a short distance from town when a busload of women stopped no more than 25 or 30 feet from us. All women were in uniform and seemed to be large and stocky in build. They got out of the bus and dropped their trousers right in front of us to relieve themselves in the snow, exposing all. They did not seem to care who watched and did not pay any attention to their own troops whistling and hollering at them. I thought, what low morals these people have! I do not know if they were prostitutes or soldiers, but they were headed straight for the front lines. I was glad to know the girls back home who had enlisted in the service were not required to be combat soldiers. It sounds old fashioned today, but I would rather see them as ladies and not placed in circumstances that would lower their dignity to the level of these German women.

Soon after we left town, new German Tiger and Mark IV tanks repeatedly ran us off the road. We also were shoved and slapped around by the fresh troops marching up to the front. Maybe slapping helpless POWs helped to build their egos. The going was slow and hazardous. The Tiger tanks were large, weighing approximately sixty-eight tons and carrying a crew of five, bigger than any tank I had ever seen.

The Mark IV was larger than our Sherman tank but not quite as big as the Tiger. The barrels of the 88mm cannon seemed to be at least ten or twelve feet long, and they were lowered so that the tanks could turn and try to run over us. The barrel, swinging around with the motion of the tank, formed a deadly weapon that we were constantly dodging. Trying to dodge the tanks and their long gun barrels on the frozen ice and snow surface was sheer hell for us. One blow from the barrel of a 88mm cannon would have meant instant death.

Snow banks were knee deep on the side of the road and when those huge tanks were turned at us, we would slip and slide out of the way while the Krauts laughed and enjoyed their sport. I really think they were trying to run over us. We were constantly pulling one another out of the way, the steel tracks missing us by less than a foot on more than one occasion. The only thing we could do was call them every curse word we could think of and be glad that they did not speak English. Whenever the column stopped, we had no way to stop the Krauts (to use one of our nicer names for them) from taking anything they wanted from us. They would push us around and, I guess if we had resisted, we would have gotten a mouthful of rifle butt, or maybe a bullet in the head. There was no discipline among the soldiers as far as molesting POW's, and they all seemed delighted with the opportunity to shove and slap us around. They took watches, rings, overshoes, or anything else that caught their fancy. I put my wedding ring in my mouth for two days to keep it out of sight and I still have it today as a result. The Kraut that took my overshoes spoke perfect English and told me how lucky we were to be captured; we were on our way to a comfortable, rear echelon POW camp and our war was over. We found out later how wrong he was.

The Kraut who took my fur-lined parka did not speak a word of English and all I could think to call him was a dirty son of a bitch; I wanted to call him a swine but had second thoughts. I thought that was a German swear word and who knows how he might have reacted if I had called him that. After losing the parka, I now had only my wool shirt and field jacket for warmth. I surely was going to miss that fur-lined parka! I wished I had worn my long handles that day. Soon we topped a high spot where we could see a long way in all directions and found that all roads were jammed with tanks, trucks, and soldiers heading for the front. Something big was clearly underway, but I, for the time being at least, was out of the action.

"The Tiger IIs of schwere SS-Panzer-Abteilung 501 filmed moving through Tondorf on their way to the Kampfgruppe Peiper assembly area on the eve of the offensive. (US Army)"

(Four stills and cut lines reprinted by permission, Battle of the Bulge, Then And Now by Jean Paul Pallud With Credits to After The Battle magazine 1984, Battle of Britain Prints International Limited, London, England, Publishers, p. 74 – 75)

"Because of the security measures then prevailing, it is surprising that the column was moving in broad daylight. No doubt all crews were alert to the danger with MG34s at the ready. (US Army)"

"On December 14 the I. SS-Panzer Division's commander, SS-Oberführer Wilheim Mohnke, called a briefing at divisional headquarters in Tondorf for his regimental commanders attended by Hansen, Sandig, Knittel and Peiper. Skorzeny was there too with some of his officers as Kamp-fgruppe X of Panzer-brigade 150 was to operate in conjunction with Peiper's forces. Mohnke announced what was about to happen and left them in no doubt as to the all-important role of the divisional units placed under their command particularly of those forming the spearhead thrust to be made by Kampfgruppe Peiper.

"Peiper, although he knew nothing of the offensive prior to this briefing, had deduced that something was in the air when he had been approached three days beforehand by the 6. Panzer-Armee Chief-of-Staff, Krämer, who asked him, Peiper

related after the war, 'what I thought about the possibility of an attack in the Eifel region and how much time it would take a panzer regiment to proceed eighty kilometers in one night.' Feeling that it was not a good idea to decide the answer to such a question merely by looking at a mat, I made a test run of eighty kilometers with a Panther myself, driving down the route Euskirchen – Münstereifel - Blankenheim. I replied: 'If I had a free road to myself, I could make eighty kilometers in one night. Of course, with an entire division, that was a different question.'

"Kampfgruppe Peiper was made up of I. Abteilund of SS-Panzer-Regiment 1, comprising 1. and 2. Kompanies with Panthers and 6. and 7. Kompanies with Panzer IVs, 9. Kompanie (engineers), 10. Kompanie (anti-aircraft) with self-propelled Wirbelwinds. To compensate for a II. Abteilung, schwere SS-Panzer-Abteilung 501 was attached with Tiger IIs; III. Bataillon (infantry) and 13. (IG) Kompanie (self-propelled infantry guns) of SS-Panzergrenadier-Regiment 2; the II. Abteilung of SS Panzer-Pionier-Bataillon 1 (engineers); and Flaksturm-Abteilung 84, a Luftwaffe Flak unit, formerly corps troops.

"There has so often been a tendency to grossly exaggerate the strength of Peiper's force, which, had his tank regiment been up to full strength at mid-1944 levels, would have possessed at most 180 tanks. At the time of the offensive, according to the various sources quoted earlier, the total cannot in fact have been more than about a hundred and was probably nearer ninety – roughly an equal number of thirty-five Panthers and Panzer IVs and about twenty Tiger IIs.

"Peiper's comments in a US Army interview after the war confirm the general composition of his own SS-Pz.Rgt.1: '(it) was supposed to have one battalion of Panthers (i.e. in addition to one of Panzer 1Vs and two of Panthers. To compensate for the shortage of tanks, my regiment was further reinforced with a battalion of Tigers which had been formerly corps troops. Therefore the regiment finally consisted of one battalion of mixed Panthers and Panzer Ivs and one of Tigers'."

The book, *Battle of the Bulge Then and Now* by Jean Paul Pallud "can claim to provide the first correct identification of both the locations and the units shown in most of the illustrations, and this applies particularly to the pictures of German origin – both photographs and stills from footage shot by German newsreel cameramen. These bore no indication at all regarding either date or place and therefore entail intensive research and fieldwork. It was somewhat easier with the pictures from American sources as they normally possess an original caption, although the details cannot always be relied upon. Easy as it is to correct the usual misidentification of virtually every German tank as a Tiger, it can be pretty aggravating to find that very nearly half the locations that are given turn out to be wrong. For instance, it transpired that a picture captioned as *Marche* was taken nine kilometers away at Hotton; another, said to have been taken at Arbrefontaine, in fact showed Vielsalm, seven kilometers away; and one of Samrée was of Amonines, ten kilometers away, and so on. It therefore seems to me that the usual procedure for an American Signal Corps photographer was for him to take a picture and then move on until he came across either a local inhabitant or a signpost to provide him with the name of 'this place', which was not always the one where the picture itself was taken! *

"I naturally take some pride in being the first person to have traced exactly where a whole host of German photographic and film coverage of the offensive was taken. Among the pictures illustrated in this book, these locations include: Tondorf (page 74, reprinted here with permission) …. where the presence of Tiger IIs and SS grenadiers .. pointed towards the likelihood that they were within the 6. Panzer-Armee sector."

* (i.e. the location of the picture of my capture, missidentified as "Honsfeld" instead of "Bülligen"!)

I, Harry Thompson, am ever so grateful to all who researched, compiled, edited and produced *Battle of the Bulge Then and Now*. It has been a great comfort to me in reconciling my memories of being a WWII POW. I again express appreciation to Jean Paul Pallud, *After The Battle* magazine 1984, and Battle of Britain Prints International Limited, London, England, Publishers for permission to use pictures and text from this fine book.

December 1944

S	M	T	W	T	F	S
					1	2
3	4	5	6	7	8	9
10	11	12	13	14	15	16
17	18	19	20	21	22	23
24	25	26	27	28	29	30
31						

My Little Bit
December 17, 1944

The countryside was covered with snow and it was very misty except at ground level. I remember thinking it was too bad that the weather kept our Air Forces on the ground that day - they could have had a real turkey shoot with all the roads clogged with enemy forces. Even though our air force was grounded by the weather, the German Air Force was able to have planes in the air all the time - the Krauts (as we despairingly referred to them) flew no matter what. They were able to help their Army obtain Hitler's objective. The American Air Force came in only when the sky opened up and the fog lifted. (Why this was allowed to happen has never been satisfactorily explained. Maybe our planes were purposely grounded to let the Germans proceed into a trap planned by our higher echelon.) Had our Air Force been flying, it more than likely could have slowed the German advance and saved lives of many American soldiers.

About eight hundred paratroops were dropped to support the German attack along the Eupen - Monchau Road (This was in our sector.) (See the official report of First Army, Volume 1 page 104.) Some were reportedly dropped near the Tank Destroyer Unit at Honsfeld at 6:30 a.m. on the 17th of

December 1944. Germans in American uniforms and gear were infiltrating through our lines in accordance with the plan "GRIEF." Parachutists roved the area of woods and bog land West of Elsenborn - Kalterherberg sector. How many aircraft did it take to drop that many paratroopers?

I was more worried about my loved ones back home than anything else. I knew they would have heard of the German breakthrough and would be worrying about me. I was almost sorry I had given them some hints of my where-abouts in my letters home. I did not want them to worry yet I also wondered if they would be notified that I was missing in action and taken prisoner of war. Would I ever make it home?

I remembered the last letter I sent home via V-mail, about a week before. I still have it, yellowed with age, in my box of war mementos.

"Dear Aunt Nellie," I had written,

"I am now located near the Belgian, German border and have been in Germany quite a few times. Little did I ever dream that I would be over here taking part in a war – course that is the way things go and I guess fate called on me. Nevertheless I am here so I will do my best and use all those years of training I have had to the best advantage . . . and not take chances. The artillery can be heard very distinctly at times and those buzz bombs pass over continuously - outside of that, there isn't much to do but work. Those buzz bombs fly low at times and several have hit rather close and believe me they have quite a punch. . . I have seen damage far beyond anything I imagined - at one large town there were homes for miles just utterly destroyed, nothing left but crushed rock just lying on the ground. I certainly am glad that such a thing isn't happening at home and I am glad to be here to keep such from happening - that is, I am glad to be doing my little bit."

My little bit. It was turning out to be rather more than I had imagined, and I had not even seen the beginning of the devastation I would behold. It was ironic, though - over three years of training stateside, thousands of dollars invested in turning me into a well-equipped, well-trained soldier, and I lasted less than a day in my first actual battle. It was something my father-in-law would use to tease me no end in years to come. That was in the future at the moment and, for now, I simply wondered if I would ever see my family again.

I also wondered where all those tanks and planes had come from and why we were not notified that so many enemy troops were so near to our position. We all had the false impression that the Germans did not have the manpower or equipment to launch such a large counterattack and that the war would be over very soon. We wondered why they did not let us move back when that anti-tank unit had come screaming through, calling that the Germans were right behind them, or during that incredible artillery bombardment. Why didn't we have any antitank weapons except for one bazooka? If we had even a handful of bazookas we could have done some damage to the enemy. As it was, there was limited action, no way small arms fire could slow those tanks down. I had one 45 Colt Automatic with one clip to use against the tanks. A pistol is no more effective than throwing a rock.

There were so many questions on my mind. There were a great many rumors regarding this offensive and I guess historians will try to figure it out for years. If rumors are true, the action by Eisenhower and his staff will be listed as secret and never released. The rumors were that the high echelons of the American Army were to lead the Germans into a trap by sacrificing the 2nd, 99th, and the 106th Infantry Divisions. When they reached a certain area, the German Army would be encircled and annihilated. The 2nd and the 99th Divisions upset their plans by stopping the fanatical German hordes to a standstill, although the American soldiers were outnumbered about fifteen to one. Some of the men of the 99th fought hand-to-hand combat.

Once the 99th Division was taken off the "secret list" in January, 1945, U.S. newspapers were filled with stories of the heroic stand of the 99th in the "Bulge" by Hal Boyle of the Associated Press, Chris Cunningham of United Press, Winston Burdett of Columbia Broadcasting System and many, many more. Another respected and outstanding war correspondent during WWII, John McDermott dubbed the 99th Division, the "Battle Babies" in his first release of the division action in the Battle of the Bulge. I still do not understand why the 99th Division had been listed as "secret". What was secret? Everyone at Camp Maxey and Paris, Texas knew that we were headed for Europe. We arrived at Camp Miles Standish and even there, everyone knew. If the secret had been lifted before we left the states a lot more publicity of action by the 99th Infantry Division would have been well known.

I wish there was some way for me to get out of this mess and rejoin my battalion. Not a chance - not only are the enemy troops on the road and beside the road, they are also in the woods and fields. I hope the bastard that took my parka enjoys it - this field jacket is not very warm and I am so cold. But wait - here I am feeling sorry for myself and some GI's are marching without pants or shirts, thanks to the Nazis. Come to think of it, I wonder where those guys are? I have not seen them since they had their clothing taken from them. I wonder what lies ahead for us? I am sure that it's nothing good, now or in the near future. If there could only be a counterattack and we could all be liberated! Wishful thinking! If there was a counterattack it would be one hell of a battle with thousands of fully armed German soldiers, tanks, and military hardware - we would be lucky to come out of it alive. And to think, just a few hours ago, I was a free person!

After three or four hours of freezing, slipping, sliding,

and struggling to stay alive, we finally arrived in Honsfeld, another small Belgian town that was a rest area for the 99th's soldiers. I wondered what the hell had happened here. Many dead American soldiers, frozen stiff, were lying all around where they froze after being shot. Some had been lined against a brick wall as we had been, but they had not been as lucky as we - they are lying where they fell, murdered in cold blood. I had seen dead Americans before, but never like this, the poor guys just left on the ground, no one even bothering to move them out of the way. I begin to wonder if they took any prisoners at all in this town. There is no way to describe the empty, sick feeling in the gut from seeing all these poor dead GI's. I had never seen anything like this before and felt like I was going to throw up. They had families and loved ones at home, the same as we did. I noticed that all of the dead GI's overcoats and overshoes had been removed. The Krauts must be poorly equipped if they have to rely on death of their enemies for winter's necessities. As it turned out, they were looking for the American gasoline storage areas to supply their gasoline guzzling Mark IV and Tiger tanks. As I saw the dead, I thought back to a time when my family drove through Camp Maxey and saw all our soldiers waiting to be transferred overseas. So sad!

After I saw so many dead I passed the point of throwing up. Nature has a way of healing. After this first time, seeing the dead never bothered me, for I saw many, many after that. It never bothered me. Of course, I felt sorry, but I could do nothing about it.

We finally were led into a building, a small, one-story frame structure - perhaps a schoolhouse at one time. Once we were inside, we were instructed to turn in all weapons of any sort that we had. I had a pocketknife that I was allowed to keep. It would have been nice if there had been some heat in the building. The Krauts did not seem to mind the cold since they all had heavy overcoats. If I were home about this time, we would be sitting down to dinner. Instead, I am wondering whether I am about to be shot or sent to a POW camp.

I was concerned for my family. Unlike today, it took weeks for families to get word from their boys at the front, even though the news of a big battle would be released within a day or two. By now I was sure they knew that I was caught up in the middle of the fight, and I wondered how long it would be before they got word that I was captured - or would I simply be labeled missing in action, with no word whether I was alive or dead? I wished I could somehow reach out and connect to them with my mind, just to let them know I was all right.

December 1944

S	M	T	W	T	F	S
					1	2
3	4	5	6	7	8	9
10	11	12	13	14	15	16
17	18	19	20	21	22	23
24	25	26	27	28	29	30
31						

The Gory Mess

December 17, 1944, a very long day!

What had happened in this town of Honsfeld? There are dead everywhere outside and quite a few here in this room. Suddenly someone yelled, "Duck! Incoming artillery!", and we all hit the floor, guards and GI's alike. Artillery shells hit outside next to the window, then another hit, quickly followed by another. The last sounded like it was right outside, and shrapnel went whizzing by, just over our heads - anyone standing would surely have lost theirs! The guards lined us up as soon as the shells stopped coming and quickly marched us downstairs to the basement - no one objected to that order! We had to step over several dead GI's lying on the stairs, and there were many more down in the basement. I noticed that the basement was full of upright two by fours, holding up the first floor. If a shell were to hit the building, the first floor would come down on top of all of us! All night long the town was shelled by American artillery, and shrapnel was flying through the basement window just over our heads. A hit by a piece of shrapnel could mean instant death, loss of a limb or a serious wound. We all knew that could happen and did a lot of praying. I do not think any of us were hit or injured, thanks to the height of the window. From the sound of the incoming artillery explosions, they must have been from our 155mm or 240mm howitzers. I do not think any of us slept that night as the shelling continued until morning. After what seemed like an eternity, dawn finally came and the shelling let up. We were led out of the building and I noticed that the roof of this schoolhouse had sustained two direct hits, tearing large gaping holes overhead. I was glad those shells did not hit the flooring! The buildings on both sides and the back had sustained considerable damage and the building across the street was completely demolished. The good Lord was on our side that night!

We then were lined up and ordered to start walking. I saw a sign pointing the way back to Büllingen. At these cross roads I saw three more dead American soldiers, still lying where they had been shot, in the road by the crossroads signs, one sign pointing to Büllingen four kilometers; the other pointing to Bahnhof one half kilometer. These men were never moved out of the road and were run over by trucks and tanks. It took years to find them. One was found some fifty years later while a new road was being built. The three soldiers and those in Honsfeld were 99th Infantry Division soldiers.

I wondered how many in our battalion were still alive and if the Germans had succeeded in breaking through to Antwerp, which they had told us was their objective. I did not think they had broken through yet because the night's artillery barrage seemed to have been coming from the direction of Elsenborn. We lined up, started marching and had gone only a short distance from Honsfeld, maybe a mile, when we saw still more bodies lying in the road. I tried counting the crushed helmets, not only American but German as well. Hell, the Krauts did not even drag the dead out of the road - tanks had driven over them all night, heads and helmets mashed flat. There were no complete bodies - just big bloody smears in the road. I wondered if the GI's had captured the Krauts or vice versa, and how many had been killed. At any rate, it did not matter now - we just had to walk over the gory mess and keep going.

Everywhere we looked, tanks and soldiers were headed for the front. At least this time, the tanks were not trying to

"An oft-published photograph, usually with the signpost censored, which typifies the battle. However these men are not Kampfgruppe Peiper as often stated but from 3. Fallschirm-Jäger-Division. (US Army)"

(Photograph and cut lines reprinted here by permission, Battle of the Bulge, Then And Now *by Jean Paul Pallud With Credits to* After The Battle *magazine 1984, Battle of Britain Prints International Limited, London, England, Publishers, p. 138.*

run over us and the soldiers were not pushing us off the road. Occasionally we saw dead cows and horses in the fields. They must have been dead for some time, they were all swollen and looked like they were ready to burst open - or maybe they were swollen from being frozen stiff. I was so hungry and cold. All I could wonder about now was when they were going to feed us. The guards had food but they damn sure did not share it with us - not even a drink! A cup of coffee sure would have been nice to warm us up, but all we had to drink was melted snow. They could have at least built a fire and let us warm up a little.

As we walked down the narrow roads through the Ardennes Forest, we saw many of the large fir trees with dynamite tied on them near the ground, so that, if needed, the explosive could be set off to make the trees fall across the road to slow pursuing tanks, sort of a domino effect.

I wondered what my family was doing. This time of the

morning, my wife should be at work - I hope everyone is warm and has enough to eat. In the last letter I had from them, they said plenty of cookies were on the way. I wonder what kind of cookies they sent. I had asked them to send me some fur-lined gloves, if they could find any. If anyone could locate them, it would be my brother; he is in the service and could get them for me at the Post Exchange. I sure would like to be back stateside right now - I could find me an overcoat and something to eat.

Someone called out, snapping me out of my daydreams. It was my turn to help carry the wounded. Those guys were much worse off than I was, and every bit as hungry and cold. At least I was able to walk - no attempt had been made to give them medical attention since they either joined us at Büllingen or Honsfeld. These Krauts simply did not care whether we lived or died. We carried the wounded until about 4 P.M. when we were told to take them inside a small building which they told us was a hospital (it did not look like one). I hoped they would be OK, some of them looked to be in pretty bad shape. One of the men I helped carry had very bad shrapnel wounds, but I never heard him complain although he was in terrible pain. We had not been allowed to keep our first aid kits, so there was nothing we could do to help him. Now it was getting dark. They herded us towards a pillbox or bunker - a large round concrete gun emplacement - about 100 yards from the road. I guess it was to be used for a machine gun or antitank battery if needed. We were told by a guard to follow a string across the field and not to step away from it, for the area around the path as well as the field all around the pillbox was heavily mined. When we got inside, the string was taken up and they left one guard at the entrance. Others relieved him throughout the night, probably so each could go have a warm dinner somewhere. They knew we were not about to try to escape without knowing where the mines were sown.

It was very cold inside the bunker. The room was about

ten or twelve feet in diameter with four to six feet of concrete overhead and three to four foot thick concrete walls. We took turns turning a wheel near the middle of the room, which was designed to pump fresh air into the windowless bunker. I had heard that the normal complement of German soldiers per pill-box is seven; there were twenty to thirty of us jammed into this one and it was still like the inside of an ice box! I am sure the other prisoners were in the same kind of structures. I imagine when German military occupied these bunkers they had some kind of heat; I do not know how they stood it otherwise.

People in the good old USA do not know how lucky they are to live where they do, and that this war is not taking place on our soil. I miss my family so very much. I am hungry and tired and hope I somehow come out of this mess alive. I am too tired to stand but I cannot lie down either, I would probably freeze to death. I am also tired of running in place to keep warm. I am tired of being tired!

December 1944

S	M	T	W	T	F	S
					1	2
3	4	5	6	7	8	9
10	11	12	13	14	15	16
17	18	19	20	21	22	23
24	25	26	27	28	29	30
31						

They Could Have Cared Less
December 19, 1944

Morning finally came and we were greeted with the now familiar shouts of "Raus!" Single file, follow the string; finally we are back on the road. Now we are going through the Siegfried Line itself - tank traps, bunkers, pillboxes, machine gun emplacements, and minefields everywhere. German troops and tanks are still on the road, headed for the front. We passed several trains loaded with tanks and soldiers going that way. Each town we passed through bore the scars of war and still more dead livestock could be seen, evidently killed by excess bombs from our air force, or just plain misses - what they today call "collateral damage". I witnessed one example of a missed bomb - we were in a small town just before dark and a bomb landed and exploded about a block from us. It must have been dropped from a very high altitude, judging from the plane's engine noise. The low hanging clouds made visibility from the air zero, and I did not see anything in the town that might have been a target unless they thought there might be a large concentration of troops there.

That night we slept in an old building that had many bunk beds but no mattresses, so I found a few wooden slats and got a little sleep. Wooden slats are not comfortable but they sure beat a frozen concrete floor! We still had not been fed - I am sure those bastards are eating something, though; they sure do not look like they have lost any weight! I lay there thinking of my mother's fried chicken and bread pudding, my absolute favorite dish, although anything would taste good right now.

After another cold and restless night, we were again awakened by the chorus of "Raus!" and put back on the road. At least I had gotten a little sleep and had not had to run in place all night. My stomach is aching, the constant dull ache that goes with real hunger. Ham, eggs, coffee - God, I hope they feed us soon! We were still seeing military equipment and supplies on the road and trains too, all headed for the front. I did not know the Germans still had that much manpower! About the only civilians we have seen since our capture are large, stocky women chopping wood and very young children. I think all the kids from age eleven or twelve on up must be in the Hitler Youth Corps. We did not see anyone in that age range. We saw no one except adult women and very young children. On the fourth day after our capture, December 21, we were loaded on boxcars early in the morning and arrived in Bonn, Germany, about three or four in the afternoon. We had walked about twenty miles or more a day! Damage by our bombers was very evident throughout the small section of town that we could see, and strangely, there were hardly any civilians to be seen. Surely they were working in some arms plant or something; a city this size must have a large population.

We were marched to a POW camp located on the out- skirts of Bonn. It seemed like a pretty large camp with a high barbed wire fence surrounding it and strategically located guard towers. Once inside, we were led to a large building where we were searched and interrogated. They asked us many questions - what division we came from, units attached, and military objectives. I gave only my name, rank, and serial number, as instructed prior to leaving the states. No attempts were made to force us to talk, nor threats made to obtain information. It was getting dark when they led us outside to one of the many camp huts, each were made of concrete blocks and cement slab flooring. There were approximately twenty to thirty POW's per hut, with a floor space measuring about twelve by twenty feet. There may have been more POW's - we were packed in like sardines, with no heat in the building and subzero temperatures outside. We felt like we were in an icehouse. We were issued half a tow sack or gunnysack to sleep on, which was a joke. There was no way we could have slept on that icy cold floor even if we had room to lie down. We tried wrapping our tow sacks around our shoulders to keep warm, but it was no use - we wound up running in place all night again to keep warm. It was a dismal night; we were all freezing and had not eaten anything in days. My teeth chattered so much it was a wonder they did not break. I had been operating under the misconception that all countries at war had to abide by the Geneva Convention but our captors did not seem to think that way. They could have cared less whether we lived or died.

December 1944

S	M	T	W	T	F	S
					1	2
3	4	5	6	7	8	9
10	11	12	13	14	15	16
17	18	19	20	21	22	23
24	25	26	27	28	29	30
31						

Crossing the Rhine
December 21, 1944

After dark, vicious dogs were turned loose in the camp. It was my first experience with German shepherd guard dogs; they were mean and seemed so fat we would have gladly settled for whatever it was they were eating. There was no restroom in the building so, when we had to relieve ourselves, we opened the door just a bit, a narrow crack so the dogs could not get through, and let fly. The dogs growled and snarled just a few inches away, and getting a hot stream of urine in the face sure did not help their tempers! We got a laugh out of watching their fierce expressions and snarl as they tried to pry the door open with their heads, and were extremely careful to hold it tight. I remember thinking when my turn came up that this was a helluva position to be in if someone lost his grip on the door. I knew what the dogs would go for first! I guess a GI will do anything for a laugh, even under these circumstances.

While running in place to stay warm, we talked about anything we could think of to pass the time - mostly about our families and homes. I recalled every detail of every date I had with my wife before we were married, where we went, who was with us, and everything about our wedding day. I wondered if my mother and father were doing OK health wise, and hoped my brother had not gone overseas and gotten into a mess like the one I was in. In camp I met up with a GI from Dallas, Texas. We talked about various nightspots, restaurants and anything else of interest. We even started naming every place of business from Akard Street east to Harwood Street. I do not remember seeing him after leaving this camp, nor do I even remember his name, just a passing acquaintance - like most of the soldiers one meets in the military.

After a tiring and miserably cold night, the doors were opened and the guard dogs were gone. My field jacket helped a little but not nearly enough; my teeth were still chattering, as it seemed they had done ever since I was captured. We went outside and walked around the camp, trying to keep warm and see whatever was to be seen, which was mainly other prisoners like ourselves. Around noon we watched an aerial dogfight overhead. At times the planes flew so low they were only about 100 feet or less over the camp. Since we could not tell the German from the American plane and their machine guns were blazing away, we stayed down while they were overhead. The American was eventually shot down; we watched his parachute land. He was unhurt and stayed with us for an hour or two before being taken off to an aviator's POW camp. I had heard that the Air Corps POW's camps were under the direct control of Reichsmarshall Hermann Goering and that they were treated a lot better than the GI's, who were under the control of the SS and Wehrmacht. Later that day we were crowded into small boxcars, about half the size of an American boxcar, packed until there was standing room only. Late that night we pulled into a sidetrack in the railroad yards; we assumed we were in Cologne but in reality we had no idea where we were.

We were running in place (again) to keep from freezing when the air raid sirens began sounding. Airplanes, British or American, started bombing the city and the rail yards and our boxcar swayed back and forth every time a bomb hit nearby.

95

We thought that a bomb would fall right on our heads at any moment and I was so miserable I found myself wishing they had gone ahead and shot us that first day. At least it would have been over. After the air raid stopped, the train pulled out for parts unknown. Sometime later, the men at the small port-hole in the side of the car said we were crossing the Rhine River. Several times during the two or three days after we crossed the Rhine, we were strafed by American fighters - at one point they knocked the train's engine out, and it took sev-eral hours for the Germans to repair or replace the engine and resume our journey. It is hard to describe the anxiety we felt being locked up in those boxcars - in addition to being cold and hungry, any American plane that happened by would find us an inviting target for strafing and bombing. None of us wanted to be killed by "friendly fire," as they call it today, al-though this happened later at Nuremberg. Little did we dream, as we crossed the Rhine in that miserable boxcar, that only three months later, the next March, the 99th Infantry Division would follow us and be the first complete American Division to cross the Rhine River on this same bridge, the Remagen Bridge.

After at least four days of hell in that jam-packed, icy boxcar, we arrived at the rail yards of Limburg, Germany. All through the trip, the train had to stop so the crews could re-pair the bombed-out rails, but we were not permitted out of the boxcars at any time to stretch, rest or eat. Now they opened the boxcar and let us out, herding us like cattle. To this day, I think we left a few men dead, starved, frozen or hit by strafing fire in that boxcar. We were massed up in a contact group and informed that we had been scheduled to go to the POW camp at Limburg, but it had been bombed the night before and there was no place there to receive us. The guards also told us that many American POW's had died in the bombing raid. Then we were led to the downtown area of Limburg and lined up in the middle of the street, where the civilians stood on the sidewalks, cursing and spitting at us. How could these nice looking people follow a mentally deranged man like Hitler, I wondered. They certainly seemed to stand behind him at the moment, although

I figured they were also angry about their city being bombed the night before. I felt they got exactly what they deserved and I did not feel a bit sorry for them. The civilians were a good example of what news propaganda can do, for I am sure the news had the madman Hitler look like a saint. I never saw these people after the war but after the war, no one who liked or supported Hitler could be found.

December 1944

S	M	T	W	T	F	S
					1	2
3	4	5	6	7	8	9
10	11	12	13	14	15	16
17	18	19	20	21	22	23
24	25	26	27	28	29	30
31						

NO Peace On Earth, Good Will Toward Men
December 25, 1944

After we had been paraded before German civilians, we were taken in groups of about twenty-five and led to an upstairs room of a building in the middle of town. As we mounted the stairs, we could see a large picture of Hitler, flanked on either side by Nazi flags with their hateful black swastikas. Throughout the room there were numerous small swastika flags and twenty-five desks, each one with two chairs. We were told to strip naked and lay our boots and clothes on the desk. Well, at least it was warm in the room and I was warm for the first time in days. They then proceeded to search each article of clothing thoroughly, examining every seam and crease, checking our pockets and even inside our boots. After the examination, they took all unopened packages of cigarettes and told us to put our clothes back on and sit down. The interrogator said he wanted to know everything about my division, unit, and what our objective had been. I gave him my name, rank and serial number. He repeated the demand sternly, slamming his fist on the desk. He looked so mad he might hit me or throw a fit. I told him I had no clue what our objective was, nor would I have known until we were underway. They never gave out that type of information. (Rumor had it we were headed for Cologne.)

"What division were you in?" he asked again.

"My name is Harry Thompson, serial number W2108690,

and I am a Chief Warrant Officer in the United States Army."

He then told me, after studying papers on his desk, that I was a member of the 924th Field Artillery Battalion of the 99th Infantry Division, that I had joined the 99th as cadre from the 7th Infantry Division. He told me everything that the division had done since activation - Louisiana maneuvers, Camp Maxey, when we arrived in Europe, etc. How did he know all this stuff? I darn sure did not tell him! Well, so much for that so called secret division. He knew just about as much as I knew - probably a little more. He released me and I joined the other POW's in the street. I had to relieve myself and there was no restroom, so I did what the others did: went in the street with the civilians lined up on the sidewalk watching. I no longer gave a damn. I had always thought that the German people had the highest morals; how wrong I was! They have no morals, and I cannot believe I have sunk this low! To me they were all SOB's, bastards, swine, and any other name I could think of at that point. Why do not they feed us? We are all so hungry and now I am cold again!

After everyone had been interrogated, we were led back to the rail yards, where the enlisted men must have been separated, since I do not remember seeing any of them afterwards. I had so many friends between the GI's that I really did not want to be separated from them. I was an enlisted man in my battalion before I was promoted to warrant officer, and never forgot the camaraderie I enjoyed among the enlisted men.

Someone told me this was Christmas Day, and it was one Christmas I will never forget. All that we had had to eat or drink since our capture was snow and ice, and there, next to us, was a water hydrant that was running to keep it from freezing. The guard would not let us have a drink from it. I told him if I got the chance I would kill him. Of course he did not understand what I said and I never saw him again. Evidently these Krauts, to use a derogatory term, did not know about Christmas, for there was NO peace on earth, good will towards men with this bunch. I think with any type of provocation they would have killed all of us.

Back in Belgium, the Germans had achieved their maximum penetration of the Allied lines without making the breakthrough that they had hoped for. Instead, on 26 December, they had created a huge bulge in the American lines, like a giant spearhead aimed at Antwerp. The entire battle takes its name from this "bulge" they had pushed into our territory. Now, the Germans had run out of manpower, tanks, planes and steam, and American divisions were massing for a counterattack that would drive the Germans back to the Siegfried line and beyond. Hitler had staked all on this last gamble, and it had failed.

Now the officers were crowded into the boxcars again. None of our enlisted men were with us - I did not see them again until after the war. In this boxcar there were many holes on each side, from six to ten inches in diameter, apparently the result of bomb shrapnel or strafing. Snow was blowing through the holes, and by nighttime the floor of the boxcar was frozen snow and ice. The snow and ice on the floor of the car was four or five inches deep, and it seemed colder inside than it was outside. We were running in place on ice.

I was so weak from hunger and tired from running in place all night that Warrant Officer James Park and I both considered the possibility that neither of us would survive another night of this. It seemed like an eternity on the rails - freezing, starving, and surviving repeated strafing by our planes. Somehow we stayed alive - at least I think most of us did, some may have frozen but I was not in any condition to notice. It is surprising, the punishment a human body can take, but I am sure that our being in top physical health had a lot to do with keeping us alive. I lost track of days and was aware of nothing but my throbbing feet and the ache in my gut.

December 1944

S	M	T	W	T	F	S
					1	2
3	4	5	6	7	8	9
10	11	12	13	14	15	16
17	18	19	20	21	22	23
24	25	26	27	28	29	30
31						

German War Bread
December 29, 1944

We finally arrived at Nuremberg POW Camp Oflag XIIID, a huge concentration camp, on December 29, 1944. I thought we had finally come to our permanent camp, where we would stay until liberation, which I was certain would come sooner or later. I do not think that any of us could have survived if we did not all believe that we would be liberated soon. We were then taken to a large stone building where we were interrogated again, but this time the interrogation went a little easier. We were once again in a warm building where we stayed for about an hour, so I was warm again, if only for a little while. All of us were weak from starvation and I was so tired that I could hardly stand. After they interrogated us, we were issued POW dog tags. Dog tags always come in pairs so that if a soldier is killed one tag stays with the body while the other is

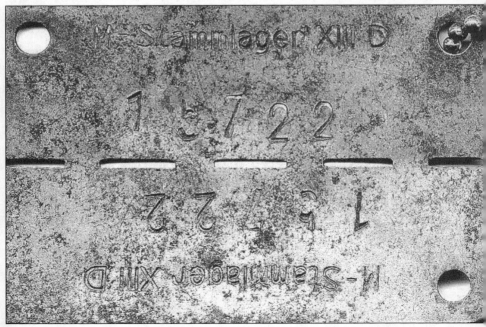

turned in to the appropriate authorities. My German POW tag number was 15722, and I still have it in my possession.

Men of the US 99th Infantry Division are marched to captivity.

They then led us into another room and told us to take off our pants and shorts. We stood there with legs straddled while a German soldier proceeded to shave off each man's pubic hair - we were all very nervous with those big electric sheep shears that close to that anatomical region. I kind of wonder about the Kraut who shaved me, he seemed to enjoy his job too much and did some completely unnecessary fondling. After being shaved, we were led outside - it seemed even colder after being in that warm building! We were told to take any money we had and put it all up in a pile. After the last bit of money was stacked on the pile, they lit a match and burned it all. I hated to see all that beautiful U. S. currency, not to mention invasion scrip, go up in flames. There must have been at least $2000 dollars gone up in smoke. I do not know what they did with the change.

Later on they gave us a large crock bowl to receive our food and eat out of. We were finally going to get something to eat, and not a moment too soon! I had eaten nothing since the morning of December 17th, and that was only a cup of coffee - some twelve days before, except for one small slice of German war bread that they gave us on the road, and I was so sick that I could not eat that. Now the crock bowl was filled with hot water with half a turnip floating in it, with no salt or seasoning of any sort. The turnip tasted good and the hot water helped warm me up, but that was no meal and I was just as hungry as I had been before. That was the full meal they promised us!

In camp, there were many sick and wounded, some in very serious condition. The other prisoners told us that there had been no attempt made to tend the wounded, walking pneumonia, and other illnesses in the camp. We were afraid some would die soon if they did not receive some kind of medical attention. Nearly all the meals in the camp were the same - hot water with half a turnip. Occasionally we had some very thin potato soup, with a thin slice of German war bread. Hungry as I was, I still could not choke down that bread. I tried and tried but could not swallow it, the bread smelled sour and each time I tried to eat a bite I would start to gag and throw up. We had heard that it was made from sawdust, acorns and I do not know what else, but if a starving person could not eat it, it must have been pretty bad. I did not know any of the men who could eat it.

In our unheated barracks, there were triple bunk beds with no mattresses, so we slept on bare boards, crowded close together. There were so many men in the barracks that a person could not get around very well, at least a hundred or so in our barracks alone. Many of them were sick and wounded, lying there in great pain. They obviously belonged in a hospital - for all I knew, some of them were dying. It was sad to see American soldiers in such a state and realize that there was not a damned thing we could do. I thought surely a camp of this size must have a hospital, but our guards seemed to care less. The SS must have run this camp! Evidently the hospital was only for their soldiers.

During roll call, which was held twice a day, all men in our compound (which consisted of quite a few barracks like our own) had to stand outside in the frigid weather to be counted; no one was excused, including the sick and wounded. They had to be helped or carried outside so the guards could count them. Sometimes they would pass out and we would prop them up to be counted. Evidently the bastards did not know how to count; it took them from about 45 minutes to an hour before they were satisfied that all of us were present. Where the hell did they think any of us could go in our condition? They did not mind the long roll count; they had on warm clothing and had plenty to eat. I do not remember seeing any of our men with overcoats.

Once, during roll call, an SS officer called an American officer, a Jew, to the front. The German was holding an American magazine in his hand (I think it was LIFE magazine), apparently showing pictures of German atrocities towards children. In a very demanding way, he asked the Jewish officer if he believed the article and when he did not answer, the SS officer slapped the magazine in his hand and screamed that they did not kill children, only Jews. All of us were afraid of what he might do to the man, but they did nothing and let the Jewish officer return to the lineup. After the count, one guard told us it was twenty degrees below zero. I believed him but had no way of knowing if it was true or not. We later found out that this was the coldest winter in Europe in fifty years. I believe that to be true! The field jacket I had helped some, but I still thought I would freeze to death - I was convinced my teeth would shatter from chattering together so much. I just hoped that our liberation would come soon, if any of us were to survive.

For a latrine we had a cement canal or ditch, about two feet wide, three or four feet deep, and seventy or eighty feet long, with swift running water going through. Ice was everywhere and the ground was very slippery. We had to be careful not to fall in, for I think a man would have frozen to death before he could climb back out. There was nothing to hold on to and no place to warm up or change clothes - not that any of us had any warm clothes to change into anyway. All of us had severe cases of dysentery, our rectums were so swollen they rubbed against the seat of our pants. You can just imagine how painful that could be. To ease the situation when we went to bed on the boards, we slept on our sides.

The main topic of conversation was food, food, and more food. I remember one officer, a second lieutenant who could not have been more than nineteen, saying how much he loved pancakes and chocolate syrup, then bursting into tears. I had never heard of such a concoction but it did sound good. Then again, at that point, anything and everything sounded good. Even lamb sounded wonderful, and back stateside, when they served it in the mess hall, I would not even go in, eating snacks at the PX instead. (I could not stand the smell of lamb cooking.) I was constantly thinking of mother's fried chicken and bread pudding. As I mentioned, that was my favorite food. I wondered if my family had found out where I was, or if they thought I was dead. They let me send a short postcard from Nuremberg after we arrived, but it would be quite awhile before my family received it. For some reason it was in French, which neither of my parents could read, although I think they quickly realized what "Camp de Prisonniers de guerre" meant. At least, when they got it, they would realize I was still alive. I had a wonderful wife, parents, brother, and sister-in-law, and I knew they were all praying for me. I just do not think anyone's parents could have been as good as mine were to me. I loved them all and wondered if I would ever see any of them again.

On New Year's eve, my mother wrote me a letter from home - of course, I never saw it until I was liberated, but you could tell how worried she was when she wrote it:

> "Dear Harry,
>   "Oh, if only I knew if you were all right since the awful battle in B. I pray that you are. Well, a new year will soon be here and even if you are so far away from home if I could only know you are safe and sound it would surely make the new year coming in much brighter. I try hard keep my chin up . . ."

I am glad she could not read my mind as she wrote that. I remember thinking: I cannot stand any more of this cold and

Kriegsgefangenenpost

Postkarte

An

MRS. HARRY A. THOMPSON

Empfangsort: 1814 Peabody Ave
lieu de destination:

Land: DALLAS, TEXAS
pays:

Gebührenfrei!

Landesteil: U.S.A.
(Provinz usw.)
départm.:

"a short postcard from Nuremberg"

Camp de Prisonniers de guerre

13 D   Date 29 Dec 44

(Seulement No. du Camp, selon les instructions du
Commandant)

Je suis prisonnier de guerre en Allemagne et en bonne santé —
~~(ou) légèrement blessé.~~

Nous serons transportés d'ici dans un autre camp au bout de
quelques jours. N'écrivez qu'à ce que je vous donnerai
la nouvelle adresse.

Meilleurs souvenirs

Prénom et nom de famille: HARRY A. Thompson

Rang: Chief Warrant Officer

Détachement: U.S. ARMY

(Aucun autre détail. — Ecriture lisible.)

starvation. I just cannot get the sick and wounded out of my mind. They are all so ill and being forced to stand out in the cold is making them worse. I wonder how many in the other barracks are in as bad a shape as we are. The Germans are crazy; they have the upper hand and are like animals - funny how some people act when they have complete control over others.

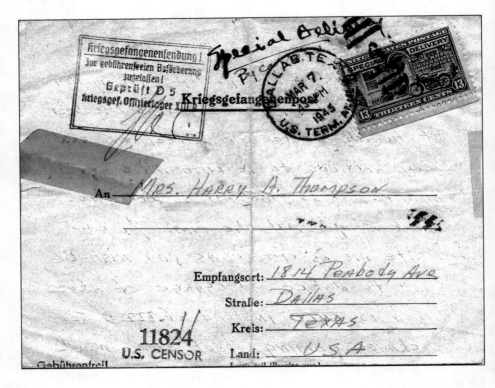

December 1944

S	M	T	W	T	F	S
					1	2
3	4	5	6	7	8	9
10	11	12	13	14	15	16
17	18	19	20	21	22	23
24	25	26	27	28	29	30
31						

This Pathetic Weary Group

December 31, 1944

On New Year's Eve, 1944 just before midnight the air raid sirens started wailing and we were led to our trenches in the compound. Some said it was the Royal Air Force releasing blockbuster (2000 pounders). The raid hit Nuremberg, five or six kilometers away. Even at that distance, each time a bomb hit, the earth would shake and dirt would fall down on top of us from the top of the trench. Each explosion lit the sky up as bright as daylight. I was so full of bitterness towards the Germans by this time I found myself hoping that everyone and everything in the city of Nuremberg would be wiped out.

The next morning many of the allied enlisted men from our camp were taken into Nuremberg to locate, dig out, and bury the dead in one mass grave. (No Americans were taken to participate in this mass burial since all Americans in our POW compound were officers and no officer was permitted to do any work.) When the recruited workers returned they said how terrible the raid was - many dead and hundreds wounded. One sergeant said there must have been two thousand killed, but I just could not believe that - maybe he meant two hundred.

————————————————

They had been made to dig one very long ditch, into which the dead were rolled and all buried in one massive grave. One of the guards in our camp had lost several members of his family in the raid and he was none too friendly towards any of the prisoners afterwards - not that he, or any of the other guards, had been friendly before.

One day while walking around trying to keep warm I walked over towards the Russian side of the compound and tried to converse with a Russian prisoner through the barbed wire. I knew no Russian and his English was so broken the only thing I could make out was that he had been captured at the battle of Stalingrad, which I knew to be the biggest battle on the Eastern Front.

About ten or twelve days after the bombing - I think it was January 12, 1945 or a little later - we were told that we officers were being moved to a permanent POW camp. All the sick and wounded were to be left behind - I wonder if a doctor ever treated them or if they were left to die. I do not see how some of them could have lasted very long in their condition. I am sure one I propped up during roll count had pneumonia, for his fever was extremely high. I have an idea that this young officer died shortly after we left. We later heard that some of the others died but I never heard the cause. I just cannot understand how a supposedly civilized country, as I thought Germany was, could allow men in such dire straits to just suffer and end up dead – leaving them to die simply because they were helpless prisoners of war. Are not we all human beings?

For the trip we were issued a number one can of corned beef for four men. Holes were punched in each can so that it could not be saved for an escape ration. We were then crowded into a boxcar that was divided through the middle with heavy barbed wire fencing separating guards and POWs. The guards' side was full of straw and supplied with blankets. Guards also had overcoats and plenty to eat for the trip, while the POW side was bare and so crowded that we had to take turns just to sit down or run in place. We had a five-gallon can on our side to use as a latrine, and when it was full, it was passed back, over our heads, to the men next to the small opening in the boxcar to be emptied. To give you an idea how hungry we were, when one of a group of four dropped their can of corned beef in the full five gallon can of excrement, one of the four rolled up his sleeves, put his hand to the bottom of the can. The can was retrieved and the corned beef eaten. The four of us sharing our can were so hungry we ate our corned beef as soon as the train pulled out - the little bit I got tasted good but I could have eaten four or five cans by myself. The label on the can said "Made in Argentina."

It was so terribly cold and so many of us were crammed together that it was not possible for all of us to run in place at the same time. We had to take turns. I think everybody in the boxcar got frostbitten feet. The guards on their side of the box-car kept warm and spent their time talking and laughing and seemed to enjoy watching us suffer. We were so hungry, cold, and tired that I did not think any of us would survive, and I am not sure everyone did. We passed the time talking about our families, homes and especially food.

The train stopped for hours, several times while railroad beds that the U. S. Air Force evidently had torn up were re-paired. The Air Force had no idea POWs were aboard and we were always on edge for fear they would strafe our train. Even if they did know, they would want to disable the train which would more than likely carry high explosives or other war ma-terials. The POWs were just add-ons.

How we ever made it through I will never know, but after three or four days we finally arrived at Hammelburg, Germany. It is amazing to me how much punishment the human body can take - I did not think my buddy Park or I would ever make it through. It seemed a long journey since the train spent so much time stuck on the sidetrack while the rails destroyed by our bombers were repaired. In reality, it was not that far from Nuremberg to Hammelburg. I think we could have walked in less time than it took us to ride the train. All of us would have

109

gladly walked rather than ride. We would have been much more safe and we could have stolen something now and then to eat.

We were unloaded at the Hammelburg rail yards, cold, tired, and hungry. We staggered, one step at a time, to the POW camp outside of town. I doubt all of us survived the trip - I do not see how some of them could have. We stumbled up a very steep hill, and as we walked we saw small children riding down the hill on sleds. The snow was only about a foot deep, but it was so cold and we were so weak we could barely reach the top of the rise where the camp was located.

There were large iron gates at the entrance of the camp. The commanding officer, General Von Goekel, an old, tall, erect standing, regular German Army Officer since 1908, whose combat injuries from WWI still bothered him, stood watching us. This pathetic, weary group of starving half dead, freezing Americans came staggering into his camp. He must have pitied us for we were marched into a large building where we were actually issued overcoats. Mine looked like a leftover French army coat from World War One, but what the hell - it was warm! Boy, I was glad to get it, even though it was full of lice!

They then led us into a nice warm building where we were interrogated once again - same old song and dance, name, rank and serial number, checking our German POW tags against information we gave them. The Wehrmacht ran this camp and our treatment was a little better than it had been before. The interrogation was not as intense, but I was taken aside and told I would be taken to another camp for further interrogation since I was a Chemical Warfare Officer. What the hell? I could not believe this! I could just see myself in some SS interrogation center and having the hell beat out of me for something I did not know anything about. I put up an argument that CWO stood for Chief Warrant Officer, not Chemical Warfare Officer. Several German interrogators got in the argument. I was getting quite concerned, afraid I was loosing the argument, when some of the others finally decided that I was a Chief Warrant Officer. They let me return to my group, ever though one interrogator did not seem convinced. Thank God I never heard anything else about this. Wow! That was close! Or was it? If I had been sent to another camp, maybe I would have been better off.

January 1945

S	M	T	W	T	F	S
	1	2	3	4	5	6
7	8	9	10	11	12	13
14	15	16	17	18	19	20
21	22	23	24	25	26	27
28	29	30	31			

Seven Small Lumps of Charcoal
January 15, 1945

General Von Goekel's men issued us a thin cotton blanket, about three by six feet, and led us through a large barbed wire gate into a compound set aside for captured American officers, then to our barracks. It was so cold that we got into groups and bunked two or three to a bed for warmth, as many of those already there were doing. Warrant Officer James Park from Burkburnet, Texas was my bunkmate. Park (now deceased) and I were drafted together, transferred around together, and wound up in this mess together. He was a close, longtime personal friend and his death about 1989 was a great loss to me.

In the bunk next to us was Second Lieutenant John Everjohn from Stephenville, Texas. He did not have a wool cap but had a gray shawl, which he wore even while sleeping. It was cold - so cold! James and I became pretty good friends with John. We talked about getting together after the war to throw a big party. Also in camp with me were five field artillery observers from 924th Field Artillery Battery: Lieutenants James Varner, Albert Balmert, Tom Andrews, John R. A. Tompkins, and Whitehurst. Captain James Cobb was also with James Park and me. How strange – three of us from Texas. Most of these prisoners, as others in our barracks, were from different states: Varner - Florida, Balmert - Ohio, Whitehurst - Florida, Cobb – Arkansas. Texas was home for Andrews, Park and I.

It was so cold that Park and I put both cotton blankets and both overcoats on top of us. The straw mattress was somewhat comfortable - at least it seemed comfortable to us - it was the first time since we were captured that we were sleeping on

something besides boards or concrete or were having to run
in place all night to keep warm. There was nothing to eat though
- no food since the one fourth of a can of corned beef three to
five days ago.

The barracks were rather large stone buildings, with
three-decker bunks lining both sides of the room. There were
fifty or sixty officers in the barracks - a lot less crowded than
we had been at Nuremberg. It was still cold, just as cold inside
as it was outside (below zero, I think) but at least we had a
place to sleep.

My hands - they were black, chaffed, cracked and very
dirty. Of course, they had not been washed since before my
capture and had been exposed to all this cold weather.

Each barracks was issued seven small lumps of char
coal once a day, so there was no warming up for us - those
little chunks would not even warm up the big potbellied stove
for a few minutes. We saved the coal for three or four days and
then lit it so that we could warm up, at least for a little while.
While the coals were hot we tried to toast the war bread to see
if that would help but the stuff was still inedible to me. The
room was so cold that we stayed in bed most of the time just
trying to stay warm. As a result of lying down so much, we
grew weak.

Each Sunday two Protestant chaplains and a Catholic
chaplain came into the barracks and held religious services.
We would lie in bed, listening to all three chaplains but, since
I am Protestant, Chaplain Moore's and Chaplain Koskamp's
services always meant the most to me. The Protestant Chaplains were Lieutenant Mark Moore and Chaplain Koskamp.
asked Chaplain Moore, a Nazarene, where he was from and
when he said he was from Dallas I told him that I came from
there too. He told me, "You can remember my name easy enough
- just mark more times." We agreed to look each other up after
the war was over. We could have talked all afternoon but I was
so cold and he had several more barracks to attend. Mark lives
in Kansas now and we still correspond with each other. I con-

sider him a good friend. We have continued our friendship by correspondence and now and then talk on the phone. Mark moved near the top of the Nazarene church organization. At the age of 72, long after retirement, he and his wife of 63 years, Clarice Moore, traveled to Kenya, where they spent four years helping establish a theological college, the Nazarene College at Nairobi, Kenya. One of their sons, Brad R. Moore, also lives in Kansas and is president of Hallmark Hall of Fame Productions.

January 1945

S	M	T	W	T	F	S
	1	2	3	4	5	6
7	8	9	10	11	12	13
14	15	16	17	18	19	20
21	22	23	24	25	26	27
28	29	30	31			

The Old French Overcoat
January 15, 1945

Inside the compound at Hammelburg there were approximately twelve barracks, each holding at least as many people as ours - six barracks on the front row and six in the back. I understood that there were about fifteen hundred American officers in the entire camp. I was in one of the barracks on the front row. The latrine (what was left of it) was directly in front of my barracks. Some time during the night some POW raided the latrine of all extra wood for their fireplace. They were kind enough to leave the front door and the toilet seats. I just wish our barracks had thought of that firewood first.

The faucet for drinking water was outside and behind us. To keep water from freezing it was left running. What a mess! If you needed water, it was very difficult with ice everywhere. You almost had to get on hands and knees and crawl to the water. We sure did not take chances of falling and breaking an arm or leg.

For meals we were again issued large crock bowls that were much more substantial than what we got to put in them. Sometimes we got half a bowl of potato soup, thin, mostly water. Occasionally it would have a few pieces of rotten horsemeat floating in it. Sometimes we were served a concoction called

————————————————

Green Hornet that looked like some kind of seaweed or just plain weeds cooked in water - it was mostly water and had a foul smell and taste. Another item on the menu was Black Death, a dark, nauseous broth with dead maggots floating in it. At first I could not believe that's what they were, but after careful inspection, we all agreed. At first I tried picking them out, but they were so small and numerous I finally said, what the hell, and ate them anyway, along with the foul smelling weeds and watery broth. None of the meals had salt or seasoning of any kind, and each was accompanied by a small slice of the war bread that I still could not eat, in spite of how hungry I was. I kept trying, even though I gagged each time.

Someone in the barracks said war bread was made with acorns, sugar beets, sawdust and straw. I know dirt and sand was also in it and I am not sure what else, but it had a kind of rotten sour smell. It should have been named GAG bread. It was awful!

When you are really hungry, you will eat anything that is edible and be glad to get it. No finicky eaters in a POW camp. You will eat anything that is edible except maybe German war bread!

Once a cat wandered into our compound and we did our best to catch him, but the guys in the other compound were the lucky ones. They got some extra meat in their stew that night.

During the train ride to Hammelburg, I worried about Warrant Officer Park for he was forty years old. I was concerned that he could not take the extreme cold weather, but he came out in about the same condition as I did.

It was about this time, on January 17, 1945, that my family finally got word as to my fate. A brief telegram from the war department arrived at 2 a.m., reading as follows:

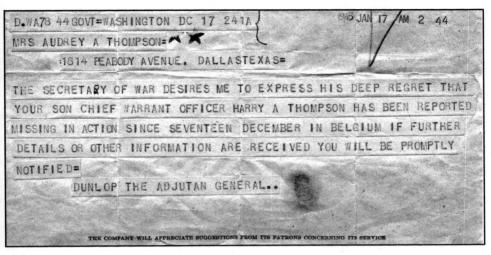

D.WA78 44GOVT=WASHINGTON DC 17 241A⎰   1945 JAN 17 AM 2 44

MRS AUDREY A THOMPSON=

:1814 PEABODY AVENUE, DALLASTEXAS=

THE SECRETARY OF WAR DESIRES ME TO EXPRESS HIS DEEP REGRET THAT
YOUR SON CHIEF WARRANT OFFICER HARRY A THOMPSON HAS BEEN REPORTED
MISSING IN ACTION SINCE SEVENTEEN DECEMBER IN BELGIUM IF FURTHER
DETAILS OR OTHER INFORMATION ARE RECEIVED YOU WILL BE PROMPTLY
NOTIFIED=

DUNLOP THE ADJUTAN GENERAL..

THE COMPANY WILL APPRECIATE SUGGESTIONS FROM ITS PATRONS CONCERNING ITS SERVICE

It was March before they got solid word that I was in fact
a POW and not killed in action:

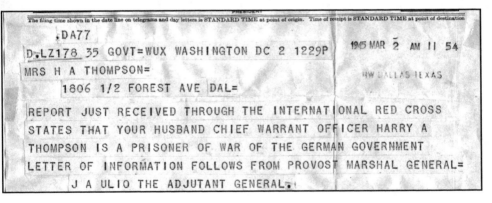

The filing time shown in the date line on telegrams and day letters is STANDARD TIME at point of origin.   Time of receipt is STANDARD TIME at point of destination

.DA77

D.LZ178 35 GOVT=WUX WASHINGTON DC 2 1229P   1945 MAR 2 AM 11 54

MRS H A THOMPSON=

1806 1/2 FOREST AVE DAL=   HW DALLAS TEXAS

REPORT JUST RECEIVED THROUGH THE INTERNATIONAL RED CROSS
STATES THAT YOUR HUSBAND CHIEF WARRANT OFFICER HARRY A
THOMPSON IS A PRISONER OF WAR OF THE GERMAN GOVERNMENT
LETTER OF INFORMATION FOLLOWS FROM PROVOST MARSHAL GENERAL=

J A ULIO THE ADJUTANT GENERAL.

Twice a day we stood outside to be counted, which took
about forty-five minutes. On each roll call it was so very, very
cold. The old overcoat helped a lot. I just do not know how I
would have endured the cold weather without the old French
overcoat. Fortunately, we did not have any wounded or seriously ill to hold up during roll call because they could not
stand. Several of the officers in our compound did have nervous breakdowns and just went incoherent. Not being a doctor, I cannot correctly identify their illnesses. They just sat in a

115

stupefied condition and did not seem to recognize anyone or talk to anyone. I do not know where they were sent or what happened to them. In front and around the compound, and in front of our barracks, there was a twenty or thirty foot space where we could walk but we had to be careful not to touch the single strand of barbed wire that was two to three feet off the ground, a yard or so from the outside fence. We were told that the tower guards would shoot anyone who touched or stepped over the single strand of barbed wire. In our weakened condition, what did they think we could do? We were pushing ourselves by just walking.

On either side of our compound were Serbian POWs from Yugoslavia. I could not converse with them because I could not speak their language and they could not speak English, but several times one of them would motion me over to the fence and give me a German cigarette. They smelled terrible (Turkish tobacco, I guess), but I was glad to get any kind of smoke. Some of the American Officers who could speak the Yugoslavian language told me that the camp contained about 5000 Serb soldiers who had been captured in 1941. They were held in two separate compounds located on either side of the American compound. The Serbs were nice and friendly and any time they caught our eye they would smile and wave and offer us a cigarette. They had been in camp longer and worked in the local fields and towns, so that they ate much better than we did from food they smuggled into camp.

The Serbs had trouble in their ranks. (So we were told by some of our officers who could converse with Serbs.) They actually had some guns hidden away within the compound to keep down any Communist attempt to take over their Serbian camp. All of the old guards from the Yugoslavian General Staff were located here and they were the ones who kept the communist sympathizers from gaining control of the camp. From what I heard, the Germans gave guns to the old guards of the Serb General's staff to keep control.

In camp there were several different compounds for different countries - Serbian, Russian, British, and American. Officers staying in "Oflag" and enlisted men in "Stalag." I never saw a Russian or British POW. The most memorable of the Russian POWs to have been in our camp was a Captain Stalin, son of Joseph Stalin, ruler of Russia. Some of the Serbs told some American officers that Captain Stalin was always fussing and arguing with his own men. He had a fistfight with an English POW. He stepped over the single strand of barbed wire next to the fence and was shot and killed by one of the guards in the tower. I have wondered how British and Russian officers got together to fight. Of course, these were all rumors, but I do believe long before we arrived Stalin's son, Captain Stalin, was killed in Hammelburg.

Our American ranking officer was a very weak camp CO. As our Commanding Officer, he had authority to talk to the camp commandant and ask for improvements, but he never did and our conditions and morale were terrible. He did not ask the German Commandant for more heat, better food or other privileges. His own men said he had been the commander of the 423rd regiment of the ill-fated 106th Infantry Division. He had surrendered his entire regiment during the Battle of the Bulge after only two days of combat. His men in camp held that against him and showed extreme disrespect in talking about him - many of the officers in camp were from the 106th. They also said that they planned to bring charges against him for his lack of leadership during the Battle of the Bulge and in camp. General Von Goekel, the Camp Commandant of Hammelburg, said later that our CO was a likable man but had no control over his troops. According to hearsay, "He was a poor commander." Also I listened to many officers of the 106th Division when they gathered together in groups and talked. They were convinced that the demise of the 106th Division was due to top brass being political appointees.

Virginia's Story, Continued

As written October 5, 2001

"We had letters back and forth and I knew where he was by the things he described, like the snow and how beautiful it was, the houses and the people. Harry had always told me not to worry because he was in the headquarters part of his unit, so I thought he would be O.K. But when I head about the break through and the Battle of the Bulge — I knew, in my heart, he was in the thick of it. Then we received the telegram saying he was missing in action. You have an empty space in your stomach and it goes up into your heart — Such a lost feeling!"

Note: My earlier statement, The Secret 99th, page 43, "I never could figure out how the soldier's wives knew where we were going. They usually were accurately informing their husbands and also telling them when they would be leaving." I still don't know how soldier's wives knew where we were going. We were the "Secret 99th!"

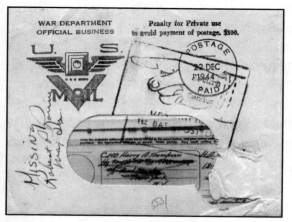

"V-mail from Mother and Dad, returned, showing me missing"

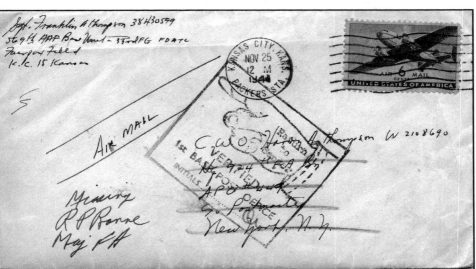

"Airmail letter from my brother, returned, showing me missing"

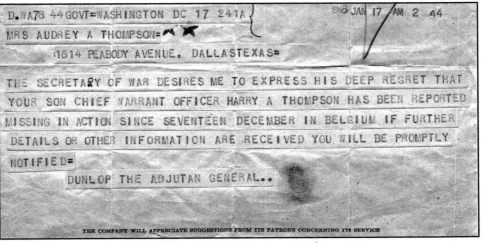

"Missing in action" January telegram

The filing time shown in the date line on telegrams and day letters is STANDARD TIME at point of origin. Time of receipt is STANDARD TIME at point of destination

.DA77

D.LZ178 35 GOVT=WUX WASHINGTON DC 2 1229P   1945 MAR 2 AM 11 54

MRS H A THOMPSON=

   1806 1/2 FOREST AVE DAL=   HW DALLAS TEXAS

REPORT JUST RECEIVED THROUGH THE INTERNATIONAL RED CROSS
STATES THAT YOUR HUSBAND CHIEF WARRANT OFFICER HARRY A
THOMPSON IS A PRISONER OF WAR OF THE GERMAN GOVERNMENT
LETTER OF INFORMATION FOLLOWS FROM PROVOST MARSHAL GENERAL=
   J A ULIO THE ADJUTANT GENERAL.

Kriegsgefangenenpost

Postkarte

An

MRS. HARRY A. THOMPSON

Empfangsort: *1814 Peabody Ave*
lieu de destination:

Land: *Dallas, Texas*
pays:

Gebührenfrei!   Landesteil: *U.S.A.*
(Provinz usw.)
départm.:

"The first notices home that I was a POW"

*" The Dallas Postmaster personally paid for
Special Delivery from all POWs.*

		March 1945			
S	M	T	W	T	F	S

The Lice Got Livelier
March 2, 1945

Around March 2, the Germans sent a group of American officers to join us in Hammelburg because the Russian army was getting too close to their POW camp located in Poland. One, a Lt. Colonel Palmer, West Point graduate and a former member of the 82nd Airborne Division, had been captured at Arnheim, Holland during British Field Marshal Montgomery's ill-fated invasion of Holland. He said it seemed that the invasion to liberate Holland was a complete disaster. It was a poorly planned offense by General Montgomery, a gung-ho affair without enough planning and intelligent information. A German Army of which they knew nothing was in their path. A complete rout! He said that they had been held in a POW camp at Szubin, Poland, but as the Russian Army closed in, 1400 American POWs were marched out of camp and started

121

their journey south and west, into Germany. Walking most of the way and covering the rest by train, they arrived at Hammelburg on March 8, 1945. He said that of the 1400 POWs who left Poland, only 430 survived the trip. (After the war was over, Col. Palmer was promoted to General and was in command of the army when American troops occupied the Dominican Republic, sometime in the 1960's, I believe.)

Enlisted men who were in the march from Poland were sent to the enlisted men's compound at Hammelburg. Most of the enlisted men captured with me were in Hammelburg Camp XIIIC which they said a huge camp, and I didn't even know it was there until after the war. I did know Serbs were on both sides of our compound. I found out after the war that all the 924th F. A. Battalion enlisted men who were parted from the officers at Limburg, Germany were sent to Hammelburg. Then all were transferred to Moosburg, Germany Stalag VIIA where the 99th Infantry Division liberated them.

Other officers transferred from Poland included Lieutenant Colonel Goode and Lieutenant Colonel Waters who were among those captured at Kasserine Pass in North Africa.

Lieutenant Colonel Paul R. Goode, ranking officer in charge of this POW group relocated from Poland, saw what sad shape our camp was in and how ineffectively our Colonel was running the place. Lt. Col. Goode, though not senior officer, somehow found a way to dismiss our camp CO and leave the impression with everyone that the change of command was agreeable to both parties. I guess the duties were just too much for the dismissed CO.

Rank did not seem to matter in our compound except to our former CO, who would not speak when passing. I saw him out walking only one time. All the other officers were friendly with one another. No names were known so we addressed each other by rank. "Hello Colonel, Captain, etc." When you are in a situation as we were, I do not think it would have been wise for anyone to pull rank, for you really never know on whom your life might depend.

Goode immediately demanded and received a few improvements. Col. Waters (General Patton's son-in-law) and a Col. Huff aided him in reorganizing the camp. Goode could not get us more food or heating, but he did demand discipline and had us all acting and thinking more like soldiers. He set up a G-2 (Intelligence) Section to monitor and observe the movements of our guards, and did a great deal to lift our morale.

As the weather got a little warmer, the lice got livelier and we all walked up and down the compound scratching. We were walking, trying to build up our strength. At least it was now warm enough to stay out of bed. I believe the lice were getting more exercise than I was. I am so glad that the last shot we got was a Typhus shot. We had been told that lice carried Typhus and from what I heard Typhus is deadly.

Lice are about the size of a pinhead, gray color, and many legs. I know of only one place where I was bitten, the inside of my left wrist where my pulse is taken. There was no way to get rid of them, for it was still too cool to remove all our clothes. Even if we removed our clothes, there would be no way to kill them. They were all over my clothes and me. A YMCA representative visited our compound (I did not know YMCA had a representative.) He was asked if any powder that killed lice was available. It so happened, he had one can, which he gave the camp - you know who got that can - our Top Brass!

As the American medical officer in our compound told us, it did not seem to him we were getting more than ten calories from the sparse food we were fed. We were literally on a starvation diet - of course we all knew that we were starving because we were all getting pretty weak. All the fat on my limbs was gone, and now the muscles were melting away - my legs were no bigger than my arms used to be. The medical officer also said that this starvation would affect all of us later in life and would ultimately shorten our life span by five to ten years. Lice were so bad that we scratched constantly. As the weather warmed up, we walked up and down our compound, speaking

123

to each other. I became acquainted and became friends with Colonel Palmer. I also spoke to Colonel Waters (Patton's son-in-law). We all greeted one another as we walked up and down in front of the barracks. While we exercised we would watch the Hitler Youth Corps drilling in back of our camp. They looked like they were well fed.

We still suffered from dysentery but were not allowed to go to the latrine when the air raid sirens were going off. One concession the new colonel got for us was permission to go to the latrine while the sirens were blowing. The day after permission was given, during an air raid, a young officer from the back row barracks was going to the latrine next to our barracks with his hands in his pockets and a guard shot him right through the back of the head. He died instantly, dropped in his tracks with his hands still in his pockets - never knew what hit him. Our new CO raised hell with the camp commandant, but of course it did no good. Their excuse was that the order had not been handed down to all the tower guards yet. The CO did get permission for us to hold a military funeral for the poor guy. Shortly after the shooting we managed to get a good look at the guard, but they had him relocated shortly afterwards. From then on we watched the towers very closely during air raids and when we had to go to the latrines, we waited until the guards' heads were turned, then walked as quickly as we could to get there before the guard could see and raise his rifle to fire.

Within a week of Col. Goode's arrival, you could tell the difference in the camp - discipline and morale were better. I never saw our former CO after Goode took over - he must have been ashamed to show himself or leave his barracks. He was probably ashamed to face his own officers because some of the officers of the 106th Division had complained about him. They thought the 106th had suffered for need of good officers from their commanding officer - General and down.

Col. Goode made a big difference when he got the Germans to issue each of us a razor, so that everyone could be clean-shaven again. I had difficulty shaving. This was the first time I ever shaved in ice cold water. Funny the difference a small thing like a razor can make. Simply being able to take a little pride in our appearance made each of us carry our heads a little higher and put a small spring back in our steps.

April 1945

S	M	T	W	T	F	S
1	2	3	4	5	6	7
8	9	10	11	12	13	14
15	16	17	18	19	20	21
22	23	24	25	26	27	28
29	30					

Talking About Food
April, 1945

We enjoyed standing in the door during an air raid and watching our fighter planes fly low overhead, circling the camp and destroying anything that moved outside our grounds - they knew this was a POW camp and never strafed us. Then when they flew away, we all wished we could get in the plane because they were heading back to base where there was plenty to eat. When the new officers marched into camp they were carrying a small radio hidden inside a set of Scottish bagpipes. Very few of us knew at the time exactly where it was hidden, but we all knew that they had a radio. Colonel Goode sent a runner to each separate barracks with news of how the war was progressing, gleaned from both the British and the German stations. We received our first news of how the war was progressing - our troops had already crossed the Rhine River and were advancing into Germany itself. Col. Goode said the German radio stations gave more accurate information than the BBC news gave.

The main topic of conversation in the camp was not the war or women or escape plans though - it was always food. Finicky eaters were no longer finicky after being held as a POW. You eat anything that is edible and are glad to get it when you are starving. Any kind of food, raw or cooked, it makes no difference, if you are starving you eat it. We exchanged recipes for our favorite dishes and planned our dream menu of what we would eat when we got back home.

Here is the menu I wrote at Hammelburg, Germany, OFLAG XIIIB, for the first meal I wanted when I returned home:

1st Dinner when I get home with my darling wife & family – dinner for Virginia & I & both our families attending – Menu made at Lager Hammelburg, Germany – Oflag XIIIB

Apetizer – Sparkling Burgundy

Menu – 3 Baked Chickens with plenty of dressing
Creamed Asparagus – young tender tips
Creamed Mashed Potatoes (plenty so no
Creamed English Peas   danger of running
Boiled Okra   short)
Fresh Corn on Cob – (if fresh corn not
  available get country gentleman corn and
  be sure enough is left over so corn
  fritters can be made next day
Cranberry Sause – 2 cans Ocean Spray opened
  and on the table
Hot homemade Rolls with plenty of peas,
  butter & peach preserves
Plenty of coffee or ice tea

Salad – Bananas, Celery, fresh Apples &
Nuts chopped & mixed together with
salad dressing – Seered on Lettuce

Desert
Peach Cobbler if possible – (Lots of it served
  with homemade vanilla icecream or cream – if
  fresh peaches not available have plenty
  of banana pudding with lots of bananas,
  vanilla wafers – seered with homemade
  vanilla icecream of cream
Chocolate pie – made good & thick – just
  have it on hand
Layer Cake – white with lots of bananas
  on icing & between layers – repeat, lots of
  bananas

People who have never starved do not know how to truly appreciate good food! We were always thinking and thinking about our families. I just could not wait to get back home to them. I was not homesick, for I got over that feeling in 1942 at San Louis Obisco, California, but I did miss them so very much. Several times back at Nuremberg we were given a small piece of paper, which folded over and made an envelope so we could send a brief message home. They told us we could ask for food, tell them we were doing O.K., and that we would be home soon, but nothing else. I still have several of these letters that I sent, both from Nuremberg and Hammelburg, folded over and yellowed with age. A typical one reads:

```
My darling wife and family,
     I am feeling all right (sic) and get-
ting good treatment so please do not worry
about me. Really will be glad when we can all
be together again. Please send me candy, pea-
nut butter, jelly, and some canned meats about
once a week by first class mail. I hope this
finds all of you in good health. I certainly
do miss your sweet letters coming in but
maybe they will be forwarded at a later date.
When I get home I want a big Xmas dinner with
all the trimmings, even to pumpkin pie and
ice cream for dessert - darling, please learn
to cook pancakes for I could eat a dozen for
breakfast . . . I know you are worried about
me but now there is no use - must close for
now - I love you darling and our families
with all my heart. Write soon.
```

That was about all we were allowed to say. We were told to tell our families that we were feeling well. As for food, we were supposed to be getting good treatment. We could not say we were hungry and if we mentioned anything about activities in the camp or about the war, our letters would be destroyed and we would be disciplined. Any attempt to convey further information would result in the letter being destroyed. I tried to be very careful in writing the letter so that they would have no excuse to destroy it. The main object of the letter was to let my family know that I was still alive. The letter would show the POW camp where I was being held. I just did not want to take any chances. Three times in Hammelburg and twice at Nuremberg we were given these small letters to send home. I think we all asked for food - I do not think it could have been sent and if it was, I imagine the Germans would have confiscated the food and eaten it themselves.

Judging from the letters we sent, everyone knew we were hungry although I doubt they realized we were starving. I had a large sore on my right foot just above the heel that would not get better - the medic said there was nothing he could do, there was no medicine to treat it and my body could not heal until I got some food and built up my body. I also had a bad toothache due to a large cavity in one of my lower molars. I did not say anything about it because I was afraid the Germans would yank it out with a pair of pliers and an infection would set in. I decided to take my chances and get it pulled by a good old U. S. Army dentist whenever I was liberated. I hoped it would be soon!

By this time, my family had received word from the War Department that I was a temporary guest of the German government. My Uncle, Rev. Bernard Thompson of Loogootee, Indiana, a Catholic chaplain, had received the mistaken word that I had been killed in action and sent my folks a letter which they got before they received the notice that I was a POW. In it, he expressed his sympathy for their loss and mentioned that he had said mass for the repose of my soul. It was an eerie feeling to read that letter after the war was over. I still have that letter to this day.

The highly prized pocketknife that I had managed to hold onto this whole time (I was one of few officers there who had one) was stolen from me about this time, not by a guard but by a fellow officer, I am sad to say. I was pretty sure I knew who it was but I could not accuse him unless I was sure that it was him, which I was not - I just had my suspicions. Once in a while, someone would be talking about food or home and just burst into tears. Everyone was on edge - captivity was telling on us. There were several fights in the barracks over the most trivial things, although the men would usually shake hands and be friends again after it was over. What a useless waste of the little bit of energy we had! Little did I realize that the dull routine of camp life was about to be interrupted by one of the most poorly planned and valiantly executed rescue attempts of the entire war - "Raid on Hammelburg."

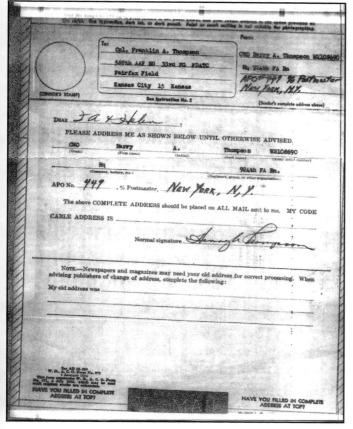

World War II APO (Army Post Office) Form sent by Harry to his brother Franklin and wife Helen.

(Bottom section was a change of address for newspaper and magazines subscription.)

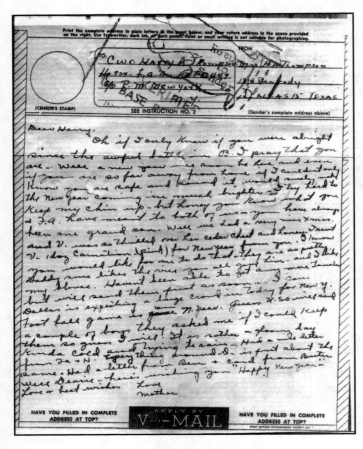

World War II
V...— mail.

Harry received no
V-Mail or packages
while a POW.

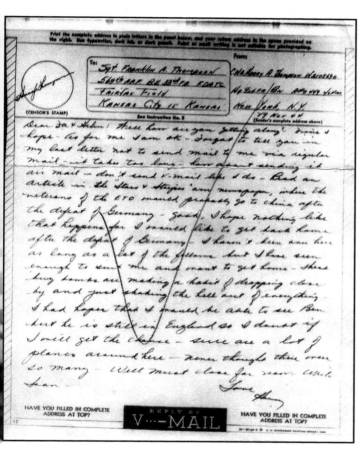

*World War II V...–
Mail from Harry to
his brother Franklin.
and wife, Helen.
"DOT DOT DOT
Dash" stood for "V
"for Victory!*

Virginia's Story, Anxiously Waiting

As written October 5, 2001

"All I could do was read the paper and listen to the radio, always hoping we would hear from him. Then, one Sunday, a messenger came with a V-Mail letter from Harry from Stalag 12 D, Nuremburg, Germany. Oh how Happy! The Postmaster in Dallas, Mr. Payne, paid the postage plus some due to deliver any mail from the prison camps no matter what time or what day it was. I called Harry's Mother and Dad – they were at the Capital Theater in Dallas watching PATHE News – and told them I had a letter from Harry and that he was alive. I wrote Adjutant General Ulio and informed him Harry was alive and where he was.

"I started writing Harry and sending food, warm gloves, socks, candy, cookies and such. Mother even sent him a roll of toilet tissue in her box.

"The next letter from him was a different address – so we sent another care package. Each time we heard from him it was a different address. I worried so about him but all I could do was pray, not knowing where he would be next time or if I would ever hear from him. This is such a helpless feeling and there is not a thing to do to help him. We sent food packages all the time but later learned he received nothing from us at all.

"I went to Red Cross meetings and read Harry's letter. One other person was there, a Goldman whose son was in the 99th. He was so glad to know some of the boys were in Prison. The Red Cross had some one there to talk to us and tell us to get our loved ones to talk when they came home."

"- Virginia."

March 1945

S	M	T	W	T	F	S
				1	2	3
4	5	6	7	8	9	10
11	12	13	14	15	16	17
18	19	20	21	22	23	24
25	26	27	28	29	30	31

Patton's Greatest Mistake
March 27, 1945

The raid on Hammelburg has been called "General Patton's greatest mistake of the war". He ordered a task force consisting of approximately three hundred soldiers and fifty-three vehicles, including Sherman tanks, half-tracks, weapon carriers and jeeps on a "suicide mission" eighty miles behind enemy lines. His son-in-law, Lt. Col. John Waters, who had been captured at Kasserine Pass in North Africa would be rescued during this raid. The task force on this mission was destroyed, as few as three and no more than fifteen of its personnel escaped being killed or captured. In addition, a large number of American POWs were killed during the attempted breakout and Patton's son-in-law very nearly lost his life. The raid on Hammelburg and its aftermath was the most remarkable event that I lived through during the entire war, although it started as another dreary day of captivity for most of us.

Around March 27, a runner from Col. Goode brought us news from the hidden radio. A German broadcast said that a spearhead of the American Army had broken through the German lines at the small village of Scheinheim, near Frankfurt, and was meeting heavy resistance near Gemunden. The rail yard at Gemunden was the unloading point for German troops resisting the advance of the U. S. Third Army. The Americans had lost fifteen tanks and other vehicles, and it appeared that the column was headed for Hammelburg. We did not believe that they had knocked out fifteen tanks though - that's a lot of tanks to be destroyed in one skirmish.

The BBC told us that Hitler had given orders for all POWs to be executed. A rumor sweeping the camp that same day said that Oflag XIIIB CO, Generalmajor Von Major Goeckel, had issued orders for all POWs to start packing because we were about to start marching to another POW camp. Later reports confirmed that the armored column was in fact headed for Hammelburg. Elation ran through the camp like wildfire as we all realized that our liberation was only hours away. The last report - all of this information was coming over the German radio - said that they were only five or ten miles away.

Soon after that radio report we heard gunfire and artillery shells going over our barracks and a real battle began raging right in front of us at Hammelburg's POW camp. I was at the window watching. We kept our heads down to avoid taking a stray bullet and thus, my description of the battle may not be as complete as it might be. It was pretty dangerous standing in front of the window with all that shooting. From all I had been through I did not want to take too many chances. The fight was tougher than they expected but the Americans prevailed and though they took some casualties they took over Hammelburg camp.

As the fighting wound down, Lt. Col. John Knight Waters, husband of Beatrice Patton, General Patton's daughter, ran out to meet the advancing troops and took a stray bullet in the hip. After the battle for the camp was over a Sherman tank came clanking up and repeatedly rammed the large barbed wire gate in front of the camp until it buckled. The battle-scarred tank came to a halt right in the middle of the compound, and cheers erupted from the POWs - what a wonderful sight to see! Immediately after he was shot, Col. Waters was carried to the camp hospital, where he was treated by the Serbian Chief Surgeon, Colonel Danovich. They say he did an excellent job doctoring Waters with what little equipment he had.

An American officer came to our compound right after the tank crashed the gate and told us to line up in columns of four. "Let's get the hell out of here!" was his precise order. We were so thrilled that we lined up in record time and about fifteen hundred American officer POWs in Oflag XIIIB marched out of the camp, happy and cheering. (Enlisted POWs were in XIIIC and were not liberated.) Boy oh boy, to be free at last - even the weather seemed warmer. The first thing we did was ask the advancing troops if anyone had any extra K rations or weapons. No guns or food were to be had. We streamed through the shattered gate of the camp and assembled about a thousand yards in front of our barracks.

We had heard from our hidden radio reports that Hitler had ordered all POWs shot, but we had beaten the son of a bitch before his orders could be carried out. We had been living on the edge for months, fearful we might be killed at any moment. There had been rumors of mass executions of prisoners at concentration camps. Always on our minds was the possibility that we would be executed. Our prayers were to live to see tomorrow.

Col. Paul Goode, our commanding officer, hopped up on a jeep and shouted for us to "listen up!" I knew something was wrong when I heard his voice - he sounded as disappointed and disgusted as I had ever heard him. He pointed ahead of us and said, "That way is west, fellows, the task force does not have enough gas to get back to the front or enough vehicles to transport all of us, so you are on your own." He jumped down, produced a white sheet and started marching toward Hammelburg, most POWs following. We could not believe it. They sent a damned task force to liberate us and did not give them enough stinking gasoline to get back to American lines!! What

135

kind of crap was this?

Later we learned that Captain Abraham Baum, the task force commander, promoted sometime later to Major, had been told that there were only about three hundred POWs at Hammelburg, and that the half-track carrying most of the extra fuel had been blown up on the way in by a German Panzerfaust. We were pretty discouraged all right, but none of us wanted to go back to the life of Kriegsgefangen or "Kriegies" (war prisoners.)

I made up my mind that I was going to escape. I climbed up on a Sherman tank, along with a bunch of other men, to ride as far as I could in the right direction. I had only ridden a short distance when I realized that the tank was so loaded with men you could not even tell what color it was, and more importantly, due to all the clinging passengers, even the gun turret could not turn. Lt. John Everjohn of Stephenville, Texas, a good friend of mine who had the bunk next to mine in the POW camp, was riding next to me.

After we had ridden about two thousand yards I got a bad feeling. "This thing's too nice a target for the Krauts with all these passengers, John," I said. "We have a better chance to make it on foot - come with me!" Lieutenant Everjohn did not want to get off. I begged him. He told me he wanted to take his chances on the tank. We shook hands and I jumped off. The tank had gone only about one hundred yards when it took a direct hit from an artillery shell.

I could not tell from that distance, but most of the twenty or so on the tank, POWs and including the tank crew, were killed. I later found out from Lt. Col. Palmer that Lt. Everjohn died instantly. Something just told me to jump off that tank and proceed on foot, because a Kraut counterattack was on the way - my only explanation to this day is that God was saving me for some other purpose.

After I jumped off the tank, small arms fire broke out all around me. I did not know what to do or where to go. I fell to the ground and flattened out while I pondered my options. My first option was to make a run for the woods a short distance away, but that would be a very stupid mistake since the Krauts would be on me before I got half way. A POW alone, trying to escape, would be shot - no questions asked.

German tanks and soldiers were moving their artillery towards Baum's Task Force, which was in front of me, so the only way to come out of this mess alive seemed to be to head back to the POW camp, as much as I hated the thought.

My escape was cut off. There was no place else to go. I started squirming along on my belly, just like the infiltration course back in the states had taught – except, in maneuvers, there was no one really trying to kill you. Bullets seemed to come at me from all sides. I cannot describe how scared I was – I think I would have just stopped and cried if I had not been so terrified. It seemed like some sort of cruel joke. When I came to a dead soldier I simply crawled across him, and I swear it seemed to me that I was four feet off the ground with a large target painted on my back every time I wriggled over one of the dead. I must have crawled over fifteen or sixteen dead. Every time I came to a dead POW or soldier I checked to see if I could snag a weapon, hopefully a Garand rifle, but I found none - I suppose all weapons had already been snatched up.

After what seemed like forever, I got close enough to the camp to make a run for it. (One account says we had been 11 or 12 miles from camp.) I sprinted as fast as my emaciated legs would carry me, afraid a bullet would come firing through the dark at any moment. I ran straight over the flattened gates and all the way to my barracks, where I collapsed, exhausted. There I found many other POWs including my buddy, Warrant Officer Park, who also had returned.

Colonel Goode had contacted the German general and asked if the POWs could return to camp. The general agreed. We heard Colonel Goode was about to explode with anger for such a botched up affair. I never saw Colonel Goode again after seeing him on that jeep yelling for us to "listen up". I guess he was sent to Moosburg Camp VIIA along with the other groups of POWs.

Captain Cobb and Lieutenant Tompkins had decided not to try to escape. They felt it was safer to return to the barracks. As it was, I suppose they were right but if I had not tried then, in all probability, I would have always thought that maybe I could have made it. Lieutenants Balmert, Varner and Whitehurst tried to escape and ended up at Moosburg POW camp. Lieutenant Andrews lived through the ordeal. I do not know where he went.

The task force commandos told us shortly before I climbed on the tank that the mission was blown, that my best chances for survival were to go back, and they were correct. I felt that I had to at least try to make a break for it though. Exhausted and discouraged, I lay down and fell asleep almost immediately. The liberation of Hammelburg had failed.

A week or so later, after the camp was liberated, General Patton himself came to visit his son-in-law in the camp hospital at Hammelburg and immediately had him transferred to a hospital in Paris, where he visited him again. General Patton always evaded the question of whether or not the raid on Hammelburg was made for the sole purpose of rescuing Col. Waters. The raid quickly became a hush-hush affair. Waters was quietly flown back to the states shortly after Patton visited him.

To this day, the raid is still seldom mentioned. I have found little in WWII history books that would go even so far as to mention "General Patton's greatest mistake of the war". Those of us who were inside POW Camp Oflag XIIIB at Hammelburg will never forget Patton's Ill-fated Raid. I do not know how many POWs were killed. I saw many dead POWs though there were quite a few who had made it to the woods.

I have no idea how many prisoners returned to camp or how many were killed or just lost in the woods, too starved and weak to return or advance. I heard that Baum's entire Task Force had been killed or captured with the exception of a tiny handful that came straggling back to the American lines. Many of us still suffer the aftereffects of the noise and horror of the day.

What a shame that so many POWs and task force troops had to die! If only the task force had brought arms for us we might have been able to fight our way out. There were only three hundred and fifty-three vehicles in the whole task force. The task force told Chaplain Moore they had expected to find only 250 POWs and brought enough vehicles to carry that number back, but since there were 1,500 it would be too dangerous and too long to march that many back even with tank protection - simply not enough men or transportation to liberate the entire camp. Was it worth it? If Patton had succeeded, he would have been considered an even bigger hero and hailed for his strategic genius. History would have glorified his gamble. As it was, the entire task force was lost, failing to liberate any POWs. About half of the men, tanks and other vehicles were wiped out before they reached Hammelburg. In reading about the Hammelburg Raid since the war ended, it appears that bad luck dogged the task force from the very outset of the mission. Patton's liberation strategy, whatever the purpose, might have worked - but it did not.

There has been much discussion among historians of what some have called "Patton's biggest mistake of the war". Intelligence about Hitler's order to execute POWs had been received. Could that have been the reason this expedition was sent to liberate a camp so far behind enemy lines? Fellow POWs generally agree that Patton sent the expedition to try to rescue his favorite son-in-law, Col. Waters. Could it simply have been Patton's intense desire to impulsively smash his way through to rescue and to win the battle? Could his caring for a son-in-law (and perhaps the rest of us) have been a new part of Patton's character not seen before?

In the Supportive Documentation at the back of this, my book, two others who were in Hammelburg tell their version of Patton's Raid as they experienced it as prisoners within the walls of Camp Oflag XIIIB. Jean Paul Pallud in the carefully researched book *The Battle of The Bulge Then and Now* published in 1984 on page 200 has written:

"The story of the 106th Infantry Division contained another unhappy twist: most of the officers captured in the Schnee Eifel were put into the PoW camp Oflag VII* at Hammelburg. In March 1945 Patton, probably because his own son-in-law, Lieutenant Colonel John Waters, was in the camp, sent a task force of the 4th Armored Division to thrust the 100 kilometres behind the lines to liberate the camp. The task force, under the command of Captain Abraham J. Baum, fought its way through to Hammelburg but was overwhelmed shortly after reaching the camp; of the 300 men that had started out, few regained the American lines, three according to some sources, fifteen according to others."

*Then and Now *book is in error. Hammelburg Officers POW camp was Oflag XIIIB. I don't think there was ever a POW Camp VII. The One at Moosburg was VIIA.

Earlier in his Preface, page 6, Mr. Pallud gave me such hope that I actually took my red pen and marked the following section in my expensive and treasured copy of his book:

"In the realm of personalities, without belittling Montgomery's contribution, the idea of his having come to the rescue of the 'defeated' Americans, transforming a shambles into victory in accordance with a meticulously drawn up 'master plan', also has not stood up to post-war scrutiny. Patton's role too has since come in for reappraisal in other than popular accounts, although this is not to say that his Third Army's knack of becoming the center of attraction has diminished in the meantime, as is shown (not least in this very book!) by the amount of coverage its operations on the southern flank inevitably receive compared with those of Hodges' First Army to the north. Certainly, in the minds of a great many people, the word Bastogne, and the image of Patton smashing his way through to relieve the beleaguered garrison and win the battle, seems to sum up the entire

Ardennes Offensive, which hardly squares with the true overall picture. Bastogne was not a prime objective for 'Wacht am Rhein' but an important road center to be taken on the way, as is clearly shown by the fact that when the 2. Panzer-Division could have easily taken the town on December 18 it was ordered to bypass it, pushing on westwards. Bastogne first appeared as a focal objective on December 27, once it was apparent that the main operation had failed and by which time the town had become a symbol for the Americans whose capture would provide at least a psychological victory. The role of the US First Army in holding and then repulsing the German attack on the northern flank of the salient is too often underestimated, and the stand of the 99th Infantry Division and the 2nd Infantry Division on Elsenborn Ridge and that of the defenders of Saint-Vith were of much greater significance for the offensive and subsequent German operations than what took place to the south. It should be borne in mind that the key role in 'Wacht am Rhein' was given to 6. Panzer-Armee."

Everybody makes mistakes, so why is General Patton's mistake so secret? Patton has been dead for over 50 years. Though Patton after fifty years still carries a great deal of clout, time is passing, some of us are beginning to tell the story as we saw it, historians continue to research and write books of the quality of *The Battle of The Bulge Then and Now* and I have hope that the real story of the Raid on Hammelburg some day will emerge.

All that aside, I can say that we were all thrilled and loved Patton for at least giving us a chance to escape from that hellhole.

PATTON'S, ILL FATED RAID

"Patton's Second Raid On Hammelburg Prison"

These two stills of a movie newsreel were made for Albert Clore, who was my corporal when we were captured and lined up, afraid we were about to be shot.

"Advancing on Prison Camp at Hammelburg"

"Entrance to Hammelburg XIIIB"

It seems Albert's brother went to the movies one night during the war. A most important part of the movie was the chance to see pictures of world news. That night, the news featured Patton's raid and successful liberation of Hammelburg Prison Camp. Albert's brother, after the movie, went to the manager and asked i there is any way he could get a copy o any part of that newsreel. Albert gave these two photos to me This is the gate I entered and the building to the right of the gate is where we were interrogated and where I was issued my old French overcoat.

As to Patton's successful raid: it came too late for me The Germans, because of Patton's Ill-fated Raid, had taken us on a 241-mile forced march, deep into German territory to keep us away from US troops and liberation.

March 1945

S	M	T	W	T	F	S
				1	2	3
4	5	6	7	8	9	10
11	12	13	14	15	16	17
18	19	20	21	22	23	24
25	26	27	28	29	30	31

Our Walk Through Hell
March 28, 1945

We fell into our bunks and slept the sleep of the utterly exhausted. About 2 a.m. the guards came through the barracks hollering "Raus! Raus!", motioning us to hurry outside and line up. It is really hard to explain the emotions we all felt. We did line up even though we were afraid they were leading us out to execute us as Hitler had ordered. We started walking, not knowing what fate had in store for us. When we got to the end of the barracks the column stopped for a moment. I saw a crate of cabbage and stepped out of line and grabbed a head, which I divided with Warrant Officer James Park.

Since Patton had sent in a group to liberate his son-in-law, we knew that American troops had crossed the Rhine River. Sooner or later we were going to be liberated. When or how was the question! If we were going be liberated in the middle of a battle, many of us would be killed. If from a skirmish, the Germans would likely kill us. Either way it looked like we were in deep trouble. Anyway, thanks to the raid, we are leaving this camp.

We were divided us into two groups, evidently because

there were so many POWs. One group went to Moosburg POW Camp. Our group left camp and walked down the same steep hill that we had so much difficulty struggling up when we arrived in that severe cold, exhausted and suffering aftereffects of that train ride from hell. I was thinking that, although I was still hungry, we were in somewhat better shape coming out of Hammelburg than we were going in. We passed through the city of Hammelburg, but it was still dark and too early for anyone to be up and about. Needless to say, it was too dark to see any of the city. I have no idea what Hammelburg looked like when we arrived. I do not remember anything except being half frozen. I looked at nothing except the road ahead. It was dark and I could not see a thing. As day broke we marched past a great number of German soldiers getting ready to head for the front - the exact opposite direction from where we were going.

Now we began our walk through hell. We marched across Germany for thirty-six days, covering some three hundred sixty-eight kilometers (two hundred forty-one miles). Little did we realize that so many officers in our group would never make it. I understand that the other groups of prisoners from Hammelburg were put back in boxcars and traveled partly by rail, then marched the rest of the way to Moosburg POW camp. We marched all the way to the Austrian border, about thirty miles southeast of Munich, apparently with no destination in mind - just walking day after day, barely covering enough ground to keep ahead of the advancing Allied front. For over a month we trekked across Germany, thanking God each day we were still alive and wondering when and if Hitler's order to kill all prisoners would be carried out.

Our group had a guard company of about fifty, both officers and enlisted men. Our captors also had a forwarding party who went ahead and made arrangements for us to sleep in barns along the way. I did not know where we were along our two hundred forty-one mile journey. Our chaplain, Lt. Mark Moore, later supplied me with a list of towns and villages where we stopped for the night or for a rest. As a chaplain, he was allowed to keep a pen and paper with him (a privilege denied other prisoners). He wrote down the name of every town we entered. He kept precise notes (towns, cities, dates, time of day, significant events) and shared his notes with me after the war.

Our captors also had a kitchen crew who went ahead to obtain a stove and have some hot soup cooked (for the guards only) by the time we arrived. The stoves were large vats with wood fireboxes underneath, formerly used to boil potatoes for hog food, so I heard. The POW had nothing to eat except what could be stolen along the way.

A Serb, who said his name was Dan, joined our column. He spoke broken English. He was with us for one day then disappeared. He could speak German so I imagine he escaped from the group of POWs and made his way back to Yugoslavia, his home.

We struggled through the night and early morning that first day, covering some sixteen kilometers. My tooth was aching and the sore on my heel was giving me a limp. After what seemed like eternity, we reached the village of Bruckendorf at nine o'clock in the morning and rested there until six p.m. How I made it through that first day is a mystery to me. A young person can do a lot of things if forced to do them - even if you think it is impossible.

During this thirty-six day trek, all I had to eat was raw cabbage, raw potatoes, a piece of limburger cheese and a pigeon which was not much. Some officers who had not attempted to escape had more than I did. They had stayed behind during the battle and had raided the mess hall at Hammelburg and therefore had plenty of food and some ersatz coffee. But if I had it to do all over again, I would still attempt to escape instead of staying behind and raiding the kitchen. I was very hungry, but there was nothing to do about that now. We had a short rest and then marched another ten kilometers and arrived at Schnachwert at ten p.m. I still don't know how we managed to cover twenty-six kilometers that first day in our weakened condition. I guess you can do lots of things you once thought impossible if you've got a gun barrel poking you in the back. Completely exhausted, famished with hunger, and emotionally wrung out, I had no trouble falling asleep that night - the hay in the loft seemed as soft as a feather mattress.

March 1945

S	M	T	W	T	F	S
					1	2	3
4	5	6	7	8	9	10
11	12	13	14	15	16	17
18	19	20	21	22	23	24
25	26	27	28	29	30	31

What The Heck
March 29, 1945

On March 29 they woke us at dawn. We were counted, lined up and ordered to march again a little after seven in the morning. The weather was warm and spring-like and I felt better, as if some of my strength was returning. Flowers were blooming all around us, but I would've appreciated their beauty more on a full stomach. All we had to eat on the march was some raw cabbage - more tasty than the "Green Hornet" we'd had at Hammelburg, but just not very filling. My foot still hurt. The toothache had died down somewhat. At least after a full day, we were still alive and had not been executed in spite of Hitler's orders.

We covered some twenty-two kilometers that day, arriving at the village of Herlheim about ten that night. It was my first good look at the countryside of Germany proper and the impressions I received were mixed. Some areas seemed devastated by bombs, others were untouched. I saw few people, mainly women, children, and old men. The war had drained Germany of her young men, as I guess all wars do if dragged on for very long. Young men always seem to pay for the ambition and greed of politicians. Hitler was ambitious. He was greedy. He was a master politician.

At Herlheim I managed to steal a few raw potatoes, which I ate with my cabbage. I tried to clean some of the dirt off the potatoes by rubbing them against my shirt as I walked. I couldn't get all the dirt off, but what the heck - I'm sure dirt has some nutrients in it. We all had tow sacks or gunnysacks which we had picked up in the barns where we slept. We cut holes in the middle and put them over our heads with the bottom of the sack in front so we could quickly stow away any food we had the chance to steal. We could also eat as we walked while protecting what little food we had from being stolen by other POWs.

We were awakened the next morning by the familiar cry of "Raus! Raus!" They did a quick count and put us on the road again by seven. It was pouring rain and we covered only thirteen kilometers by noon, when we stopped, shivering and soaking wet, at Obershargack. The weather was getting warmer, which I didn't mind, but the lice were getting more active, which kept us scratching all the time.

I stole more potatoes and a couple of eggs right out from under the hens while the guards were outside. We couldn't cook the eggs, so I just sucked them out of the shells raw, giving my body some much needed protein. I also swiped a large piece of Limburger cheese and kept it in the sack right under my nose. It stunk to high heaven, which may be why it was so easy to steal. I tried trading it to the other POWs but got no takers. At least it did not taste as bad as it smelled, although it's not something I would eat by choice. Still, it was better than that awful German war bread!

We dried out in the barn that night, sleeping with our clothes on in the warm hay. How we kept from getting pneumonia I don't know, but God apparently still had his eye on us.

On March 31, we started walking again at eight in the morning. It was misting rain as we started out, but as we marched, the weather cleared and we dried out while walking. I saw a German plane that day - it was one of the new Messerschmitt 262 jet fighters, the fastest plane in the world at that time, and the world's first combat jet. We were amazed at its speed, as it roared overhead. We noticed German planes were getting to be a rare sight as the Allies won control of the skies over Germany. Day after day, we saw wave after wave of

147

———————————

U. S. bombers going overhead, sometimes far off and sometimes quite close. I wonder how these people can stand the constant bombing, night and day? Still, I've never seen as many bombers at once as I did back in November at Elsenborn. Germany deserved the bombings for electing that crazed Austrian (Hitler) as their leader. As gruesome as it may seem, I just cannot make myself feel too sorry for them. Anyway, the German people seemed to love that man. If there ever was a devil on this earth, it had to be Hitler.

We covered twenty kilometers that day and called it quits about three in the afternoon when we reached Wasserberndorf. We were all pretty tired - we were eating more, but our bodies were burning more calories due to constant marching. At least it wasn't cold anymore. Here, like nearly everywhere else, the guards had our slit trenches (latrines) dug out in front, next to the street. We had to relieve ourselves in full view of anyone who was watching. Sometimes small children would come up and giggle at us. I was embarrassed at first and tried to hold it in as long as I could, but eventually reached the point that I simply thought, "to hell with them". I just didn't care anymore.

April 1945						
S	M	T	W	T	F	S
1	2	3	4	5	6	7
8	9	10	11	12	13	14
15	16	17	18	19	20	21
22	23	24	25	26	27	28
29	30					

Safer In Numbers Than On Our Own
April 1, 1945

The next day, April 1, 1945 was Easter Sunday. We got to rest all day, no walking! I ate raw cabbage, potatoes, and some of that foul smelling Limburger cheese. Every time I ate it I was reminded of that damned town of Limburg and how rude the people there were to us. It wasn't fried chicken and bread pudding, but it was food. Since leaving Hammelburg, we had marched eighty-one kilometers in four days. We could hear artillery booming in the distance behind us. Judging from the direction, I'd say Hammelburg had been liberated again for good. I hoped. I only wish I had been there to see it.

April 2, 1945 - after roll count, we began trudging through the rain again, covering twenty-five kilometers before stopping at Weisendorf at four in the afternoon. I was wringing wet with water sloshing even in my shoes. I had my usual meal of raw potatoes, cabbage and Limburger cheese, and then went to sleep in my wet clothes. By morning they were dry and the weather was pretty - no rain, lots of sunshine and warm. For some reason the guards quit counting us - I guess they figure that we are so far inside Germany it would be foolish for us to try to escape and most likely be executed by the SS troops who seemed to be everywhere. Either that, or they realize, as we did, that the war was nearly over and when we were liberated anyone of us could have a say in how they would be treated as POWs. We were up and moving at five in the morning, heading east as we had been ever since leaving Hammelburg.

Even though we were marching through rural country, we could see the results of the Air Corps' bombs all around us - craters in the road from strafing by fighter - bombers, destroyed houses and businesses in nearly every village, and occasionally the smoking wreck of a shot-down aircraft, German or American. The damage in the villages now seemed worse than when we first started walking. War is truly an engine of destruction. I still do not understand why people let some idiot, mental derelict like Hitler in office. It is beyond me. Their country was being demolished. Hitler thought, with a powerful army, he could rule the world. He never gave a damn for all the dead and injured and destruction left in his path.

We arrived at Vaca at 11:30 in the morning and halted for the day, having covered sixteen kilometers. I ate my usual meal and rested for the remainder of the day. That night we slept on the floor of a Lutheran church. We started walking at six-thirty and stopped at Furth, only eleven kilometers away, before noon.

We still could hear the rumble of artillery in the distance, growing closer now. We all knew the war was nearly over and liberation was drawing closer day by day. Even the guards knew. You could see a look of uncertainty on their faces. We spent the afternoon and evening on the outskirts of Furth,

149

a fairly large German city.

When we entered the city, I could not believe my eyes. There was damage, far more than I had ever seen. The city was demolished. It is hard to describe the damage. It seemed as though every house and all the buildings were just shells of what they used to be, old beautiful stone buildings. It was hard going through all the rubble. The city was just a pile of rubble.

Once while pausing inside Furth to rest, I saw several hiding places in the rubble. They looked like caves. We could slip off to hide and wait for our army to come and liberate us. Park and I decided not to hide. We realized several days ago that, with the whole mess nearly over, we would be safer in numbers than on our own. The Air Corps' bombs had done heavy damage to Furth - an excellent job. How this country could ever be cleaned up and repaired was utterly beyond me! I couldn't see a single building that wasn't heavily damaged by bombs. We walked and crawled over and around rubble in every street as we cut through town. I was glad our country was not being devastated like that!

That afternoon and night we stayed in a huge barn. I found several grain bins still full of oats and wheat, and a grinder too. I ground enough oats and wheat to fill all my pockets and moved on before the guards caught me. The meal I'd ground was dry, but it was the best stuff I'd had in months. We had to be very careful when pilfering food - the guards evidently had the authority to shoot any one of us at any time. They gave the death penalty to be carried out the next day to one POW for milking a cow. I'm not sure if it was ever done.

On April 5, we left Furth and after a few kilometers we marched through Nuremberg. It was the largest city we had seen in Germany, and it was a beautiful mess. Our Air Corps and the British RAF had done a real "bang-up" job here - block after block of rubble where the factories that fueled Hitler's war machine once stood. Most of the rubble had been cleared out, but I don't remember seeing a single building in the downtown district that didn't show some bomb damage. We passed block after block of hollow blackened shells where buildings used to be - bare brick walls were all that was left standing on most blocks. I saw one block of apartments that Hitler had built for show before the war - I remembered seeing them in a newsreel back in the states in the thirties, a newsreel showing what great things Hitler was doing for Germany. I also remembered a soldier collecting cans of grease to be used for explosives from the apartment. Now these apartments were all scarred and cratered - complete devastation. This is war. As far as I was concerned, Germany deserved all that they got. Still, I was so glad this wasn't happening to the U.S.!

There were very few people in the city, and they were all on bicycles. I saw one funny looking car that looked as if it were using firewood for fuel. It must have been some kind of steam engine. Just a short way out of town our captors let us stop next to the rail yards and an ammunition plant to rest and eat any food we might have under a small grove of fir or pine trees about fifteen of twenty feet high. We were feeling somewhat better with the warmer air, exercise and more food. My tooth was still hurting pretty bad and the lice were really running wild with the warm weather.

The German officer in charge said that the break would be ten minutes but changed his mind and said we could stay thirty or forty, so we took advantage of the opportunity and swapped food with each other. James Park and I felt pretty lucky, since we had a couple of potatoes and grain in our pockets from the day before. We had stolen all our food from the barns where we stayed for we were never issued any rations at all on the entire thirty-six day march. I traded some of the grain for half a cabbage, and then mixed the grain up with cold water to form oatmeal-like paste that tasted downright delicious - to me, at least.

April 1945

S	M	T	W	T	F	S
1	2	3	4	5	6	7
8	9	10	11	12	13	14
15	16	17	18	19	20	21
22	23	24	25	26	27	28
29	30					

Huddled On The Ground
April 5, 1945

As we finished eating lunch at Nuremberg, the air raid sirens from the nearby factory started blaring. The steady droning whine brought up goose bumps on my skin. The American Airforce (Germans called them AMIS.) started dropping bombs on Furth. We could tell at a distance it was Furth. Too bad the Airforce did not know Furth already lay in ruins. Even though we were on the other side of Nuremberg, we could see the explosions. We were all excited. Give 'em hell! We were all in awe. The day before it looked like the city of Furth was a pile of rubble. Bombs hit something! We could see resulting explosions! American or British intelligent agents were doing one helluva good job in finding a munitions plant in that bombed out city.

People from the ammunition plant about a hundred yards more or less from us came running out in all directions, hollering at us even though we couldn't understand a word they said. We got the drift all right, but our guards would not let us move! Moments later, a reconnaissance plane dropped a flare over the factory, designating it as the target for the bombers following behind. Then the first wave of B-24's came roaring into view.

Five hundred pound bombs began dropping on the factory about a hundred yards away from us. Nearby, anti-aircraft batteries opened up on them - the falling shrapnel from their shells came wailing down from the sky, sounding like a pipe organ in the sky. It was sheer chaos – eighty-eight millimeter shells arcing into the sky and five hundred pound bombs screaming down and shaking the earth when they hit. It felt like an earthquake. We were both excited and scared stiff from being so close to the action, but cheered our bombers anyway and told them to give 'em hell! We were all giving each other play-by-play descriptions of what was happening.

Another recon plane appeared and dropped more flares, even closer to us this time. Seeing those flares drop, we knew what was about to happen. A second wave of bombers appeared, and we watched their payloads come shrieking down - too close for comfort! We could see the buildings just disintegrate when hit, but we weren't looking up as much now - no words can describe our terror as wave after wave of bombers continued to drop their deadly cargo closer and closer to where we lay huddled on the ground. Smoke and fire are everywhere in the air. The next two waves are again hitting the plant. Hell is breaking loose all around us, heaven and earth have been reduced to a creaming universe of battle where the greatest danger comes to us from our own side and we are helpless to fight back even if we could.

God, this is getting close - men were lying down, praying that they had not come this far to die by the hand of our own airmen. The sixth wave struck a more distant target. Dare we hope the raid was over? No! Another wave comes roaring in, hitting the nearest plant with bombs and incendiary shells that create a huge fireworks display in the sky, a spectacle that we were too scared to appreciate. The plant was reduced to a huge fountain of flame that continued to explode and burn for hours, a pillar of fire with continual explosions marking the wrath of the Allies.

Another recon plane approached. Flares dropped right on top of us and on the rail yard which was next to us! Still the guards would not let us move! None of us had helmets. Shrapnel, jagged shards of metal from exploding anti-aircraft shells that can cut right through you, was raining all around us. We could hear the deadly, screaming, swishing sound as they spun overhead and among us. Being hit by shrapnel is almost always fatal, or at least results in dismemberment. Now the eighth wave of bombers appeared, and instead of coming from left to right they headed straight for us. They were directly overhead when they released their bombs. I'll never forget the horrible screaming noise the bombs made coming down. I was lying face down with my head in my hands. I thought the earth would never stop heaving and bucking under me - it was like trying to ride a giant Texas Mustang. I was certain that my time at last had come. The five hundred pounders were hitting all around us, and now another wave of bombers came thundering and hit the rail yards. The noise was deafening. I had trouble hearing for days afterward. I was bouncing like a rubber ball from impact tremors. It was hard to keep lying down. I wanted to get up and run like hell, but the shrapnel I could hear whizzing overhead would probably kill me before I got ten feet. I could hear men all around me screaming their prayers - "Our Father who art in Heaven," etc. Shells from the ammunition plant and trains were exploding and going off like giant firecrackers from the blaze our bombs created. The sheer force of the sound was buffeting me like knockout punches from Joe Louis. This was such a tragedy. I wanted to scream out, "Hey, we're Americans down here!" Men were screaming, cursing, and praying, sometimes all in the same breath.

It was just so indescribable, the sheer force and the noise those bombs made. The earth rolled and heaved like an earthquake. Every time a shell hit I felt like a giant hand was lifting me by the nape of my neck and seat of my trousers and slamming me back into the ground. Dirt, rocks, boards and debris showered down over me, nearly covering me, then another ear-splitting explosion, with metal, wood and other debris - probably some human body parts as well - flying overhead with a deadly whistling sound. This is hell, I thought - it couldn't get any worse.

Thank the Lord it did not! The last wave of bombers flew off, and I finally stood and looked around, my knees shaking so badly I nearly fell. The carnage was sickening. Dead and wounded men lay all around, some crying in pain, some with arms and legs blown off, bodies blown apart with intestines and organs on the ground, all covered in blood, either their own or that of stricken comrades. Some of us had bits of human flesh all over us. If I had any flesh or blood on me, it was on my back where I could not see it.

Such a terrible, sickening sight. I shuddered at the thought that I could have been one of those dead, or worse yet, dismembered. I thought I might faint. At that moment I felt a fleeting sympathy for the German people. However horrible their government might be, women and children don't deserve to live through this kind of stuff.

The bombs stopped falling. Before we stood up, James Park and I reached down into a crater and tried to pull out an officer we thought was wounded. He was totally mutilated – only his clothes were holding his body together. We rolled his remains in a blanket and laid him with the other dead, for the Germans to dispose. We could see that he was a 2nd Lieutenant and looked to be just a young boy about nineteen or twenty years old. I shuddered to think that this man was no more than ten or fifteen feet away from me, and the bomb that killed him could just as easily have struck me. Why am I continually spared? We gave his dog tags to Chaplain Mark Moore, who kept track of all our dead and wounded. Chaplain Moore is a true American hero and I am still proud to have him as a friend. After the war he wrote a narrative of his experiences, called *Prisoner of the Germans*, which I quote here by his permission:

> *"I wondered how I would feel being torn apart or dashed out into eternity. During it all I knew whether I lived or died I would be in the hands of my God. I opened my eyes but dust and smoke limited my vision to fifteen or twenty feet. Then the ninth wave moved in and hit the target, and then the tenth wave repeated what the eighth had done. This time I got into a bomb crater and it was not as bad although several bombs hit nearby. After a few seconds I crawled out and looked around. I saw a number of lifeless bodies. I wanted to run, hide, fly, or anything to get away. I didn't think I could stand it - then someone called out "Water,*

*Water!" I thought, "I can give him my water," and I
started. After that everything became natural. ... The
guards moved all the able-bodied out and left thirteen of us to care for the deceased - four chaplains,
three medics, and six others. We worked for an
hour and a half and got about forty men on trucks
and back to a hospital where we knew an American medic was stationed. Then we worked for two
and a half hours on identification of the dead."*

As for me, I walked around the many dead and wounded,
thanking God that I was still alive. How many of us had lived
through it I don't know, and I certainly don't want to seem
arrogant, but even during the worst of it I had the strangest
feeling. I knew that God was with all of us but some were spared
and some were not. I like to believe that prayers from home
plus my own saved me. I am sure that all the brave men killed
and wounded also had those from home praying for them. As
I was lying there during the bombing, all kinds of debris were
falling on me. I was covered with rocks, wood and dirt; yet it
was such a strange feeling that it is hard to explain. During
the bombing, it felt like something was protecting me. I like to
believe that it was my guardian angel. It had to be more than
just luck. It is a strange feeling that I cannot describe. I am
fortunate to be alive when so many others or not - for some
reason, God is still watching over me.

About fifteen or twenty feet away lay the mangled body
of a captain with whom I'd been talking shortly before the raid
began. His leg, with the boot still on, was hanging in a nearby
tree - my God, how horrible! My legs were still shaking so badly
I could hardly walk. Here just a few minutes ago he and I were
talking about something. Of course, we had no idea what fate
had in store for us. I often wonder what his name was and
where he was from. I thought of that old saying, "You will not
die until your time comes."

Park and I sat on the edge of a crater, along side Lieutenant Bob Everly from Chicago, whom we had pulled out of the crater. The man was trying to talk, but was bleeding from his mouth, nose, and ears. I thought he must have internal injuries and later I wondered if he lived. I remember him so well. He said that his name was Bob Everly from Chicago. He said that the singer Bob Eberly was spelled with a "B" but his name, EVERLY was spelled with a "V". He was just a young boy, a second lieutenant. I believe he must have died from his internal injuries within a day or two. After the war, I tried to locate him but had no luck, so I still wonder about him.

April 1945

S	M	T	W	T	F	S
	1	2	3	4	5	6	7
8	9	10	11	12	13	14
15	16	17	18	19	20	21
22	23	24	25	26	27	28
29	30					

Chaplain, Are You Jumpy?
April 5, 1945, a long day

Among the dead found after the Nuremburg and Furth bombing was the senior Protestant Chaplain, Lieutenant Roland Koskamp - someone had drawn a cross of dust on his forehead. I had met him in Hammelburg. He was not only a good chaplain but also an exceptionally fine gentleman.

I am forever grateful for our chaplain, Mark Moore, a Nazarene preacher, who was in the POW Camp Oflag XIIIB Hammelburg. He was in the two hundred forty-one mile march with us from beginning to end. He also endured the terrible bombing at Nuremburg. After Chaplain Koskamp was killed during the bombing, Chaplain Mark Moore became senior chaplain in charge of all dead and wounded. First Lieutenant Moore describes his duties well in his book, Prisoner of the Germans, and has given permission for me to quote a passage here:

> *"I was put in charge and it never occurred to me that I was senior chaplain until I reached down for a dog tag. When I held it in my hand I read, 'Rowland A. Koskcamp.' I dropped it on his chest and took hold of the left side of his shirt collar. There was the cross! I looked into the face and surely enough there was Chaplain Rowland A. Koskcamp!*

157

"Just a few days before, he had shown me his New Testament and had told me how much it had meant to him. He said that the pages were coming apart from wear. He took his billfold out and showed me his wife's picture and the picture of his little girl, and one of his church and one of the parsonages in Holland, Michigan. Chaplain Stonesifer and I took his personal possessions so I could return them to his wife. I found an American blanket and I wrapped his body reverently, as I breathed a prayer. We had worked together and now he had preceded me to his reward. I realized it could easily have been I.

"During the four hours the ammunition plant had been on fire shells were exploding by the hundreds. In fact, as I worked trying to identify a body, a delayed action bomb went off (it may have been a large powder room) and a piece of four-by-four came buzzing through the air and over my head, causing me to duck. Several of the fellows said, 'What's the matter, chaplain? Are you jumpy? That missed you!' I guess I was jumpy. I was tired and ready to move on.

"I had the personal belongings of twenty-four officers who had been killed. They amounted to about fifteen pounds of extra weight. We couldn't get them to the Red Cross or to our lines, so I gave them to the officers who knew the men. They promised they would see that the belongings were returned. At times we were so tired we couldn't take another step, and because I knew I could not carry that extra weight, I had to do the next best thing.

"Twenty-four officers were killed the first day. We heard that five died the next day. Three Germans also were killed.

"The civilians acted differently during the

hours following the bombing. Some came and laughed. Some asked how we liked the bombing by our comrades.

"A few of the civilians wanted to help us and I talked to some who stopped me as I went from man to man. They said Hitler was the cause and he should be hanged. They were careful when they spoke such words for they were afraid of the guards and their fellow civilians. One man said he had lived in America twelve years and hated Hitler and wanted to leave Germany and return to the States. However, the guards moved the civilians back and we worked without their sarcasm or sympathy."

Chaplain Moore, now the ranking chaplain in our group, went from one lifeless body to the next, praying for the souls of the dead and comforting the wounded as much as possible. He too was shell shocked from bombing and every bit as weak and scared as I was, yet he had time and a kind word for everyone. He worked tirelessly among the wounded and was still at it when we who were able walked away from the scene of carnage. My thanks to Reverend Mark Moore for excerpts from his book and copies of letters about notifications of death he received after turning in the dead soldiers' dog tags. He is a dedicated minister, and should have received a medal for his actions, not just that day, but throughout the long march, for his ceaseless work under incredible pressure. Looking back as we left Nuremburg, I noticed that so many trees had been knocked down, their limbs severed by shrapnel, craters all over the place - it's a wonder that there weren't a hundred of us instantly killed.

It is hard for me to believe that I (or anyone, for that matter) could survive being so close to a five hundred pound bomb when it exploded. Perhaps if the ground had been hard instead of soft everybody might have been killed. Before we moved on, I counted twenty-four American officers killed outright and over one hundred and five wounded, plus a few guards. Five or six more officers died the next night. I'm sure some of the more seriously wounded did not recover. I'll never know just how many died. Mark told me a couple of days later that the total death toll rose to thirty-five, but I imagine that after a month or so it might have risen as high as fifty, there were so many gravely injured. I am sure some were blown to bits or buried in the rubble of the bomb craters - the young officer Park and I pulled out was almost completely covered with dirt. Someone said they were near the German guards that died, and that the guards had tried to make a run for it and been slashed to death by flying shrapnel. I don't know of any other time during the war in Europe when that many American officers were killed and wounded at one time. The bombing raid at Nuremberg haunts me to this day.

I should add that the Air Corps should not be blamed for this tragedy. The raid had been planned long before we got near Nuremberg, and the bombers were flying so high over us there is no way they could have seen us. I blame it on the horror of war - an unfortunate accident. In fact, the bombers did a very good job of striking their targets that day - the factories and rail yards were completely wiped out.

With tears in my eyes, I looked around the area. A cold chill went through me - men lay dead, the wounded had been moved together and lay there, moaning in pain, the captain's leg still in the tree. Trees knocked over with limbs severed by shrapnel lay scattered about. Ammunition from the flattened factories was still exploding. Rail yards were demolished. Some bombs were still going off - I just had to see it again one more time before I left - a memory that I do not want to, nor will I ever, forget. War is so terrible - fifty years have passed and I can still close my eyes and see it all over again. What next, I wondered as we staggered away from that blood bath.

As we left, debris from the exploding factories was still flying all over the place. I hoped that Mark would be able to make it. As I reminisce this day, with tears in my eyes, I do not know how I survived such a catastrophe!

At least I knew that our liberation could not be far off. We won't have to endure another winter in captivity, anyway. As I began to file away from the rail yards, a Lieutenant Colonel, who looked to be about forty-five years old, with shrapnel wound in his leg asked if I could help him along. With his wound and in my dazed and shell-shocked state, we straggled along behind the column as the German trucks arrived to evacuate the dead and wounded. As we walked away, we took one last look at the carnage behind us. Tears came to our eyes. I never knew this Lt. Colonel's name, never asked him. He seemed like a beaten dog, seemed more like he was following me. I had to tell him what to do on the walk. He was in a complete daze from the bombing and just as scared as I was.

		April 1945				
S	M	T	W	T	F	S
1	2	3	4	5	6	7
8	9	10	11	12	13	14
15	16	17	18	19	20	21
22	23	24	25	26	27	28
29	30					

Bombed By Our Own Planes
April 5, 1945, a very long day

The guards did not care how quickly we moved now - they just wanted to put Nuremberg behind them as fast as possible. Warrant Officer Park with Captain Cobb and Lieutenant Tompkins were right behind us. None of them had been hurt in the bombing.

As we left I noticed a secondary string of explosions coming from the ammunition plant and rail yards as buried ammunition, powder and fuel caught fire. Debris was still flying around us as we hobbled away, and I couldn't see how the rail yards could ever be cleaned up and used again. Trains and boxcars were twisted, mangled, and stacked on top of one another like giant building blocks. We could have escaped, but where could we go in this wasteland? If we escaped and they caught us, the SS would execute us in a heartbeat - unless the relatives of those in Nuremburg, who'd been killed in the bombing, got to us first. As we struggled past an anti-aircraft battery, I heard the crew laughing at us for being bombed by our own planes. I can still hear those SOB's laughing at all our fine officers being killed. We consoled ourselves with the thought that they failed to shoot down even one American bomber. I wonder if some of the anti-aircraft shrapnel killed some of the POWs. We could still hear the explosions rocking the ammunition plants and rail cars long after we left our scoffers.

Later after leaving Nuremberg, I could see birds but couldn't hear them singing. Many noises I used to hear I no longer hear, my eardrums shattered by the concussion of all those bombs. We were far behind the column now, and about three miles outside of Nuremberg we stopped at a house for water and to see if there was any food. When we came upon the house I asked Colonel if he wanted to stop and try to find something to eat. His answer was, "yes sir." Boy he was confused. I was just a Warrant officer. The old lady and her husband gave us a cool drink. She spoke broken English and beamed when I told her I was from Texas. She told me her son's name and said that he lived in New Braunfels, Texas. She asked me if I knew him - naturally I answered "Ja!" She was so pleased I knew her son that she gave us a small piece of cheese - probably all the food that they had. I felt badly about that afterward - she seemed so nice and seemed very proud to have a son living in the states. I felt pretty guilty for lying to her and wished that I had really known her son so that I wouldn't have had to lie. Whoever he was, he should be proud to have such decent parents. They were the first Germans to treat me nicely since I was captured. When we were ready to leave, I asked the Colonel if he was ready - his answer, "Yes sir." Later on, we caught up with the rest of the group at Sevcht - a small town not far from Nuremberg. In spite of it all, we'd made eighteen kilometers that day. I fell into the hay as soon as we arrived and slept like the dead. The war might be spinning out of control to its fiery finale, but the walk through hell couldn't be stopped for any reason it seemed. I'd had a bellyful of war. I couldn't help but remember that I had worried back in Belgium that it might all be over before I had a chance to participate!

All along the route of this march I noticed German civilians, young and old, pushing carts ahead of them as they carried all their worldly possessions west, ahead of the approaching Russian army. The carts were two wheeled. The wheels looked like they might be bicycle wheels. I could not hear any Russian gunfire but evidently they were pretty close or these people would not have been in such a hurry. What a shame. However it was their fault for letting an insane man control their destiny. It was so strange. When the Germans were winning the war people thought Hitler was wonderful, but when Germany was being defeated, you could not find anyone who liked him. I guess that the Russians were about the only thing that the German people really feared.

There is an old saying "I will see you tomorrow." I thought it would be a wonderful day if only we could live this day to welcome tomorrow. This had been my prayer. With Hitler's orders to kill all POWs, I felt fortunate to be spared today, so we could see tomorrow. I thought if we could see another tomorrow and yet another then maybe this damn war would be over. After we stopped, I never saw the Colonel again. Where did he go? Even after liberation, I never again saw the wounded shell-shocked Lt. Colonel whose name I never asked.

Before

After

"*Germany deserved the bombings for electing that crazed Austrian (Hitler) as their leader. If there ever was a devil on this earth, it had to be Hitler.*"
–Harry Thompson

April 1945

S	M	T	W	T	F	S
1	2	3	4	5	6	7
8	9	10	11	12	13	14
15	16	17	18	19	20	21
22	23	24	25	26	27	28
29	30					

Keeping Just Ahead of American Forces
April 6, 1945

The morning after the Raid on Nuremberg was April 6 - the guards did not even wake us up. I slept till noon and woke with every muscle sore. I ate raw potatoes and some grain mixed with water. The guards waited until three in the afternoon to line us up for the forced march they were planning. I guess they were just as hurt, dazed and tired as we were. There were not nearly as many men with us as before, in fact, there seemed to be only about a fourth of the group who had begun the march after Patton's Raid on Hammelburg. I did not see the prisoner who was to be shot for milking the cow or the guard who caught him. I suppose that they may have been killed or wounded in the bombing. Several guards had been killed. We knew that the American troops were near because we could hear the roar of artillery close behind us. Why not just let us go? Germany is finished.

Shortly after setting out on our forced walk, fleeing further away from Patton's advancing troops, going further behind German lines, we saw an American bomber flying a short distance away blow up in mid-air and, though we watched anxiously, we never saw any chutes - an entire ten-man crew killed! What a terrible tragedy! I am sure that most of the Airmen were only youngsters in their teens or early twenties. Grief stricken parents hung ten more gold stars on front windows, not to mention equally grief stricken brothers, sisters, girl friends and other close friends.

It was the same old thing when we stopped at barns for the night. Our guards always asked the owner of the barn where they wanted the latrine ditch dug and the owners always wanted them dug out front, next to the road. I could never figure out why they were always in front and not around back, where we at least could have a little privacy. Was it a deliberate policy to humiliate us or did the Germans simply have no decency about such things? Anytime we went to the toilet we had an audience of young boys and girls, sometimes grown women, standing and watching us urinate - hardly my idea of great entertainment, but none of us cared anymore. I really was not embarrassed even a little bit. To hell with them! We did get a laugh at their reaction to Larry, a black officer. We went out to the toilet and he attracted quite an audience. They had never seen a black officer and probably wanted to know if he was black all over. I teased him about it for quite awhile afterwards.

We made only fourteen kilometers that day and stopped four hours after we stayed at the town of Buch. I was tired and still shaky from the bombing. On April 8 we got an early start and made eleven kilometers, spending the rest of the day and night in a large barn. The farm was located next to a large stone bridge over a cement canal. I think it was the Ludwig Canal. There was a huge explosive charge shaped like a gigantic bomb in the middle of the bridge, ready to be blown at a moment's notice to slow down American troops, who were very close now. I had the jitters just walking by it. Artillery shells were landing less than a mile away.

On April 9 we stayed near the cement canal all day, too weak and tired to march. I was hoping maybe we could hide in

165

the cellar or something and let our troops overtake us, but no chance - the guards were too alert now. The artillery was now landing about half a mile away. How I wish our GI's could break through and liberate us.

On April 10 we were up early and marching by six in the morning - keeping just ahead of the American forces. At one town we were assembled in a big circle around a German general who spoke to us in English. He said that he commanded this district and had received orders from Hitler to execute all POW's. He went on to say that as long as we were in his district that this order would not be carried out by any troops under his command. Well, we had finally found one good German, I hoped. More likely the Americans were so close he did not want to harm us, lest he be executed by our own forces when captured. Still, we wondered what would happen when we left his district and if he had authority over the SS troops. Guards for stealing food along the road had shot several of our men. Once, we passed a big stack of sugar beets (I think that's what they were), each beet shaped somewhat like a carrot and as big as a small log was stacked like cordwood. One young officer wondered aloud if they were edible and went to pick one up. He was shot by the guard and died instantly.

After making some sixteen kilometers before noon that day, we stopped at Braubach, another small village. I traded my fountain pen for an egg from one of the guards. After dark I managed to steal a few more potatoes and another head of cabbage - was that all the Germans had left to eat? The lice were getting livelier and more numerous every day. My foot was much better but now the tooth was aching again.

Three or four days before being captured, I had gone to Division supply to get three pairs of new combat boots, a pair for Tech. Sergeant Carl Leibrock, Sergeant Burrel Hartley and myself. We were lucky, for all three of us were captured and those boots protected our feet. They were definitely obtained at the right time.

On April 11 we hit the road at six in the morning and

headed out, once more barely ahead of the American lines. My toothache is becoming unbearable. One American fighter plane made a strafing pass over us and we hit the ditch. Luckily I do not think anyone caught a bullet. The pilot fired only one brief burst before realizing we were prisoners, then did a fly-by and tipped his wing in recognition. He never came back to bother us and neither did any more planes, but we all envied the lucky SOB as he winged his way back to the nice American airfield and some hot coffee, a good meal and a warm bed.

We saw another German jet shortly after that - I do not remember the precise date. The Messercschmitt 262 was an experimental aircraft that could fly faster than anything we had ever seen. If Hitler had gotten those secret weapons to the front a little earlier in the war it could have been disastrous for the Allied cause - I do not think we developed any aircraft during the war that could equal the German jet. One second it was directly overhead, the next it was out of sight. We watched it make four of five passes.

I guess the American Army had taken Nuremberg by now - they were so close behind us. We were constantly just outside their artillery range and if our column lagged, the shells sometimes got too close for comfort. The guards would speed us up whenever that happened. At ten-thirty, after walking fifteen kilometers, we arrived at Kelterbell. So far we have traveled some two hundred seven (207) kilometers since we left Patton's Raid at Hammelburg. We spent the day in and around another huge barn filled with pigeons - tried all day to catch one, but we had to be very careful, for the penalty for killing any stock or fowl was a bullet in the head.

One day, as we were marching, I do not know the date, I remember seeing one of our guards stare intently at a house we were passing with an expression of deep sadness. He could not take his eyes off it and kept staring as if he were looking for someone until that house was out of sight. I guess that might have been his home and his superior would not let him leave the column to check on his folks. I kind of felt sorry for him - maybe he was wondering if he would ever see his family again.

April 1945

S	M	T	W	T	F	S
	1	2	3	4	5	6	7
8	9	10	11	12	13	14
15	16	17	18	19	20	21
22	23	24	25	26	27	28
29	30					

Pretty Nasty Broth
April 12, 1945

Guards on April 12 told us that we would be given a day off from marching in celebration of Hitler's birthday. They heated up a fifty-gallon drum of water and told us that when it boiled we could boil our socks. I can still hear artillery, but not as close as yesterday. I wonder what happened?

I had not had clean socks since capture, and the chance to boil them gave me an idea. I went up to the barn loft for one more try at a pigeon, and caught one! I hid behind the hay and plucked the feathers out of it, gutting it with my bare hands and hiding the evidence in the straw. Then I removed my shoes and socks to put the pigeon in one sock and a potato in the other. By this time the water was boiling, so I tied the socks together and, while the guards were not looking, I threw them in the boiling water with all the other socks. The dirty sock water made for a pretty nasty broth, but the pigeon and potato were edible all the same, even if the pigeon and potato tasted like dirty socks. I divided both pidgeon and potato with James Park - it was the first hot meal we had had since leaving Hammelburg.

The Air Corps and the RAF were out in force with some fireworks, evidently helping Hitler celebrate his birthday. This was the first time I had seen the new B-26 Marauder bombers. They were flying over at low altitude, maybe five or six hundred feet. They made no passes at us but shot the hell out of every German military vehicle they saw. What with a hot meal, air show, and clean (if pigeon-scented) socks, I was feeling pretty good - except for that blasted toothache.

April 13 - today the guards woke us with the news that President Roosevelt had died. I was not sure whether to believe them or not. We started walking at six in the morning and, to my surprise, we stopped after cresting a large hill - we had only made twelve kilometers for the day. We have been walking since Patton's Raid on Hammelburg. I wonder if they even have a destination for us, or just intend to walk us around till the war ends? We spent the day at Machbell. All the small villages are alike, it seems - located in a valley near a small river with a white-steepled church at the center of town. The steeple is always the tallest object around. In most of the small towns there are few signs of the war - no military vehicles, bomb damage, etc. The larger towns and cities are all heavily damaged. What a shame that the people of Germany have allowed one lousy leader to bring so much death and destruction on this once great and beautiful country. We spent the next day resting there at Machbell, wondering how much longer the war was going to last. We headed out on April 15.

We left Machbell at six in the morning, making only seven kilometers before arriving at Schafshill a little after eight. The guards must be as tired as we are, and our troops are so close they do not know which way to take us. It's funny - the closer our troops get the nicer our guards become. We all now were getting the hell scared out of us. The American Army was right behind us. Some artillery shells were landing no more than fifty to one hundred yards behind us. For some strange reason we did not even move. We stayed where we were. The shelling soon stopped. The next day we did not walk. We ate our cabbage and potatoes raw and I ate that stinking cheese. I could not even give it away. I still have to say it was better than the German bread.

On April 17 we left Schafshill at six in the morning and walked eighteen kilometers, stopping at Breckendorff. Then we walked the short distance to the Danube River, near Regensburg and they paddled us across the river. The paddle, a large oar mounted on the back of the small boat, propelled the boat by moving back and forth. We kept a sharp eye out for airplanes because, if our airplanes mistook us for Germans, we would be sitting ducks for a strafing run. Once we were safely across, the boat returned for another load of POW's.

169

PATTON'S, ILL FATED RAID

After we crossed we heard small arms fire behind us - American patrols must be right behind us. The guards are marching us farther and faster behind German lines.

The next day we marched another eighteen kilometers, arriving at Scheldenburg, where we spent the rest of the day and that night. The guards were keeping us just ahead of our troops. Artillery fire was getting closer every day. Some of the shells were really too close. I could not understand why they did not just let us go unless it is due to the fact that we were all officers, most ranked no higher than Captain though we did have one or two Lieutenant Colonels. Could they have been holding us as some kind of hostages? Then I thought, if they release us, they will have to go back to fight our advancing columns - and guarding a pack of weakened, hungry prisoners is a lot easier than trying to slow the advancing forces of General Patton!

On April 19, 1945 we stayed at Scheldenburg. The artillery was still very close. I hoped our troops knew where we were - I hated to think that one of our own artillery barrages or an open firefight might kill all of us now. It kind of looked like it might be, and many would be killed. Hundreds of our airplanes were flying around but we had not been strafed since a few days ago or bombed since Nuremberg, so they must have known where we were - I HOPED!

We rested all the next day at Scheldenburg, and the shelling got closer and closer. Our troops must have been almost on top of us. Trying to avoid our own troops, I was so shell shy that every time one landed nearby I hit the dirt. Artillery shells landing less than fifty yards or so from us were too close for any peace of mind. Were they going to let us be killed by our own artillery shells? God, I wanted to live. I had been through just too much to be killed so close to liberation. I had too much reason to look forward to going home - I hoped! The front lines had gotten so near that we were moved during the night. Not one person objected to getting the hell out of the way of the fighting, even if we moved at night.

On April 21, we arrived at Bogenhausen at five in the morning after marching fourteen kilometers in the dark. The guards issued Red Cross boxes to us. Warrant Officer Park and I had to split one between us. Nothing against Park, but I would love to have a whole box to myself. While we were prisoners, we received only three Red Cross boxes and Park and I had to divide each one. Our troops were getting closer and closer and our air force was very active. The next day we left Bogenhausen at six in the morning and walked twenty kilometers, arriving at Silstater which is very near a large POW camp at Moosburg - we were now far ahead of the front. Evidently our last march must have led us in the opposite direction from the advancing American Army.

April 1945

S	M	T	W	T	F	S
1	2	3	4	5	6	7
8	9	10	11	12	13	14
15	16	17	18	19	20	21
22	23	24	25	26	27	28
29	30					

The Guards Were As Scared As We Were
April 22, 1945

We stayed at Silstater for the next four days and rested some. I thought staying in one place for four days was very boring after so many days of marching and being on the move. Boy, was I ever mistaken. Suddenly artillery seemed to be all around us: in front of, in back of, just everywhere. We also could hear rifle and machine gun fire all around.

German troops were all around us, and they were as scared as any Germans I had seen yet. Those scared Germans were a great sight. They were nothing like those cocky bastards we had seen before and during the Bulge. They were getting badly whipped and they knew it. I am sure they all knew Germany had lost the war and wondered why they were forced to continue fighting. I wondered what they were going to do with us. Maybe they were taking us to Moosburg to be liberated! Germany was almost finished. Why were they still fighting? The country was in shambles. Every place you looked the scars of war were evident and still soldiers were supporting Hitler one hundred percent. How could they continue their support? Hitler was solely responsible for the country being devastated! Hitler was the cause of creating nothing but ruins everywhere you look!

I kept thinking that maybe we could hide in this hayloft - it is just full of hay - I started to hide there but twenty or thirty other officers had the same idea. Park talked me out of it, fortunately. The other officers buried themselves in the hay before we left. There was so much hay that no trace of them could be seen. The guards did not even notice that they were gone, or maybe did not even care.

On April 27 we walked a fast pace only a few kilometers to Auerbach, still only a few short miles from Moosburg. The shelling was back again very, very close, maybe two or three hundred yards away. There were German troops everywhere. These German soldiers are not grinning and laughing the way those were during the Battle of the Bulge. They were all grim faced and worried looking. Our troops must be coming, for the Germans were running around instead of walking, as if they could not make up their minds what to do.

We left Auerbach at ten PM and marched all night. Shelling was everywhere, all around us. Some artillery shells landed as close as twenty-five to thirty yards from us, so they moved us again. Just at daybreak a B-24 Liberator flew over very low - must have been a cripple returning from some air raid trying to get back to base. I hope he made it but I do not know - we are in the foothills of the Alps and I do not know if this guy had the power to get over the mountains.

After marching all night we arrived at Kinderbaum a little after seven in the morning on April 29. We got out just ahead of one helluva scrap between our forces and the Germans in our rear - shelling and small arms fire everywhere. I was glad to move out - as hard as it was for me to walk on my crippled feet. I was moving rather fast compared to some of the others. We spent this night in a church - shells dropping all around us. We later heard that on April 29, none other than my old outfit, the 99th Infantry Division, liberated the POW camp at Moosburg.

On April 30 we left Kinderbaum and arrived at Inning, then walked on to Moosen. We moved quickly, stop, then start, then stop again. The guards were so hesitant. Then we marched fast again. We were all nervous and scared. It was impossible to know just how scared we were. Artillery was landing around us like we were Germans. Our own artillery or the crossfire could have killed us at any moment. The guards were as scared as we were. They moved us out of the way as soon as possible.

The country was now very hilly. We were getting close to the Alps Mountains. By the end of the day we arrived at Oberlataufkirchen.

I later heard that this was the day Hitler blew his brains out while hiding in a bunker in Berlin. It was too bad that he did not blow his brains out years before. Many lives would have been saved. I wish that he had lived so that the Russians could have captured him. He would have been tortured and never made it to Nuremberg to be tried for his war crimes.

On May 1 we arrived at Gars on the Inns River. On the way, we walked through a deep ravine and could hear shells and rockets passing overhead. The guards later told us that we had marched right through the middle of a tank battle. We topped a large hill and could see the town of Gars down below. The road down was very steep and ran through town, across the river into Austria, but the bridge guards mistook us for advancing American troops and blew the bridge up a quarter mile in front of us. We were pinned between the river and the advancing American troops. We were going to be either liberated or we were going to be killed.

We later heard that on April 29, none other than my old outfit, the 99th Infantry Division, liberated the POW camp at Moosburg.

173

May 1945

S	M	T	W	T	F	S
		1	2	3	4	5
6	7	8	9	10	11	12
13	14	15	16	17	18	19
20	21	22	23	24	25	26
27	28	29	30	31		

I Gave The Prearranged Signal
May 1, 1945

We were half way down the hill when the bridge into Austria blew so they stopped us at the Burgermeister's house (the mayor) and we bedded down in his barn. There were so few of us now that we could all get into the barn and have room to lie down. When we started on our forced march late the night of Patton's Raid at Hammelburg it would have taken several barns of this size to accommodate all of us. Now we all fit into one barn.

There was no place other than this barn for us to go. The only way out was straight into the arms of our own Army something we just could not do. We kept close together, afraid of getting caught in a cross fire or artillery barrage. Gars was a very old town - the only thing of interest was an old international cathedral and that did not interest me at all - the only thing I wanted to see at that point was home. Still, a lot of the prisoners were fascinated by that old church for some reason - maybe it was a reminder of the faith so many of us leaned on to get us through the whole mess.

As far as I could tell, the plan was to sit in the

174

Burgermeister's barn until we were liberated. We were all a little worried that the SS might find us before our troops did. I heard that the twenty or thirty POW's who hid, waiting there in the hayloft while we marched out a few days before, were discovered by the SS, who raked the hay with machine gun fire and killed nearly all of them. Of course, that may have been nothing but a rumor, but I would not put anything past the SS after seeing what they had done on the first day of the Bulge. I was glad Park talked me out of hiding in the hay!

On the night of May 1 a member of the French underground approached us and told us that we would be liberated the very next day, May 2, 1945, by American troops who were only a short distance away. A short distance, hell! They had been on top of us for about a week. The next morning, May 2, I was walking in the yard in front of the house, near the road, when I spotted a jeep in the middle of the road and American soldiers, crouched and walking single file on either side of the road. My God, what a wonderful sight! I gave the prearranged signal and we all casually walked into the barn and reclined on the hay.

We were officially listed as being liberated by the 14th Armored Division and the 86th Infantry Division, although the soldiers who actually freed us were from the 86th Infantry Division. Our German guards must have been expecting our troops, for as soon as they saw our soldiers, they threw down their guns, raised their arms to surrender without offering any resistance and hollered whatever their word for surrender was. They were all smiling and seemed glad it was all over. All their rifles were all piled up. I had not realized how many guards there were, for there must have been forty to fifty (40 to 50) rifles with bayonets in that pile. I picked up the best rifle I could find, dismantled it, and kept it for a souvenir. Also, a few days earlier, I traded my fountain pen to a guard for an egg; now I got that back from him. I still have both the rifle and my pen.

It was ironic that Chaplain Mark Moore's brother was a

member of the 86th Infantry Division. The 86th Division soldiers took Mark with them when they left and reunited him with his brother. The powers to be were good to both Mark and his brother. Both had been through the war and had been spared!

Soldiers in charge told us we would have to stay put till the next morning - May 3, 1945. They had no way to transport us but would call for trucks to come pick us up. American troops marched the German guards away. We now had a chance to go into town but there really was not anything to see except for that old church. It was an international cathedral - those men who went inside told me it was very beautiful.

Even though we were liberated, there was still that creeping, uneasy feeling that some wandering, fanatical SS unit might find us and gun us down. I hated those black-uniformed bastards - they were Nazis to the core, whereas the Wehrmacht were more everyday soldiers. I disliked them also, but for them, I had at least a certain amount of respect.

The next morning American trucks came rolling into town and I knew this time we were truly liberated. One of our men broke down completely when the trucks arrived. I do not know how to describe what I call breaking down. Men looked like they were in a daze and did not seem to recognize anyone. They cried and had to be led around like babies. I saw quite a few in this same condition at Hammelburg and Nuremberg. What a shame to see an American soldier having to go through this illness. All of them were First or Second Lieutenants, ages ranged around nineteen or twenty years old. What a shame. Maybe after some hospital treatment they got well. I often wonder whatever happened to all of those sick and wounded soldiers at the hellhole POW camp at Nuremberg. I just cannot see how any survived if they were left at that camp for any length of time. What a shame; they were all just young boys.

Our truckload left and other trucks full of POWs joined us. There must have been at least forty truckloads in all. Some POWs in the convoy were full of anger. They were ready to fight anyone at the least provocation. They were a very unruly bunch. I wondered where they came from. The rifle I had taken as a souvenir was dismantled in my gunnysack but many of the others had also taken rifles and ammunition and they were firing into the air or shooting any animal they saw. The POWs who were shooting the rifles just did not give a damn. I have no doubt that they would have shot any German soldiers they saw out in the open. I guess they probably would have shot any German civilian too but fortunately we did not see any.

The transportation officer in charge of the convoy stopped many times to try to get them to stop shooting, but to no avail. Though he stopped the convoy quite a few times and begged, they continued shooting. He sometimes seemed as if he was a little uneasy around them.

When the convoy stopped in a town I heard someone call my name. He hollered, "Hey Harry!" It was an old friend of mine, Major Tom Grace.

First thing I said was, "Congratulations, Tom. They made you a Major."

We talked until our convoy started moving. He told me the route the 99th division had taken and said that the 99th had liberated POW Camp Moosburg VIIA. He said when they retook Büllingen all men of the 924th just knew we were all dead because the same group that captured us killed our men at Malmédy. They looked in every hole and ditch, looking for our bodies.

The 99th Division took part in the liberation of Dachau Concentration Camp. I wish that I also could have had the honor of liberating people in the concentration camps. May Hitler still feel the fires of hell for causing all the grief people throughout the world have suffered!

May 1945

S	M	T	W	T	F	S
		1	2	3	4	5
6	7	8	9	10	11	12
13	14	15	16	17	18	19
20	21	22	23	24	25	26
27	28	29	30	31		

What The Heck Was Going On?
May 3, 1945

As we were being transported back by our American liberators, we saw one barbed wire enclosure, which looked to be about a half-mile square, full with thousands of captured German soldiers. There were many thousands of German prisoners; this was only one of many such enclosures.

Finally, we arrived at the POW camp at Moosburg. Guard towers and fences had been removed. Most of the POW's in Moosburg had already been sent to the rear. We could pick any place we wanted to stay. Instead of staying in those POW barracks, Park and I decided to stay in a brick building next to the camp. The prisoners had been told it was a cheese factory, but it was a ball bearing plant. Evidence of this was obvious: the place was full of machinery and the floors were covered with ball bearings of all different sizes. There must have been quite a fight here because the place was pretty well torn up.

While at Moosburg I saw some of the enlisted men from whom we had been separated back on December 25, 1944. Some of the enlisted men from the 924th Field Artillery came over and took a picture of Warrant Officer Park and me. I still have this picture. We were told that the 99th Division had liberated Moosburg on April 29th. They also told us the route the 924th had followed to Moosburg and, sure enough, they had been right behind us the whole time. My old outfit had been lobbing those shells that fell all around us! We had gotten out of their path when the POW column turned south toward Austria. I asked what happened to the 99th during the Battle of the Bulge. He said that on December 17 all of the 924th FA Battalion had been shelled unmercifully all through the morning - thanks to that phony Lieutenant and his unwitting ally, our Service Battery Captain, no doubt! The entire battalion had pulled out and the 99th regrouped on Elsenborn Ridge in Belgium, along with the 2nd Division.

The battles that raged on Elsenborn Ridge were termed the "North Shoulder of the Bulge" by the army historians who reconstructed the entire battle. The role of the U. S. First Army was initially to head back and repulse the German attack on the Northern flank, better known as Elsenborn Ridge. The importance of this area, Elsenborn Ridge, the "North Shore of the Bulge", has too often been underestimated. The heroic stand of the 99th and 2nd Infantry Divisions and the gallant stand of the U. S. First Army at St. Vith should go down as of great importance to the history of "The Battle of The Bulge". Elsenborn Ridge was of a much greater significance than the German action to the South. The elite troops of the German army could not break through on the road to Antwerp so their attacks turned toward the South at Bastogne.

After the Bulge, the 99th fought to the Rhine River and became the first complete Division to cross the Rhine and hold the beachhead at Remagen. I talked to the CO of A Battery of the 924th Field Artillery and asked him how many shells a day they had fired, on average, during the Battle of the Bulge. He said that on the one night when the Krauts attacked all night long, A Battery alone fired thirty-five hundred (3500) rounds of 105mm howitzer shells. The next morning all the firing tubes (barrels) had to be replaced! The artillery units of the 924th Field Artillery Battalion are enshrined in the Hall of Fame at Fort Sill, OK, the artillery center of the United States Army today.

While at Moosburg, we were told by the few remaining POW's that when the camp there was liberated, the Russian POW's went down into the town of Moosburg and raped every female in town, young and old - horrible! The U. S. Army had no control over Russian POWs after they were freed. Yet, from what I read, that was the norm wherever Russian troops overran enemy territory. Our soldiers would have been court-marshaled on the spot!

I am told that Hammelburg and all the other area through which we marched - some three hundred seventy-eight (378) kilometers or two hundred forty-one (241 miles) - are all part of Bavaria. At the time I did not understand what Bavaria meant, although now I am told that it is one of the southern states or provinces of Germany that used to be an autonomous kingdom. There were several large castles in Bavaria. I just never saw any. There were no cattle to be seen there except for a few dairy cows and the fences were all of brick or stone - I guess Hitler reserved barbed wire for prison and concentration camps.

After arriving in Moosburg on May 3 the first thing I did was to go look for a dentist. To my surprise, I found that the dentist had a trailer in which he simply followed the front lines so that he was able to treat our GI's. He pulled that infected tooth, a great relief to me!

We stayed in Camp Moosburg until May 8, with no guards and nothing to do but eat and rest. During this time I had an actual slice of white bread, which tasted like angel food cake to me after that horrible German war bread! We were issued one can of C-rations (beans) a day. C-rations were cans about the size of a number one can today. They were afraid to feed us too much because many POW's had gotten sick and died from overeating after liberation. I was happy with that can of beans - it was a lot more than I had been used to in months. The second day in Moosburg I heard shots and instinctively dropped to the ground - what the heck was going on? For a moment I thought that the fighting had broken out again. Then I discovered that the repeated shots were from some German ammunition that was burning in a concrete trash pit.

May 5, 1945 was my birthday - how lucky I have been to live to see it. I truthfully can say that many times I thought I would never live to see the war end. I just lay around and rested, I know for at least three days. Now that I was back at Moosburg, I was afraid to leave the camp, in case my name might come up to be transported back to France. Three days after my birthday we were transported to Inglestat right on the Danube River. I had always heard of the beautiful blue Danube, but take it from me, it is just another muddy, brown river. At least it was during the war. We stayed right on the bank of the river. Next to where we were waiting was a huge room about half a block in width, dug out in the hill and containing nothing but leather gear for horses - no saddles, only harnesses and bridles for wagons. We were then transported to the airport, which was located in the middle of town, many houses right next to the runway. American C-47 cargo planes were transporting only POW's, no other passengers. As soon as one cargo plane left, another landed. I was told that the orders were to shoot down any aircraft flying over the airfield. Trucks with machine guns mounted on top were parked facing the runway, lined up side by side for about a hundred yards.

After one C-47 had taken off and before another could land, a German Stuka dive bomber with bombs attached tried to land and every single machine gun opened up on it - we all jumped into bomb craters for protection - nobody wanted to die from a stray bullet after being liberated! The plane circled around and barely cleared the row of houses, then landed with both bombs still attached. I went over to the plane and the German pilot and passenger both said they were trying to surrender. It's a miracle that plane managed to land with its bombs intact. I cannot imagine how both pilot and passenger escaped injury. That German Stuka was riddled with bullet holes made from machine guns mounted on our trucks.

All Allied aircraft had been warned not to fly over this airfield at Inglestat. Orders were that any aircraft flying over the base would be shot down. This airfield was used exclusively to transfer Allied POW's. Some time before we arrived, a British Mosquito bomber flew over and, even it, a British plane, was immediately shot down, its wreckage remaining fully visible at the end of the airfield.

We later boarded a C-47 transport that, by evidence of the seating arrangement, had been used as a paratroop transport. As we flew and I looked out the window of the plane, I noticed that there were circles along the countryside. I asked the pilot and crew what those circles were and was told that the farmers tied their cows to a pole, when they had eaten all the grass in the circle as far as the rope would reach, they were tied to another pole.

A CONFIDENTIAL order announcing Germany's UNCONDITIONAL SURRENDER was issued 7 May, 1945 from Hq 99th Inf Div with a note at the bottom signed by Maj Gen Lauer, Commanding:

"I added the following remark to the order: Monday. 7 may 1945. D-335; 298th Week of War; 177th Week US Participation. My sincerest congratulations to each and everyone of you on this historic occasion. Every member of the 99th Infantry Division can be proud of his combat record, in having aided materially in defeating the Nazi beast and gaining this VICTORY!"

quoted by permission from 99th Division Battle Babies
by Maj. Gen Walter E. Lauer. 1951, Halldin Publishing Company, p. 318

"Germany is finished." –Harry Thompson

James Park, Warrant Officer 924ᵗʰ F.A. Service Battery (with cap) And Harry Thompson, 924ᵗʰ F.A. Headquarters Battery, Both Liberated at Gars, Germany on Inns River on Austrian Border on May 2, 1945.

Picture taken at Moosburg POW Camp, Germany May 3, 1945
by friends of Harry, enlisted men from the 924ᵗʰ Field Artillery, from whom Harry had
been seperated back in December 25, 1944

May 1945						
S	M	T	W	T	F	S
		1	2	3	4	5
6	7	8	9	10	11	12
13	14	15	16	17	18	19
20	21	22	23	24	25	26
27	28	29	30	31		

Not Even A Dime To Buy Coffee Or Doughnuts
May 8, 1945

We flew to the military airport at Rheims, France. When we landed there were many generals, colonels and newsmen at the airport and, also, lots of dignitaries. We did not realize what was going on until someone told us that the Nazis had surrendered - it was V-E day! Victory in Europe! The Red Cross was even there, giving away free donuts and coffee, in my opinion, as part of their publicity. The Salvation Army had repeatedly come close to the front to serve coffee and donuts to GI's. The only free coffee and donuts we as military usually had received was from the Salvation Army. When we boarded the LST back in England, where there were many newsmen and a lot of publicity to be had, the Red Cross provided free coffee and donuts. Now, V-E Day, and again, the Red Cross, free coffee, donuts and much publicity! I do not understand why the Salvation Army did not get as much publicity as the Red Cross for serving donuts and coffee. I have never seen one picture or heard mention of the Salvation Army and what they did for us during the war. They should have been given as much credit as the Red Cross. Why not?

After debarking from the planes and having our one cup of coffee and one donut, we were loaded into trucks and taken to Rheims to a large brick building with spacious, well-kept grounds bordered by a brick wall. Across the street and down the block was the famous Rheims cathedral that I had read about and seen pictures of while still in school - but I did not even walk down the block to see it! All I wanted to see was my transportation home!

Outside the building, we were deloused with DDT with our clothes still on - down the back, sleeves, pants, both legs and in our hair. I was glad to be getting rid of those pesky lice once and for all. About one hundred feet from the shower, we shed all our clothes and shoes, leaving everything in a large pile. We walked from there straight to the showers. I can hardly describe how good that shower felt. We were not rushed, and my stay under the nice warm water felt so very, very good! I am sure those in the building were glad to get us cleaned up. I had not had a bath in about five months, with dysentery most of that time. Nearly all of us were in the same state - smelling like an open-air privy! I wonder how they got the odor and lice out of the airplane. After taking our showers, we were issued clean clothing and new boots - what a relief! We must have smelled awful.

The next day we were sent to Camp Lucky Strike, a processing center for all prisoners of war, where we had our first good meal. We were given only a small helping of food - boiled chicken with no seasoning, a small helping of mashed potatoes and one slice of white bread. We were kept on a strict diet at first; they were afraid that too much food too soon would kill us. We thought the chicken was delicious but wanted larger portions. That night the garbage was raided and all the chicken entrails and leftovers were stolen and eaten by some of the prisoners - goes to show you how hungry we were. I can truthfully say that I tried to abide by the diet the whole time I was there. At the camp a booth was set up. I do not know whether the USO, the Red Cross or the Salvation Army operated it, but it served delicious non-alcoholic eggnog. I managed to obtain several cups and heard from the gossipy waiter that some POW's who had come in several weeks ago had been served coffee and many donuts, and several of them had died from eating too many of those greasy donuts.

The next day, after we were issued new officer uniforms, we were sent to interrogation and debriefing. The debriefing officer asked me if I knew of any atrocities committed, at any time, by the Germans. "Sure", I said and then tried telling him about the shootings at camp and on the road, but he wanted to know the names of the Germans involved. I told him every-

185

thing I knew, but how was I to know their names? You do not exactly run up to a guard who has just shot one of your buddies and say, "Excuse me, what is your name?" - Better yet, should I have given him a piece of paper and asked him to write down his name? Heaven knows I could not pronounce, much less remember, German names. I told them that I would recognize any of the murdering bastards if I ever saw them again. Even if I had known the names and they had been caught, it would not have done any good in my opinion because later some were caught and tried.

After liberation, the war crimes interrogation of SS Col. Peiper and Gen. Deitrich, the SS group who captured us, proved futile. General Deitrich, Colonel Peiper and the rest of the SS group who murdered all those American soldiers at Honsfeld, Büllingen and Malmédy were given the death sentence during the Nuremberg trials. A short time later, they were released. What a tragedy. They should have been shot. Peiper was eventually shot and killed at a villa in France during the 1970's.

For some reason, Park and I got separated at this point - I do not remember why, he probably had to go to the hospital. I did not see him again until later when we ran into each other at Fort Sill, Oklahoma.

After debriefing interrogation, I went to see a medical officer who asked me what was physically wrong with me. It was very hard for me to walk due to my still-swollen, frostbitten feet and I had some trouble hearing. He told me that my temperature was 102 and that he needed to send me to the hospital. I did not want to go so he gave me a small sack of aspirin to take for the fever - two aspirins every fifteen minutes until my ears started ringing. Fortunately the aspirins worked and I did not have to go to the hospital, which might have delayed my departure for home. We had physical examinations for several days after that. Each day we were taken in for a complete physical - blood tests, urine sample, etc. They gave us paper cups to pee in while we stood in line, but invariably some of us could not go and passed the cup to a buddy for a fill up – don't you know the doctors had a time figuring that one out! I found that my weight was only 105 pounds.

Before capture I weighed 150 or so. Now my abdomen was bloated from malnutrition and I actually looked a little heavier. There was not much else to do at camp for the next week or so, so I just lazed around, resting and eating and letting my body recover. For a week to ten days at Camp Lucky Strike, we were quartered in squad tents, four men to a tent - just like Fort Ord, four years and a lifetime ago. We slept on folding canvas cots - what a relief to get a good night's sleep without scratching the whole time!

After a week or so, we were transferred from Camp Lucky Strike to our port of embarkation area at Le Harve. The area was full of squad tents like Camp Lucky Strike. While at Le Harve I wrote a letter to my brother, which showed not only my frame of mind, but also that of most war veterans I know:

"Dear F. A. and Helen,

"I am now at Le Harve, France - I was flown in from Rheims. The liberated POW's have priority over all except sick and wounded so I think that I will be back stateside shortly. I may get transportation by C-54 but that remains to be seen. I just want to get back and I am not particular how just as long as I start. There are so many horrible memories I want to leave here too - anyone who thinks that war is not hell is just plain crazy! I used to think that I would like to get into combat but of course I never knew what I was talking about. I hope that a peace settlement will be so damn severe that the goons will never have another factory for making firearms - not even water pistols or BB guns! I am lucky, for 8 different times I do not know how I got out alive. I was fired at by burp guns and had dirt knocked in my face. I hugged the ground so darn close that I felt like I was part of the ground! Well, enough for that..."

I did not look around Le Harve very much. I sure did not want to miss our ship when it came in and, besides, we were warned to stay out of some districts of Le Harve for there was a good chance of being shot by Nazi sympathizers and some Frenchmen who had lost their families to American bombs. I was glad to stay in camp; I have never liked France much anyway. You could tell the French people did not like Americans. It was surprising to me that France had so many communists - I do not know why they disliked the U. S. so much after we had saved their country twice in thirty years. Maybe they were jealous or angry that they seemed unable to save themselves. I wondered if France had ever won a war by itself, I doubted it.

One thing I did do was ride the escalator up to the top of a steep hill overlooking the bay and back down. The ride took about fifteen minutes each way. I just was not in a mood to do much of anything except board that ship and get back home. We had not been paid since liberation, so I did not even have a dime to buy the coffee and donuts that the Red Cross was selling. While in captivity, the Germans took all our money.

At long last our transport, the SS Sea Robin, docked for our voyage back home. The Sea Robin was an old U. S. Merchant ship, converted to a transport. As soon as I boarded the ship I was handed a cold Coca-Cola. It sure tasted great, and the radio was playing the Andrews Sisters' new song, "Rum and Coca- Cola." The SS Sea Robin was an American ship and there was no stench below decks as there had been on the British ship Exchequer that we sailed in on our way to Europe.

May 1945						
S	M	T	W	T	F	S
		1	2	3	4	5
6	7	8	9	10	11	12
13	14	15	16	17	18	19
20	21	22	23	24	25	26
27	28	29	30	31		

Oh If I Only Knew If You Were Alright
May 10, 1945

I was on my way home. How I longed to tell the people back home what was happening. How I wondered what and how they were doing.

My darling Wife and my family back home also were longing and wondering where I was, what I was doing, how I was. A few letters, post cards and telegrams had been all the news either of us had of each other since the day after I married Virginia and left for overseas. An ocean separated us and, on both sides of that ocean, we were trying to imagine what was happening on the other side. V-mail letters and letters written in pencil on paper provided by German prison camps remain, carefully preserved, as evidence of how we were holding on to hope and encouraging those on the other side to do the same.

V-Mail letters were a new experience. Each V-Mail actually measured four and a quarter inches wide by five inches long and our letters were written on special paper, then placed on microfilm and processed by the United States Post Office especially for military personnel overseas. The tiny letters had to be carefully folded so the address would show through the window cut out of the envelope. Each V-Mail was subject to censorship and some of the letters arrived with a large check across them and a signature or notation by the censor.

Reading the few letters, telegrams, Kriegsgefangenenpost Kriegsgefangenenlagers, Postkartes, and V-Mail reveals the emotions my family was experiencing while I was over seas.

Aunt Nettie Thompson whose address was simply "1100 Hawthorne St, Ft. Worth, Texas", received and kept two letters. V-Mail letters had very limited space to write and since I did not use any space to date the letter and her letters were not preserved with the envelopes designed for them, it is impossible to tell the exact date.

Aunt Nettie saved one of the first letters I wrote. I wrote to tell Aunt Nettie about my marriage to Virginia.

> "Dear Aunt Nettie,
>
> "Well I am now located in England for the time being – certainly is a long way from home – in fact it is much too far. The country isn't so bad, in fact I think it is very pretty except I don't like the weather –

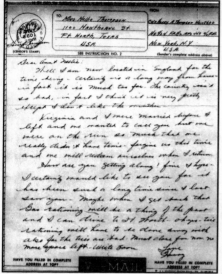

Aunt Nettie saved one of the first letters I wrote. I wrote to tell Aunt Nettie about my marriage to Virginia.

"Virginia and I were married before I left and we wanted to call you but we were on the run so much that we really didn't have time – forgive us this time and we will redeem ourselves when I return.

"How are you getting along? Fine I hope – I certainly would like to see you for it has been such a long time since I last saw you – Maybe when I get back that Gas rationing will be a thing of the past and I can drive to Ft. Worth – oh, yes – tire rationing will have to be done away with also for the tires we had – Must close for now. No more space left – write soon.

"Love
"Harry"

A Second Letter Was Also Saved By Aunt Nettie

The first V-Mail letter was sent to Aunt Nettie in Fort Worth, prior to my capture. My next letter to Aunt Nettie was written as I was nearing enemy lines and still had not seen any real action.

"Dear Aunt Nettie: I hope that this letter finds you in the best of health – as for me, I am feeling fine – I am now located near the Belgium, German border and have been in Germany quite a few times – Little did I ever dream that I would be over here taking part in a war – Course that is the way things go

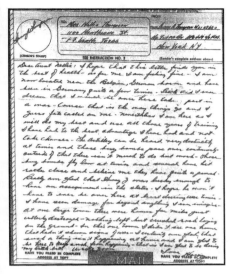

and I guess fate called on me – Nevertheless I am here so I will do my best and use all those years of training I have had to the best advantage I have had and not take chances – The Artillery can be heard very distinctly at times and those buz bombs pass over continuously – Outside of that there isn't much to do but march – Those buz bombs fly low at times and several have hit rather close and behind me they have quite a punch – Really am glad that Henry J was lucky enough to have an assignment in the states – I hope he won't have to ever be over here at least during war times – I have seen damage far beyond anything I ever imagine – utterly destroyed – nothing left but crushed rock laying on the ground – In this one town I didn't see one home that hadn't shown signs of war – I certainly am glad that such a thing isn't happening at home and I am glad to be here to keep such from happening – that is I am glad to be doing my little bit. Write soon.
" Love, Harry."

There was no Limit to the amount of V Mail a soldier could send at no charge and the Dallas Postmaster, Mr. Payne, gave them special attention.

A Letter to My Parents

"Dear Mother & Daddy: I go into occupied Germany quite often but am anxiously waiting the day that I

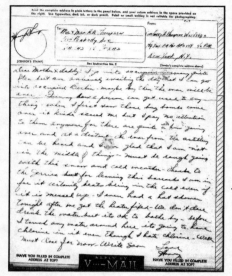

can go into occupied Berlin – maybe by then the war will be over. Funny how a person can get used to anything – when I first saw those buz bombs come over it kinda scared me but I pay no attention to them anymore for there are quite a few going over and at a distance – The war from the Artillery can be heard and I am glad that I am not in the middle of things – must be rough going with this snow and cold weather - Thanks to the Jerries but for leaving this barracks I am in for it certainly beats being in the cold even if it is messed up – I even had a hot shower tonight after we got the heater fixed – We don't dare drink the water but its ok to bathe by – before I touch any water around here its going to have chlorine in it even though I hate chlorine – Well, must close for now. Write soon.

> Love
> Harry"

The following letter, written jointly by my Mother and Dad, was marked "Return to Sender" and returned to them unopened. After I was captured, all my mail was returned unopened to sender "Missing in Action" "R.P. Ronne, Major FA.". Major Ronne was the executive officer of the 924 F.A., a friend of mine. Mother's letter probably was about December 20, 1944 because she must have just heard of the Battle.

> "Dear Harry,
> "Oh if I only knew if you were alright since the awful

battle in B. I pray that you are – Well a new year will soon be here and even if you are so far away from home if I could only know you are safe and sound it would surely make the New Year coming in much brighter. I try hard to keep my chin up – but honey you know what you and F.A. have meant to both of us as you have always been one grand son. Well we had a very nice Xmas and V. was as thrilled over her cedar chest and honey I sent V. 1 doz carnations (pink) for New Year from you. I know you would like for me to do that. They are so pretty. Daddy sure likes the vise you all gave him – and I like my blouse. Haven't been able to get any more Tamales but will send them just as soon as I can. Dallas is expecting a large crowd in today for New Y. Football game is on N. Year. Guess U.S.O. will send a couple of boys they asked me if I could keep them so guess I will. It is rather a gloomy day. Kinda cold and trying to rain . Had a nice letter from F.A. – H. Everything around D. is just about the same. Had a letter from Ben & card from Buster. Well Dearie – here's wishing you 'Happy New Year's'. Love and best wishes. Love.

Mother."

Three letters written by my brother, Franklin A. Thompson, a Sergeant serving with an Intelligence Unit at Fairfax Field in Kansas City, Kansas were all returned to him, each marked in pencil, "Missing …(signature)", "Verified – 1st Base Post Office".

A letter, written by Franklin from Kansas City and mailed Nov. 25, 1944, was returned, unopened, postmarked on the back "U.S. Army Postal Service A.P.P. 448 Jan 7, 1945". Handwritten on the front was "Missing R P Ronne Maj FA" and rubber stamped across the address to C. W. O. Harry A. Thompson was "Return to Sender, VERIFIED 1st Base Post Office". The unopened letter, marked "Missing" reads:

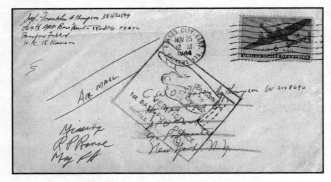

Letters from Franklin

Nov. 25, 1944

Dec. 23, 1944

Dec. 30, 1944

All letters returned un-opened!

"Friday Nite
"Dear Harry:

"Thanksgiving was yesterday and of course we
thought of you – wondering how you were –
whether you were able to keep warm and if you

had any sort of special meal for that Special day. I have quite a lot to be thankful for even tho' I do get discouraged at times over my not getting anywhere – Am so thankful that you are still ok physically and haven't suffered any of the physical horrors of war and I trust that we can all be together again in the not too distant future celebrating our return to civilian life – but I personally am not in favor of reverting back to a civilian way of life until the Germans & Japs are crushed.

"From your last letter I draw the conclusion that you are very very close to the heavy fighting. All hell no doubt will break loose on the Germans before long – same for the Japs – it was announced this AM that a heavy force of B-29's raided Tokyo – and that is just a sample of what is to come for those   b——ds. Raids will come oftener & oftener now that the new landing strips on Saipan have been completed.

"Helen received a letter from her home today & was told that word had been received from the War Department that her cousin, Andy, whom you met last summer was killed in action in France on Nov. 3 – too bad.

"Harry before I forget it – the main purpose of this letter is to ask you to please & pronto send me a letter requesting that I send you a carton of cigarettes and anything else that you might need. In fact in the next several letters you write how about asking me to send something whether you need it or not – at the end of the letter you can indicate whether you really need or want it – in this

195

way I'll be able to send you a few things – now and then – such as cigarettes – the papers here in the States indicate that you boys across are having a hard time also in getting cigarettes & I've been saving some up for you when I'm able to get them which isn't too often but then I personally don't use them & Helen has enough – At our PX I'm allowed 2 packs a day when we have them. So don't forget. Too Harry, anything you might really need & can't get it don't hesitate to write me & I'll try & get it.

"Harry don't have much to write about so will be closing for now – Helen said she would write tomorrow – her day off –

"As Ever
"Franklin

"P.S. Yesterday I had 2 turkey dinners – one at the post & the other that nite when Helen had hers – I took her to a restaurant for her dinner – I had intended getting only a very light dinner but had to order turkey or nothing as that was the only thing they had – just the one choice – turkey dinner.

"Write soon Harry – Best of luck. Be careful. Maybe your next letter you'll be telling me you're in Germany"

One of Franklin's letters which I read after returning from overseas helped me understand what my family had been feeling and doing while I was gone. That letter, written December 22, 1944 and postmarked from Kansas City, Kans. Dec 23, 1944, was also returned unopened with the word "Missing" penciled in the left corner and a rubber stamp mark across my address "Return to Sender, 1st Base Post Office" reads:

"Friday   22 Dec 44
"Dear Harry:

"I have a few minutes to spare so thought I'd drop you a few lines. Really don't have much to write about today and too I'm not in much of a mood for writing – I still have a terrible cold and you know how that can make one feel. Last Friday and Saturday I could not talk above a whisper – Harry, hope that you are able to keep warm and protected enough to miss catching a cold – With all that snow, sleet and rain in your part of the world it's a wonder all of you are not down with one – of course the top physical condition of you soldiers go a long way in keeping you well – Here at our base and in others like it the men are soft so to speak since most of their work is of an administrative nature and consequently insufficient exercise.

"Next day – didn't get very far on my letter yesterday – got busy and had to lay it aside – I still have my cold only it seems worse this day – my head feels like a balloon and it is stuffed up very badly – If it was not so close to Xmas I'd go to the dispensary but I'm sure they'd put me to bed and I can't afford to let that happen.

"Harry, being on the spot you know of our unexpected setbacks of the 1st Army – from the papers here it must be a costly one to us and no doubt it is even worse than the papers play it up – Of course I believe the German offensive will be halted and others armies defeated but I am disappointed that they should catch us off guard as they did and make such a break through. I feel so sorry for our

197

boys that are catching the brunt of the German offensive. I'm sure that Mother worries about you – which is quite natural for a mother to do – She is afraid you are in the first army – the one catching hell now. However I've written her and told her it was my opinion that you were in the 9th Army. Of course neither of us know as you say you are not allowed to disclose that information – My guess as to the 9th Army is due to the fact you've mentioned V-1 or buzz bombs so often – The local papers say that only the 9th Army is troubled with those weapons – In any event I hope you are well and safe and that Germans fall will come soon and that we can all be together again. Take good care of yourself –

"As I mentioned in an earlier letter Mother wrote to me to see if I could find some good warm boots or shoes for you – I looked and looked and finally found some which have been sent – I tried to get a pair of Air Corps flying boots which would have been just the thing but could not get a hold of any – After so long a time I found some that thought may keep you warm – As well as the fur lined boots I sent along some inner boots or bootees whatever they are called. I sent them 1st class mail thinking they may get to you quite a bit sooner and when they do get to you let me know approx. date – just a matter of curiosity – had I sent them parcel post I'm afraid the package would have gotten mixed up with the ordinary Xmas package and you wouldn't receive them for another couple of months – when you get them don't thank me for them – it is Mother that you owe thanks to for she is the one that wanted me to get them for you –

"Harry I am so glad you are able to write to mother so often – and to me too – you have no idea *how much we like to hear from you – its been several days now since I've heard from you but will look for a letter tomorrow – Tomorrow is Sunday Xmas Eve and it is my day off but I guess I'll come out to the post to pick up letters that we may have. Harry wish I could have sent you something for Xmas but of course you know postal regulations – without a request from you I can't send anything – Helen & I were just talking about your Xmas will be so bare – and she said lets let the boots be Harry's Xmas present but Mother wanted so much to pay for them that I thought she wanted to send that for your Xmas too Harry, Helen and I are going in on half the costs of the boots for one boot and one bootee will be our Xmas present to you – I'm sure that Mother and Dad won't have any objection.*

"Wish you could be here with us to open packages – she wants me all time to let her open them up – even opening one would please her but I'm letting her wait til at least Xmas eve nite – Sunday nite our Group is having a big party at the NCO Club and the party is for everyone whether members or not – guess we'll go to it – Xmas day 3 couples including ourselves are having dinner at one of the couples house and the girls are going to cook it all and everyone split expenses which will be nice and of course will beat eating at a café .

"Not much else to write about for the present time so will close for now with a wish for you for A Very Merry Christmas and A Happy New Year And that you will be back Soon So we can celebrate a belated party.

"Franklin".

December 30, 1944 yet one more of Franklin's letters was returned, unopened bearing the penciled words "Missing" and the rubber stamp saying "Return to Sender VERIFIED 1st Base Post Office":

"31 Dec 44

"Dear Harry:

"Today is the last day of 1944; the past year has seemd incredibly short – so much has happened tho! The war fronts have changed considerably – you got married – and you left for Overseas destination and find yourself in the midst of the battle – I've never yet been able to guess as to which Army you are in – I hope it isn't the 1st Army – that is the one Mother thinks you might be in and she is naturally quite worried about you since the papers here have been full of the German offensive successes thru the 1st Army. Wish she wouldn't worry so but I realize that its not possible to keep mothers from worrying about their children.

"Harry I know your Xmas was not too Merry but maybe the spirits you were saving helped it to make it a little more Merry – I know that you are glad your loved ones – Mother – Dad – Virginia and others are safe – well and far away from the war – that in its self should make Xmas something more than just another day – of course actually to all soldiers fighting it was just another day –

"To get off that subject I might write you a little about our Xmas – we both received nice things – Helen got a sweater and a blouse from

200

Mother & Dad – from Virginia she got a very nice pin – or I should say 3 pins – each was a flying fish – and each larger than the other – they look very nice on her blouse - ….. – Virginia sent me a very nice men's nail set in a leather case – So all in all our Xmas was nice – Sunday afternoon we went out to eat at a couples house – Xmas Eve nite we went to a party at the NCO Club and everyone had a good time.

"Its Sunday morning and I'm at work so I'd better close for now and get to work – Haven't received a letter from you in about two weeks plus so here is hoping I'll hear from you in a few days – Will close for now – and I wish you all the luck possible in the coming New Year and before its end I hope we are all re-united and in good health and again Good Luck to you, Harry.

"Your brother

"Franklin."

It was after Franklin had received three of his letters unopened that a letter Mother and Dad wrote to me was returned to them: postmarked on the back, "U.S. Army Postal Service Jan 16 1944, 640", and in an envelope which, instead of a return address, was marked "War Department, Official Business, V Mail" and the handwritten word "Missing" followed by a signature. Three letters from Franklin returned and now this, Mother's letter.

How does a parent feel when a letter they have written to a son is returned marked "Missing"? This one was written more tiny than usual because Dad and Mother were sharing one V-Mail, both wanting me to know it was Christmas:

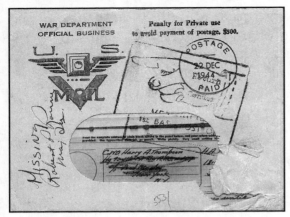

"*Dear Harry – Just a few more until Santa shows up. My how we all miss you and Franklin. Memories still revert to the times when Mother and I had a time keeping you boys in bed until we thought the room to be warm enough – The past is more cherished the memories more glorified in knowing we have raised two fine young men in whom mistrust or worry has never caused us a moments uneasiness –*

"Hope you don't think you are exclusive in that cold weather stuff – Believe it or not, since Dec. 1st we have had from 24 degrees to 50 degrees (now 20 degrees) and I will also add that I am in no way crowing about it. Wish it would settle on about 78 until next 4th of July. Going to leave some space for Mother – So Adios, Dad.

"Old Sweetie Pie – Well how is you this cold Tues A.M. This is our first really cold spell and it isn't so bad. Harry. I know you are homesick and a long way from home but if you can just keep well and be safe that will be the best wish I could ask for Xmas. You know how I'll miss you without me telling you – In fact I haven't got use to some one else being a head of me but I am trying hard to adjust myself to it. You know how close we have been. Love & best wishes Love, Mother."

Then came the letter, addressed to my parents, "Mr. And Mrs. H. A. Thompson, 1814 Peabody Ave, Dallas Texas," post marked Feb 1, 1945, which gives me chills to read. An uncle

who was a Catholic Chaplain for the Department of Justice
United States Penitentiary at Terre Haute, Indiana wrote:

WARDEN

J.E.Overlade

DEPARTMENT OF JUSTICE

United States Penitentiary

TERRE HAUTE, INDIANA

Office of
Catholic Chaplain

February 1 1945

Dear Austin and Audrey;

I learned yesterday that your Harry had been killed in action and
I want you to know that to have received such bad news was indeed
heartbreaking.In this hour of sorrow for you I certainly want to
extend to you my sincerest sympathy.In a time like this human
words are most inadequate to express our feelings.We do know
that Harry could not have done a more noble deed than to have
given his life for his God and Country.I offered my Mass this
morning for the repose of his soul.You know that Christ one time
said #Greater love than this no man has that he lay down his life for
his friends"!

All the family is well.I get down to Loogootee about once a month
to see the folks.Paul is doing very well in the Navy and Margaret
is working all the time at the Burns City Naval Ammunition Depot.
Helen has three boys in the service,all over seas.

With kindest regards to you all and wishing you all an abundant
share of God's blessings during this year,I am

Very Sincerely

Bernard J.Thompson

"Dear Austin and Audrey;

"I learned yesterday that your Harry had been killed in action and I want you to know that to have received such bad news was indeed heart-breaking. In this hour of sorrow for you I certainly want to extend to you my sincerest sympathy. In a time like this human words are most inadequate to express our feelings. We do know that Harry could not have done a more noble deed than to have given his life for his God and Country. I offered my Mass this morning for the repose of his soul. You know that Christ one time said 'Greater love than this no man has that he lay down his life for his friends.'

"All the family is well. I get down to Loogootee about once a month to see the folks. Paul is doing very well in the Navy and Margaret is working all the time at the Burns City Naval Ammunition Depot. Helen has three boys in the service, all over seas.

"With kindest regards to you all and wishing you all an abundant share of God's blessings during this year, I am

"Very Sincerely

(signed) "Bernard
"Bernard J. Thompson"

At the bottom of the page was the patriotic and urgent plea to "BUY WAR BONDS".

HARRY A. THOMPSON IS MISSING IN ACTION

Chief Warrant Officer Harry A. Thompson, has been reported missing in action in Belgium since Dec. 17, the war department has notified his parents, Mr. and Mrs. H. A. Thompson, 1814 Peabody.

With the headquarters unit of a field artillery battalion, Warrant Officer Thompson entered the service in 1940 and has been overseas since September, 1944.

Prior to enlistment, he was employed by Continental Supply Company. He is a former Forest Avenue High School student and a member of Tannehill Masonic Lodge.

Thompson

Chief Warrant Officer Harry A. Thompson, son of Mr. and Mrs. H. A. Thompson, 1814 Peabody, has been reported missing in action in Belgium since Dec. 17, the War Department has advised.

He enlisted in March, 1940, and has been overseas since September, 1944, with the 924th Field Artillery. Prior to enlistment he was employed by the Continental Supply Company. He is a former Forest High School student.

THOMPSON.

The filing time shown in the date line on telegrams and day letters is STANDARD TIME at point of origin.   Time of receipt is STANDARD TIME at point of destination

.DA77

D.LZ178 35 GOVT=WUX WASHINGTON DC 2 1229P   1945 MAR 2 AM 11 54

MRS H A THOMPSON=   HW DALLAS TEXAS

        1806 1/2 FOREST AVE DAL=

REPORT JUST RECEIVED THROUGH THE INTERNATIONAL RED CROSS
STATES THAT YOUR HUSBAND CHIEF WARRANT OFFICER HARRY A
THOMPSON IS A PRISONER OF WAR OF THE GERMAN GOVERNMENT
LETTER OF INFORMATION FOLLOWS FROM PROVOST MARSHAL GENERAL=
        J A ULIO THE ADJUTANT GENERAL.

January 17, 1945 Virginia and my Family were notified of my official POW status by a brief telegram from the war department and in March Adjutant General Ulio sent solid word. In addition to two U. S. Dog Tags, I now was wearing a break-away German made POW tag designed so that, in case of my death, half of it could be broken off and used for official purposes with one of my U.S. Dog Tags while the remaining half and one U.S. Army Dog Tag remained with my body. Captured Dec. 17, 1944 my family did not really know until March.

After notification that I was a prisoner of the Germans, I was able to write what seemed to be called a Kriegsgefangenenlager to family. Unfortunately, most of the letters Virginia and I wrote during my overseas experiences were lost when we stored them for safekeeping and rats had other ideas. Please note that the letter was marked by hand, "Special Delivery By Carrier" because Mr. Payne, the Dallas Postmaster, personally paid for "Special Delivery" when all letters from any POW arrived in the Dallas Post Office.

March 1945

S	M	T	W	T	F	S
				1	2	3
4	5	6	7	8	9	10
11	12	13	14	15	16	17
18	19	20	21	22	23	24
25	26	27	28	29	30	31

A letter from Harry written to Virginia Jan. 7, 1945, received March 7, 1945

My Darling Wife & Family

The following letters from me to my family will give an idea of how little my family was able to know – and how little I knew about what they knew:

Kriegsgefangenenlager
Datum: 7 January 1945
"My Darling Wife & Family
I am feeling alright and getting good treatment so please don't worry about me. Really will be glad when we can all be together again. Please send me candy, Peanut Butter, Jelly, and some canned meats about once a week – by first class mail. I hope this finds all of you in good health. I certainly do miss your sweet letters coming in but maybe they will be forwarded at a later date. When I get home I want a big Xmas dinner with all the trimmings even to pumpkin pie and ice cream for Desert – darling please learn to cook pancakes for I could eat a dozen for breakfast. Please write and tell Logan Clarke that I am ok. – I know you have

worried about me but now there is no use – Must
close for now – I Love You darling & our families
with all my heart. Write soon.

"Harry."

Kriegsgefangenenlager
Datum: 25 January 1945
"My darling: I am alive and well – Be so glad when
I return so we can be together again – Please write
regular and keep food coming also cigarettes –
check with the Red Cross on how to write me – I
love you so much darling and long for you – Tell
all hello – I can write 2 letters & 4 cards monthly –
Love Harry."

Kriegsgefangenenlager
Datum: 9 February 1945
"My darling Wife & family: Here's hoping this finds
all of you in the best of health. I am feeling fine
and very anxious to get home. I am being treated
alright and fed as well as can be expected. I lay
awake at night darling thinking and planning on
the day I return – Would like for us to make that
trip to Kansas to see Franklin and Helen if they
are still there and you want to go. The weather is
much warmer so it isn't as bad as it was for
awhile. Tell all to write – Give our Mother & Dad
a big Kiss for me – Write often even though I can't
Love Always Harry."

Auf diese Seite schreibt nur der
Kriegsgefangene!
Deutlich nur mit Bleistift auf die Zeilen schreiben!
Na tej stronie pisze wyłącznie jeniec wojenny!
Pisać tylko ołówkiem, wyraźnie i nad liniami!

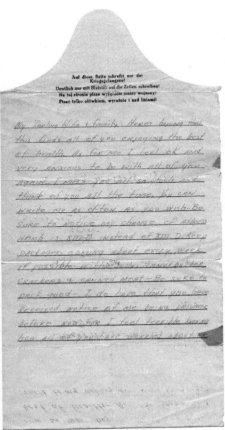

+++
Another letter, a new
format, date of the letter
not marked.

"My Darling Wife & Family: Here's hoping that this finds all of you enjoying the best of health. As for Me I feel ok and very anxious to be with all of you again. I miss you all so much and think of you all the time. You can write me as often as you wish – Be sure to notice my change of address which is XIII B instead of XIII D. Keep packages coming about every week if possible with Candy, Jelly, Peanut Butter, Crackers & canned meat – Be sure to pack good – I do hope that you have received notice of me being prisoner before now for I feel terrible knowing how all of you have worried about me. Again I wish to assure you that I am feeling ok – I will write just as often as possible which will be 2 or 3 times monthly – My letters are limited so they will be for all of you – must close for now so heres hoping all of you the best of health - All the Love in the world to my darling wife and our family – Harry

Still another letter, date unknown:

Auf diese Seite schreibt nur der
Kriegsgefangene!
Deutlich nur mit Bleistift auf die Zeilen schreiben!
Na tej stronie pisze wyłącznie jeniec wojenny!
Pisać tylko ołówkiem, wyraźnie i nad liniami!

"My darling Wife & Family: I hope that by now you know I am a prisoner of War and that I am well – Really will be glad when I can return home to you. Would like for you & I to take a trip to Kansas City if you want to. I certainly hope that everyone is feeling ok – It certainly is consoling to me knowing that I have such a sweet wife waiting for me and that we have so much to look forward to. It has been rather cold but today it is a little warmer so am in hopes that it stays warm. Am looking forward to a letter from all of you and also some packages of candy, peanut butter, Jam and canned potted meats. Tell Mother that I have a menu filled out for my first meal at home when I return and will mail it as soon as possible – Would like both our families to be present for the big feed – Darling I must close for now. I love you so much and hope to see you soon – Tell all hello & write soon – Love Always – Harry"

I faithfully wrote letters to my family. I hoped they were receiving them. Though I now know they were writing letters and sending packages, I received nothing. I received nothing until I returned home.

May 1945

S	M	T	W	T	F	S
		1	2	3	4	5
6	7	8	9	10	11	12
13	14	15	16	17	18	19
20	21	22	23	24	25	26
27	28	29	30	31		

It Was Just Wonderful
May 30, 1945

Shortly before we left France they issued me a partial payment of twenty dollars, so I had a little spending money on the way home. Even after I finally had a few dollars, I would not give the Red Cross the dime for a donut. Right after being paid, I bought a quart of Chanel #5 for my wife for five dollars from a French merchant. I wonder what that would cost in the U. S. today. It was stolen by an air corp First Lieutenant whom I had known for a couple of weeks. I had already been issued all new uniforms, plus any toiletries I might need such as toothbrush, razor, etc., so the only thing I needed to buy while on board ship was cigarettes. There was no tax on them aboard the ship, so I could get them for fifty cents a carton. I bought ten cartons for five dollars. The ship's skipper told us we could go on deck any time we wanted, weather permitting, there was no blackout now that the war was over. I remember thinking that, with my luck, we would run across the only U-boat that had not heard the news yet, but no such thing happened.

Once, on board ship, a captain who was an old friend did pull a practical joke on me. He went to the ship's recreational officer and told him that I was a former professional boxer and was ready to take on all comers for the entertainment of crew and passengers. This was announced on the loud speaker, and I had to do some fast-talking when the recreation officer came to sign me up. To my relief, I finally convinced him that it was a practical joke. I could not fight my way out of a wet paper bag, then or now.

Below deck in the recreation room, the personnel of the ship tried to keep us entertained with games, lots of magazines, etc. There were several tables of soldiers playing poker. Some had been POW's for a couple of years with no allotment to deposit money back home and were paid all their back salaries, so they had a lot of back pay with which to gamble. One of the games had huge stakes, and the ante was twenty dollars - not much now, but a hefty chunk of cash back then. How foolish! I did not have to worry though; I had spent my twenty dollars and did not have enough to get into a game unless the ante was a penny.

It seemed like the first day of the voyage lasted more than a week. I was so anxious to get home. I thought that this was a very slow ship at first, even though we were making pretty good time by the second day.

After several days, the ship's crew told me we were getting near New York. Suddenly it seemed as if the skyline of New York City just popped right up out of the ocean. I could see the beacon of the Statue of Liberty in the distance - what a beautiful sight! On June 11, 1945, we entered New York Harbor - tears welled up in my eyes as we passed Lady Liberty and I realized at last that I was truly, finally home in the good old USA. New York really went all out to greet the returning soldiers. We were told that ours was the first ship to enter the harbor after the nets were lifted. A huge sign on the shore read "Welcome Home" and people lined the piers and shoreline, waving. The noise was incredible - horns from the ships and tugboats, one smaller ship pulled up alongside ours with a band playing popular tunes on the deck, which was filled with pretty girls waving - it was the most wonderful welcome you could ask. Tugboats following us in were blowing their horns, and other boats were sending up huge sprays of water - what a great welcome it was! Our only regret was that we could not thank everybody personally.

After the ship docked, we were transported to Camp Shanks, New York. They issued us ID cards that afternoon and showed us to our quarters and - best of all - showed us where the telephones were so we could call home. It was just wonderful to talk to my wife and family - we all bawled.

Later that afternoon they took us into a huge mess hall and told us we would have our best meal since we left the states. Appropriately enough, the waiters were all German

POW's. Camp Shanks provided any kind of American food we wanted and cooked it however we wanted. All this was followed by whatever kind of dessert we requested. It was one of the best meals I have ever had.

The next day we started a series of physical examinations and a dentist checked our teeth. After several days we boarded a train headed for Fort Sam Houston at San Antonio, Texas – a train occupied by ex-POWs from Texas. Our train must have had at least fifteen cars of POWs. We lost about half the POW's on the way down. Anytime the train stopped near a tavern we would lose some passengers who went out for a drink and decided not to come back. Also, once in Texas, anytime we passed near someone's hometown he, too, would "abandon ship".

The train had a kitchen car and, all through the trip, we had good meals. Although the coaches were very old, no Pullman cars, it did not matter to me. Once we stopped for a few minutes at a rail yard and beside us, going in the opposite direction, was a trainload of German POW's. I suppose they were headed for some point of embarkation to go home too - I would hate to be in their shoes, for when they get home they will find so much of Germany in complete ruins. How odd: they were riding in new coaches and we were in the old ones. Who cares - we were nearly home!

We arrived at Fort Sam Houston around noon. We were immediately taken by truck to camp headquarters, where we were told that each of us would be given sixty days temporary duty for further recuperation at our homes, which would not be deducted from our leave time. Then we were told to sign up for some Rest and Recuperation accompanied by our wives at Hot Springs, Arkansas or Miami Beach, Florida for two weeks! After we chose our R & R site, orders were immediately typed and we could leave for home. I selected Miami Beach, Florida and got two weeks there, plus eight days travel time each way. I left camp for home about five that afternoon. At the rail station in San Antonio, I found there were no trains till morning, so I got a motel room and called my family the next morning and told them what time I would be home. I boarded the train and arrived in Dallas that afternoon. All my family and my wife's family were there to meet me - what a happy reunion! We all had a good cry that day - to be perfectly honest, I never thought I would come back from the war alive. Somehow I managed to beat the odds.

It's so strange, while overseas, locked up in a box car, running in place to keep from freezing, constantly exposed to cold weather, marching through Germany soaking and drying in the freezing rain, sleeping in damp haystacks, sometimes warming up then going outside again, all that time I never had a cold. Shortly after I arrived home I caught a cold.

I had a great time at home. Just to be with my wife and family made it special. While still in Hammelburg I had filched a page out of one of the three books in our library (a book on plastering, of all things!) and had written out the menu for my first meal at home. I don't remember if my first meal at home had everything on the menu I made up or not - I had listed sparkling burgundy, baked chicken, creamed asparagus, mashed potatoes, creamed English peas, boiled okra, fresh corn on the cob, cranberry sauce, hot homemade rolls - you get the idea. I can't remember the meal. Just being back with my family was good enough.

We visited old friends where I used to work; so many people came by to see me! The sixty days passed too quickly, but then we packed up and headed for Miami Beach. We had eight days' travel time, so no rush - we were issued sufficient gasoline coupons for the trip and were in New Orleans on V-J Day, when Japan surrendered and the war in the Pacific ended. There was a wild celebration in New Orleans that night, and the next day gasoline rationing was ended. When we got to Miami we stayed at a beautiful hotel - no room charge for my wife and me, and my meals were free while hers cost only a dollar a day, and the meals were all excellent. A dollar a day was our total expense for a trip, other than gasoline. The Army had even chartered a deep-sea fishing boat. We caught a few fish. My wife caught the largest. While fishing, a sudden storm brewed up. The ocean got very rough. Everyone got seasick except my wife and I. Even the men running the chartered boat got sick. Not us though! Ha!

The second day at Miami Beach, I was ordered to report in full uniform to Army headquarters a few blocks away. There I stood in military formation and received the Purple Heart for the injuries I had received during my service in Europe.

Time just flew by - after the two weeks were up I took my wife home and headed for Fort Sill, Oklahoma, where she later joined me. She stayed at a hotel in nearby Lawton. At Fort Sill, I found several officers who had been transferred from our battalion while on Louisiana maneuvers and assigned to division just before they left to participate in the D-Day landings on June 6, 1944. They had all been injured and shipped home. After a brief stay at Fort Sill, I was sent home, and once my two months' accumulated leave was used up, I was automatically discharged from the Army, effective December 9, 1945, having served four years, nine months, and four days. I was drafted for one year. That old song "Be Back in a Year Little Darling" sure did not apply to me.

THE UNITED STATES OF AMERICA

TO ALL WHO SHALL SEE THESE PRESENTS, GREETING:

THIS IS TO CERTIFY THAT
THE PRESIDENT OF THE UNITED STATES OF AMERICA
AUTHORIZED BY ORDER OF
GENERAL GEORGE WASHINGTON, AUGUST 7, 1782
HAS AWARDED

THE PURPLE HEART

TO

Chief Warrant Officer Harry A. Thompson, W2 108 690, United States Army

FOR

WOUNDS RECEIVED IN ACTION
European Theater of Operations, in January 1945

GIVEN UNDER MY HAND IN THE CITY OF WASHINGTON
THIS 9th DAY OF June 19 50

Virginia's Story, "I Would Do It All Over Again"
As written Dec. 5th, 2001

"Harry came home June 11th and called me late that night to say that he was back in the USA and was coming home. I was so emotional I could hardly talk. I kept thinking of all I wanted to say but didn't after we hung up.

"Mother Thompson and I met trains all day when we thought he would be passing through to San Antonio but to no avail. He called the next day from San Antonio and said he would arrive in Dallas at 2 o'clock.

"We were all there to meet him. I never knew anyone could be so handsome. I had expected the worse but I got the best, all in one piece and healthy looking. Little did I know it was unhealthy puffiness. Later he was down to about one hundred forty-five (145) pounds. He ate a meal and in one hour he could eat again.

"We had R and R in Miami Beach, Florida from the goodness of Uncle Sam for two weeks and then Harry had thirty day temporary leave at home. After that we went to Fort Sill at Lawton, Oklahoma from where he was later discharged and we returned to Dallas.

"In Dallas we could not find an apartment — then the lady that introduced us called to say that the apartment next to her was vacant, so we moved there. We could not find a stove (none to be had), so I learned to cook on a two-burner hot plate and we borrowed a bedroom set from my Mother. Later we bought both a stove and a bedroom set and a nice little home.

"I have been happy now for 57 years and would do it all over again if I could."

Virginia.

December 1945						
S	M	T	W	T	F	S
						1
2	3	4	5	6	7	8
9	10	11	12	13	14	15
16	17	18	19	20	21	22
23	24	25	26	27	28	29
30	31					

I Did Not Know What I Wanted
December 9, 1945

The war was finally over and I was so happy to be home with my wife and our family. However, everything was not as rosy as I had hoped. Night and day, I relived my captivity. Even to the present day, I relive my experiences in the military. If it had not been for my wife, I do not know how my life would have turned out or would be today.

Medical exams revealed my eardrums had been burst. I guess the process of eardrums healing and knitting back together caused my earaches off and on for five or six years following discharge. My nose had been broken. I do not know how, but suppose it happened during bombing. I had it straightened by Dr. Knowles, a Dallas Nose and Throat doctor. The slightest unexpected noise caused me to jump. I could not concentrate. I do not know how to explain it, but a person could talk a few minutes with me and, later, I could not relate any of what was said. My swollen feet and legs turned out to be artery problems that have affected me later in life. Artery problems caused two strokes in 1969 and I spent two months in a VA Hospital in Dallas. They also caused a heart attack in 1995 and hospital time in Bonham, Texas. My stomach bothered me and the doctor said I had severe bleeding ulcers caused by malnutrition. My feet had been frozen, causing my foot problems and my ears still hurt. Some veterans reacted to problems such as mine by turning to drink. I never found alcohol much of a solution for physical problems that developed as a result of my military service.

Working inside no longer appealed to me. I did not know what I wanted. Even though college would have been free and I could have obtained subsistence moneys while attending, that also just did not appeal to me. I used to love working at Continental Oilfield Supply Company in Dallas, but I no longer desired to return, although they called me several times.

217

I went to work as Sales Supervisor for Blue Cross. I just could not concentrate. Once, while I was on the phone talking to a customer, a bolt of lightning hit next to the outside of the building. I threw the phone and dived under the desk. I was so embarrassed and had the shakes for the rest of the day. After six months this Blue Cross job did not appeal to me, so I obtained a position with the insurance division of Veterans' Administration and then spent eight long miserable years working for them, without a doubt the worst years I have ever worked. I kept staying, not knowing what else to do, until the V. A. announced that the insurance division was moving out of state and we could move with them. I thought, "No way! Too much time has already been wasted."

I then went to work as a salesman for Sunshine Biscuit Company. I liked the work and, after three years, was promoted to Sales Supervisor. After a while I got tired of that and started selling insurance stock out of state. The money was good, so I had my wife move out of state with me. When she became pregnant, I quit and moved back to Dallas before the baby was due.

Our baby girl was born February 19, 1960. It had been fifteen years since I had been discharged from the Army. Fifteen years before our first and only child was born! A couple years after being discharged from the Army, my wife and I went to a doctor to find out why we could not have children. An examination was given and the doctor told us that, due to malnutrition, my sperm count was very low and it would take ten or more years before I could have children. He was so right. It took fifteen years! We have really enjoyed our baby girl. Today, as I write, we have three grandchildren - all girls!!!

Shortly before our daughter was born, I was forty-five years old, back in Dallas, and had no job. I took a job as a grocery store manager. A year later I returned to Sunshine Biscuit Company for whom I had worked before my insurance job out of state. Once again I was not satisfied, so I bought a bar. Since I did not drink alcohol, the bar turned out to be successful. A year later, due to an electrical fire, the bar burned up. I rebuilt it from insurance money, sold it and opened a nightclub at a better location. This turned out to be very successful, so I incorporated, forming Thompson Enterprises, and branching out to carpet business. I then purchased an eighteen-wheeler and also started a trucking business with my nephew driving the truck. The trucking and carpet business turned out to be a disaster so, next door to the night club, I opened a cafeteria which did not make money. I changed it to a recreation hall with coin operated pool tables. I owned eight pool tables, two new juke boxes, three pinball machines and two cigarette machines.

I was being successful until the local Mafia got a few state representatives to pass laws whereby no one other than a vending company could own vending machines. When the Alcoholic Beverage Commission told me I could not own machines in my own place of business, all I said was, "The hell I can't!" I then hired a lawyer, put my machines under a grandfather clause and got an injunction against the State of Texas, winning each court case all the way to the Texas Supreme Court. Next I successfully lobbied the Texas Legislature, getting all vending laws changed to the way they should be. All vending laws in the State of Texas now read "Thompson vs. State of Texas".

During this time, my daughter was in junior high school. Dope had become a problem in the school and within our city. I also had begun to fear for my family's safety. It had been years since discharge and, still, I did not know what I wanted. Gradually I began to realize that what I wanted was a safe environment for my daughter and for my family. We decided to buy a farm near a small town with a better environment. We moved.

Finally I knew what I wanted: I wanted the same things I valued when I proudly registered for the draft to join the U.S. to fight for the land I love, the home of the free and the brave.

Outside my medical problems, I am now in fairly good shape, thanks to God and the V.A. Thank God: I did not lose an arm or leg, or my life. I have so much for which to be thankful and I am very proud to have had the honor and privilege of serving my country.

Harry Thompson

IN RETROSPECT

It seems strange. While in the service I knew and talked to hundreds of men from I guess every state in the union. At the time and in those war circumstances, I considered them good friends. Now, while I vividly remember a lot of them, I can recall very few of their names. I guess the really few remembered were true friends.

Also, I would like to note: the incredibly vulgar, filthy language supposedly used by the soldiers in today's army was not used by the soldiers of World War II, at least not in my experience. We uttered "hell" and "damn" pretty frequently, but I never heard the words used in today's movies and books, not even during some of our closest calls.

Actually, officers are not really discharged with the same stipulations as enlisted men. We, as officers, receive a certificate of service, but are liable to be called up at any point in the next seven years. If I had not gone overseas, I think I might have stayed in the army. After going to Europe as I did, I had had enough of the army to last me a lifetime.

Someone told me that, as a result of reading "General Patton's Papers" which told about the 99th Infantry Division and their heroic stand in the Battle of the Bulge, he requested the 99th be transferred to the third Army in order that they also might have the privilege of going through the middle of Bavaria.

You know, it's funny. During and before the war, it seems everyone in Germany thought that Hitler and his Nazi party were great for the country, but once it was all over no one would admit that they had ever supported him. I guess no one likes to admit a mistake. When I came home, I said that I never wanted to return, but now that time has passed by, I think I

221

would like to go back one last time - to see England, Belgium and Germany (but not France) free from the scars of war. I know that things must have changed a lot, but I would like to see how those places look today, to see if the house where I was captured still stands, maybe to try and dig the blade of my dagger out of the cellar wall, and walk through the Ardennes and see the flowers blooming in a peaceful spring. Before I leave this earth, I would like to walk those old battle fields again, before the years sweep away the memory of that dark and turbulent time when so many young men gave their lives so that my children and grandchildren could grow up in peace and freedom.

Now, as I finish this book, America is again at war.

I wish I were young enough to do it again.

Harry Thompson

Virginia and Harry
POW Reunion, Barksdale Air Force Base, Louisiana, 1998

SUPPORTIVE APPENDICES

Related Books:

Battle Babies, The Story of The 99th Infantry Division in World War II. Published by The A. G. Halldin Publishing Company, Indiana, Pennsylvania. 1951. Maj. Gen. Walter E. Lauer, U.S.A. (Retired).

Battle Of The Bulge, Then And Now by Jean Paul Pallud. Battle of Britain Prints International Limited. 3 New Plaistow Road. London, E15 3JA, England. An *After the Battle* publication.

Prisoner of the Germans by Chaplain Mark R. Moore. Beacon Hill Press, Kansas City, Missouri. 1945.

Related Articles:

Greenville (Texas) Herald Banner, Sunday, July 2, 2000, P. C1. "The memories of war" by Carol Ferguson, Herald Banner Staff.

Chaplain Mark Moore's Bronze Star

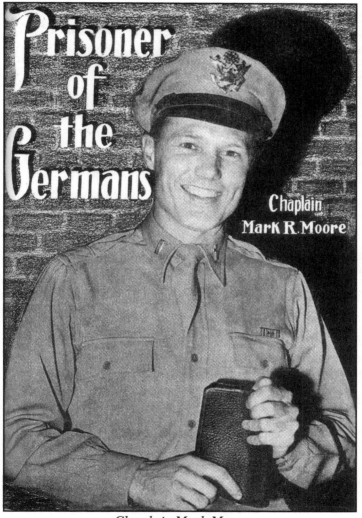

Chaplain Mark Moore
U. S. Army, O 50265

PATTON'S, ILL FATED RAID

Excerpts from *The Overland Park (Kansas) Sun,*

September 5, 2001

Chaplain Mark Moore was captured December 19, 1944 during the Battle of the Bulge, while he was serving as a chaplain for the field artillery of the U.S. Army's 106th Infantry Division. During his first few days of captivity, he and about 3,500 other POWs were transported by crowded boxcar to POW Camp in Bad Orb, Germany. Later, because R.A.F. planes blew out all the windows in Bad Orb prison barracks, "Moore and about fifteen hundred (1,500) fellow POWs were moved to the prison camp in Hammelburg, Germany, which had previously hosted Russian prisoners. As they arrived, they learned that the bodies of 40,000 Russian soldiers were lying in a long trench near the camp. Unlike the Russians, however, the Americans at Hammelburg had one thing going for them: Among the Americans' ranks was Gen. George Patton's son-in-law.

"Patton later denied knowing his son-in-law was in Hammelburg, Moore said. But the Allied tank contingent that arrived to liberate Hammelburg on March 27, 1945, had traveled past two other POW camps to get there.

"Unfortunately, Moore said, there were too many prisoners for the tanks to transport back, and shortly after the liberation, an entire German division arrived and recaptured most of the Americans, including Moore.

"From Hammelburg, about 500 American POWs, mostly officers, were marched for 36 days through Germany, toward the Austrian Alps, where the Nazis planned to hold them until they could be traded for German Pows. But Moore and the other officers were liberated, this time for good, by Americans near Gars, Germany, on May 2, 1945."

Mark R. Moore

11925 West 109th Street
Apt. 303
Overland Park, KS 66210-3985

Phone: (913) 338-4758
Fax: (913) 663-3757
E-mail: markrmoore@aol.com

January 31, 2002

T0 WHOM IT MAY CONCERN:

RE: Harry A. Thompson, Chief Warrant Officer
SN W 2108690
924 F.A. BN
99th Inf. Division
Captured 17 Dec. l944
POW CAMPS: Bonn, Nuremberg, and Hammelburg

Mr. Thompson was in Hammelburg POW Camp with me when a detachment of General George S. Patton's Army came in and liberated us on March 27, 1945. The following day we were recaptured. We were then marched for 36 days across Germany. Mr. Thompson was in the group, which was marched to Furth, just outside of Nuremberg, where we were bombed by our own Air Force.

On April, 5,1945, the German guards stopped the column of 500 American prisoners at Furth (Neuemburg) for a 10 – minute break. The German Colonel extended the break to forty minutes. Soon we heard air raid alarms. For the next thirty to forty-five minutes, our heavy bombers dropped bombs in ten waves on the freight (marshaling) yards and nearby ammunition supplies and buildings. We were so close that the debris from the buildings was hurled over us.

The last two waves of planes came from a different direction. Ten of the bombs released by the bombers fell into the midst of these 500 Americans and their 60 guards. One bomb fell within a few yards of me. One man, about fifteen feet to my right was killed and one about the same distance to my left had his arm blown off. In my conversation with Mr. Thompson, I learned the same thing happened to him. He was within a few feet of those exploding bombs.

My Commanding Officer had me remain behind while most of the men were moved out and on to a farm barn for the night. He put me in charge with the responsibility to prepare the forty or more wounded and identify the twenty-four officers who were killed. There were twelve of us who took care of the wounded. The Germans transported the wounded to a nearby hospital. Then I identified those who were killed. I submitted the list of the deceased to the proper sources after I was released. I also wrote to the next of kin of each of our comrades.

After we had completed our assignment with the wounded and dead I rejoined our group. Mr. Thompson was among those who were marched away from the bombed area. I could not give an exact appraisal of the more than 400 men who were moved out yet I know many could be classified as "walking wounded."

As we continued our march often we could hear exploding artillery shells exploding behind us. Our march from Hammelburg until we were freed by American troops took 35 days.

Attached are pages 52-57 of a book I wrote which was published in 1945. I submitted five copies to the War Department at that time for approval. This book, PRISONER OF THE GERMANS, gives many details of this bombing. I include these statements as part of my affidavit.

Sincerely,

Mark R. Moore
Former Chaplain, U. S. Army, O 550265
11925 W.109th St. Apt. 303
Overland Park, KS 66210

State of KANSAS
County of JOHNSON
Signed or attested before me on 1 day of
February 2001

(Seal)   Notary Signature

My appointment expires:
5-3-2003

KAREN WALLACE
Notary Public - State of Kansas
My Appt. Exp. 5-3-2003

Note: *Pages 55-57, three of the pages to which Chaplain refers in the above letter, do not appear in the book, but are available to interested researchers through Historical Resources Press.*

Bombing at Nuremburg

This bombing at Nuremburg was such a catastrophe that our chaplain, 1st Lieutenant Mark Moore included a whole section on it. I quote from the chapter of his book Prisoner of the Germans which he mentioned in his affidavit:

DEATH UNDER OUR BOMBERS

On April 5 we were marched near Nuremburg and were taking a ten-minute break. The German colonel extended the break to forty minutes and we started eating a few items of food, which we had. I had a raw cabbage, which had been given me. Stoney and I took some of the cabbage, some raw carrots, onions, and beets and cut them up in a salad. We also had bread and water.

As we finished we heard the air alarm and then saw our B-17's and B-24's coming our way. We all hit the dirt and waited. The first wave moved in and dropped their loads about five hundred yards from us. We could hear the bombs rushing down and felt the earth tremble when they hit. I got up and seeing Lt. Johnson from Birmingham, Alabama, who was formerly a radio announcer, standing there I walked over and asked him, "Is it easier sweating it out if you can see them?"

He said it was, so I stood by him during the next few minutes.

We gave a play-by-play description of what took place. The second wave moved in and we saw the marker leave the plane so we hollered, "Bombs away!" and then

"Down, down, down they hit." We could see the trail of smoke from the planes to the ground.

The second wave hit nearer. We could see the trail of smoke made by the bombs. The third moved in nearer and then the fourth and fifth came quickly. Each time we saw the marker and then down, down, down and then the explosion. The earth would shake, the buildings would fall apart and smoke rise up in the air. The fifth wave hit an ammunition plant about one hundred fifty yards away. The sixth wave dropped back on one of the other targets. The seventh wave hit the ammunition plant again and must have had all incendiaries for the plant caught on fire. It looked like a fountain of fire for many hours.

The eighth wave, instead of coming in from the left to right, came in from the front. Ack-ack had been breaking around the planes and some of our number were ducking the falling flak. We stood there and called to this wave of bombers, "Move over, move over," for they were coming straight at us. Then we called out "Drop them, drop them," but we never saw a marker and then the planes were over us and we could hear the bombs coming down on us. The shrill, whistling noise will never be forgotten.

There were several bomb craters near by but I did not have time to get to one so I stayed on top of the ground. I hit the ground near a tree and everything broke loose. The earth shook! I went up and down and it seemed my ear drums would burst. I could feel rocks and dirt being thrown over me. The bombs hit hard and fast around us.

Quoted with permission from
PRISONER of the Germans, p. 52-54
By Chaplain Mark R. Moore
Beacon Hill Press, Kansas City, Missouri 1945

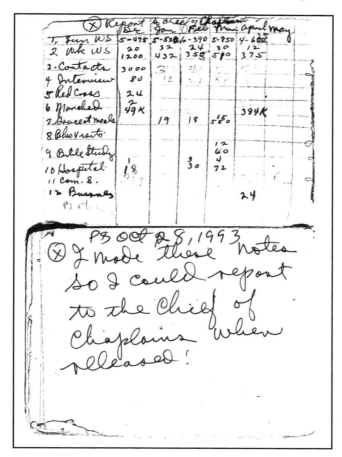

A "Page" from Chaplain Moore's "Book"

(made from 2 sheets of typing paper)

The notes, made by Chaplain Moore, reveal the variety of tasks he conducted as a POW without a chapel or office: Sunday worship, weekday worship, contacts, interviews, Red Cross, <u>Marched</u> (Item 6, previous page "2 + 49 + 384 Kilometers, Dec. - Apr."), Grace at Meals, Visits, Bible Study, Hospital ... ... In his book he states, "The work of the Chaplain did not stop when a Chaplain became a prisoner. It increased rather than lessened our responsibilities for doing spiritual work."

Notes Chaplain Moore gave Harry October 25, 1993 proved invaluable in writing this book. Chaplains were allowed to keep pens or pencils (a privilege denied other POWs) and, with his pen and "two pages of typing paper", writing on both sides, carefully using all space, he recorded information which allowed us to identify, sort and date memories which otherwise would have been lost. On two pages of typing paper he recorded names of places, villages, towns; kilometers marched (information he obtained from road signs later identified in famous pictures), what he ate (mostly soup: "Hot water", "Slaughter House Soup", "Bad Soup" [POW Camp Bad Orb], "Green Hornet" or "Green Death" made from everything green.)

From Chaplain Moore's book, Prisoner of the Germans, his Hammelburg barracks must have tried to be creative with German War Bread. One chapter is entitled "Recipes New and Different":

"Neither time nor space would allow me to list all the concoctions or recipes we figured out in the months of prison life. The desire for food was the strongest one among most of the men. The talk, dreams, and thoughts had food as the theme. Can you imagine your stomach gnawing with hunger for five long months? That's the way it was with us. We tried many dishes but regardless of failure or success we always ate it. Whenever the dish happened to be a new one there would be an audience to see the expression of satisfaction or displeasure on the face of the 'chef of the moment'. ...We all learned the art of taking the 'goon bread' and making things out of it. 'Goon bread' was the Nazi G.I. ration ... It might have been baked months before but regardless of mold we ate every crumb. We used it as the base of all our cooking. We made pudding, cake, doughnuts and pies out of it.

"Our food was cooked in the (camp) kitchen and a detail from our room went after it and brought it back to the room in a large tub vat. I was on detail several times and it was a job to carry the vat just one block. Once the food was in our room, we had one man to dish it out. Each man lined up in his place

233

Communions
1 april 150 { Stonisifer / Moore

19 april 50 { Stone, Custer + Self
22 april 35 { Stone Custer + Self
21 may 85 { Custer + Self
3 june

Men Killed april 5 1945
Nurnburg Germany
4 Harold F Nonamaker 0292219
2 Thomas L Corlett 01322977
3 F C Feiken — 0286459
4 Leon Kastenbaum 01314146
5 Willis K Burke 01167344
6 Francis L Reardon 01287240
7 George J Bowlery 01548358
8 W C Grimes Jr. 0542810
9 Carl O Butcher . 01311113
10 Thorold J Charity 0299691
11 Lou F Leibbrand 01556730
12 Carl K Luck 01313623
13 Leo Rabinowitz 01296742
14 William H Gordon

and carried his bowl by the vat and received one cup of soup.
Always there would be another half cup each so we went around
twice. There were times even after that when there would be a
little left so rather than try to give every one a third helping
we had voted to give another cupful as long as it held out. ...
We always had a problem with the soup. ... There were not
many solids and those would go to the bottom ..."

Perhaps the saddest pages in Chaplain Moore's book-
let: a list of the 24 who died at Nuremberg plus "5 German
dead, 5 American dead later, 5 killed on Tanks".

Chaplain Moore continued his pastoral concern even
after discharge. He wrote the War Department requesting the
home addresses of the twenty-four deceased military personnel he attended at Hammelburg. The reply from Major General Edward F. Witsell, Acting the Adjunct General of the Army,
concludes: "Your desire to write to the families of those personnel is most considerate and very much appreciated."

18 Ronald H Daniels
01049785
19 Rowland A Koskamp
0517319
17 Francis L Buttrick
01306238
18 Nick Vitale #
20304413
19 John L Scully 01015252
20 Norman A Engle 01324831
21 Charles F Devlin 01109893
22 Harold L Smith 01308771
23 Robert C Payne 0405639
24 C C Reily (USN 25595)
3 German dead
5 Am. Dead later

5. Killed on tanks
Seer
Pettijohn
Holstein
(EM) Incomm?

Mark Moore provided a copy of "My Little Book" October 25, 1993 as help in writing this book. His notes have proven invaluable: providing dates, details and names of places neither of us could have remembered. His notes also made clear how much Mark had done "above and beyond the call of duty"– standing up, exposing himself in order to assist the wounded and dying. When I realized that he had never been honored, never publicly been recognized for bravery above and beyond the call of duty, I sent a letter and an affidavit April 29, 2000 to the Honorable Sam Brownback.

Response to my letter, which I had thought too late to request a decoration, was more than I had dared hope. I had presented my reasons for honoring 1st Lt. Mark Moore:
- a Prisoner of War in German P.O.W. Camp XIII B

Oflag Hammelburg, Germany.

- During extreme cold (temperature 10 – 20 degrees below zero), no heat in any barrack (approx. 10), he went to each barrack and gave religious services each Sunday.
- Around early March 1945 a failed expedition by General Patton to liberate his son-in-law Lt. Col. Waters caused Hammelburg Camp Commander on March 28, 1945 to put all American officers in the camp on a Forced March, which lasted about 250 miles and ended May 2, 1945.
- on April 5, 1945 on the outskirts of Nuremburg, Germany the POW column on Forced March was severely bombed by American planes, 500 pound bombs by B24s hitting a German munitions plant, large rail yard with box cars loaded with high explosives and our POW column resulting in death

"It is my pleasure to introduce my friend, Chaplain Mark Moore".

Kansas City Bronze Star Ceremony

Harry Thompson, Chaplain Mark Moore and the Honorable Sam Brownback
September 4, 2001

of 24 American officers killed instantly and approximately 105 wounded.

- Immediately after the bombing, ranking Chaplain Mark Moore stood up, exposing himself regardless of his life to extreme danger and extra ordinary heroism, ran to each dead giving last rites and caring for many wounded.
- German soldiers (2 German soldiers also killed) led all POWs away, but Chaplain Moore stayed, helping put dead and wounded on trucks while all the time terrific explosions were still hurling all types of debris throughout the area.

I was pleased that Tuesday 4 September 2001 (twenty months after my letter and 56 years after his heroics at Nuremberg), Mark R. Moore was awarded a Bronze Star. I was able to introduce Chaplain Moore before U.S. Senator Sam Brownback (R-Kansas) who made the official presentation of a Bronze Star during a meeting of the Heart of America Chapter of the American ex-Prisoners of War in Kansas City, Missouri.

Better late than never

Bronze Star awarded 56 years after chaplain's heroics

BY ROB ROBERTS
SUN STAFF WRITER

An 84-year-old Overland Park man's heroics as a chaplain and prisoner of war in Nazi Germany went unheralded for 56 years but were never forgotten by one of his comrades.

On Tuesday, after the comrade had gone through U.S. military channels to set the record straight, Mark R. Moore received a Bronze Star Medal for his actions in the wake of an April 5, 1945, Allied bombing raid that left dozens of American POWs dead or wounded near Nuremberg, Germany. The medal was presented to the retired Nazarene Church official by U.S. Sen. Sam Brownback during a meeting of the Heart of America Chapter of the American Ex-Prisoners of War in Kansas City, Mo.

"Personally, it's very rewarding," said Moore. "But what's more meaningful is that it provides some recognition for the entire chaplains corps."

Moore was taken prisoner by Germans on Dec. 19, 1944, during the Battle of the Bulge, while he was serving as a chaplain for the field artillery of the U.S. Army's 106th Infantry Division.

Nearly five months later, Moore and about 500 fellow U.S. officers were in the midst of a 36-day forced POW march through Germany when wave after wave of Allied B-24s began unloading their 500-pound bombs during a raid on a Nazi ammunition factory and railyards near the POW column. Some of the "blockbuster" bombs fell right on top of the Americans.

Harry Thompson, a veteran of the 99th Infantry Division now living in Wolfe City, Texas, witnessed Moore's actions in the bloody bombing aftermath. And upon learning recently that Moore had never been honored, Thompson lobbied the Army on Moore's behalf and described the clergyman's valor via a written affidavit in May.

"The devastation and noise was terrible, with high explosives going off in railyards and the munitions factory," Thompson wrote. "All types

See BRONZE STAR, Page 2

Mark R. Moore

BOB JOHNSON/THE SUN

Mark recently told me "often a relative will write a letter requesting a medal." "I am honored to have a friend like Harry Thompson recommend me for this medal."

The Sun Newspapers, Midweek Edition, The Overland Park Sun (Kansas), "Better late than never, Bronze Star awarded 56 years after chaplain's heroics" by Rob Roberts, Sun Staff Writer.

My Buddy Park

"I miss him so much."

- Harry.

NOTE: *The original of the following "AFFIDAVIT OF FACT", signed and certified by the Notary Public of Wichita County, Texas the 7th day of October, A.D. 1983, was in the possession of the family of James W. Park.*

A copy of the document, made on legal size paper and too fragile to scan, is in my possession. This document was originally made for the purpose of establishing my medical problems encountered a result of service with the Army. A copy of the notarized document was placed on file with the U.S. Army to document my medical needs.

For reproduction and readability in this book, the document was re-typed in a different font (and with a few suggested corrections of fact which are indicated by endotes at the end of the document) and only the final page with the signature was scanned.

AFFIDAVIT OF FACT

To whom it may concern:

I, James M. Park, of 210 Preston St., Burkburnet Texas, acknowledge that I am acquainted with Mr. Harry A. Thompson, formerly of Dallas, Texas, but now residing at Rt. 1, Wolfe City, Texas 75496.

I first met Mr. Thompson on March 6, 1941, at Fort Sill, Oklahoma, the day after we were drafted. We served in the same organizational units during World War II.

After completion of basic training at Fort Sill, Oklahoma, we were sent to Fort Ord, California, as filler troops in activation of the 7th Infantry Division and assigned to the 57th Field Artillery Battalion.

In October of 1942, Mr. Thompson and I were sent as cadre to Camp Van Dorn, Mississippi to form the 924th FA Battalion of the 99th Infantry Division. We remained with this unit until we were captured.

We went overseas in September 1944. We moved into Belgium to back up the 1st Division. On December 17th, while Billeted in Bullingen, near the front lines, our service battery was overrun by the German Army, and the ones in our organization that were not killed in the fighting were captured and marched behind the German lines.

Walking, plus short rides in boxcars, we arrived in Bonn, Germany late in the evening of December 23. During this trip, the only food received was small portions of dark German bread and water melted from the snow. The snow covered the landside from 12" to 18" deep during this forced march. We spent the night of December 22 in a bombed out building, with little protection from the severe, cold wind.

On the evening of December 24, we were loaded into boxcars for an unknown trip. These cars had been bombed and had many holes in the tops and sides, allowing the snow to filter in and cover the floor, 4 to 6 inches deep. The boxcar that Mr. Thompson and I were in was overcrowded and very little room for movement was available.

We remained in the boxcars without any exercise until about eight o'clock in the morning of December 29. Many of our men received frozen or badly frostbitten feet during this trip.

After unloading in Nuremberg, we were taken to a prison camp that was holding Russian and Polish prisoners.

During the next ten or twelve days that we were held in this camp we were given no medical treatment for our feet condition except bathe our feet in warm water twice each day, morning and evening.

Just before our arrival, Nuremberg had been bombed and the German guards told us that some 3,000 German civilians lost their lives. The American officers were not permitted to leave the camp, but our enlisted men were placed in a work force and worked until all recovered bodies were buried.

We, again, were placed in boxcars and moved out. Around January 12, 1945 we arrived at OFLAG 13B at Hammelburg on about January 16, 1945 and we remained until the latter part of

March, when we were liberated by a task force sent in 90 miles into enemy territory by General Patton to liberate his son-in-law Col. Waters. Col. Waters was injured during the fight to take the prison camp, and had to be taken to a hospital - after the battle. The prisoners were rounded up and taken about a mile into a wooded area. Here the task force surveyed their damage, and decided they could not take any prisoners with them, but they could try to get through enemy lines some 90 miles away or go back to camp and await the arrival of the German guards. I decided to return to camp along with some one hundred other prisoners to await our fate. Many others took off.

We returned to camp around 10:30 at night, and the guards rounded us up soon afterwards, and gave us 15 minutes to be ready to march out. Around 11 o'clock that night we marched out of camp to be on a forced march through southern Germany until May 2, 1945, the day of liberation.

On April 5, 1945, we were marching through Nuremberg, and crossing the railroad yards, where many boxcars were on the rail siding. The air raid sirens sounded and the German guards marched us into a wooded park paralleling the rail tracks. The planes were flying at very high altitude in flights of five. As soon as the plane flights zeroed in on the marshaling yard, flight after flight dropped their bombs on the box cars—within seconds after the bombs began to land among the boxcars, a wall of fire developed with heavy explosions, a dense wall of heavy smoke and concussion waves passed over us one after another, with the soil shaking under us.

On the last wave of planes in the formation, they dropped their bombs in the park where the prisoners lay on the ground. The holes made by these bombs were about 8 feet deep and 20 feet in diameter. Mr. Thompson and I were laying about 2 feet from the outer perimeter of one of the bomb craters, covered with sand and gravel. I personally assisted in removing one POW body found in the bottom of the crater by where I was lying. His body was mutilated from the sand and gravel blown through his body, until only his underware and o.d. trousers and shirt held the body together. The remains had to be rolled on to a blanket and carried to the roadside to be hauled away for burial.

Of the near one hundred prisoners taken into the park, 25 or 27 were either killed or had to be sent to a hospital. I know that Harry Thompson complained of his ears ringing, back and feet bothering him during the long daily forced walks.

James W. Park
WOJG, Supply Officer
924th FA Battalion
99th Infantry Div. WWII

JAMES W. PARK

THE STATE OF TEXAS
COUNTY OF WICHATA   BEFORE ME, the undersigned authority, in and for said County, Texas, on this day personally appeared JAMES W. PARK   known to me to be the person whose name is subscribed to the foregoing instrument, and acknowledged to me that he executed the same for the purpose and consideration therein expressed.
GIVEN UNDER MY HAND AND SEAL OF OFFICE, This 7th day of October ,A.D. 1983.

(L.S.)   Barbara Bilyeu
Notary Public Wichita   County, Texas
My Commission Expires 9-1-86

Note: *At the bottom of the document, marked in red ink, are the words "ears ringing (underlined), "back" (triple underlined) and "feet" (underlined).*

A POW

Working *In A German Bakery in* 1945

by

**ROGER V.
FOEHRINGER**

WW II POW

2-6-02

Re: Black Bread/Schwartz Brot

Harry

Schwartz Brot / Black Bread was a staple of the POWs diet. It also was used by the German Military.

whether it was a source of vitamins or was a nourishment leaves much to the imagination, but it did provide a "food" intake.

Having worked as a POW in a German Bakery in wurzburg, Germany, I now attest there was not an ounce of white flour in a loaf of this so called bread. It was black OK because the ingredients were all dark, nuts[1], corn husks, poor grades of wheat/rye and probably some saw dust.[2]

The German Bakery I worked at was named Heeresbäckerei. we five American POWs moved heavy burlap bags of so called flour from one side of the second-floor warehouse to the other side, a distance of about 50 feet. we wondered what this was all about and were told this moving prevented infestation (bugs, mice, rats).

we were running short of these bags of ersatz flour. So one day, in early March, 1945 two Germans and three of us POWs got into a steam driver truck and drove out into the country side to a very small flour mill, where we picked up their small in-stock burlap sacks of ersatz flour. These mill workers asked me where I was from and I told them Chicago. They replied, Al Capone and The Stockyards. Sounded strange coming from these country farm/mill workers.

Ersatz meant/means "artificial". Therefore, "artificial bread".

Enclosed is a blown up picture of the remains of Heeresbäckerei approximately April of 1945. The English and Americans as you see bombed the hell out of Wurzburg and in particular the Bakery. Sure glad we were not working that night. My German friends sent this to me about 10 years ago.

[signature] [3]

Roger V. Foehringer

[1] He told me that "nuts" were acorns (he thought).

[2] He also told me that dirt was also mixed in.

[3] Hand-written letter on lined notebook paper from Roger Foehringer has been transferred to computer for ease in reading. The signature has been scanned.

The 99ᵀᴴ
Infantry Division

By
Dick Byers

99ᵀᴴ IDA ARCHIVES CMTE.

DICK BYERS
99ᵀᴴ IDA ARCHIVES CMTE.

ANS·R·GRAM ▆▆▆▆▆

FROM:
M   MDICK BYERS
     5884 THUNDERBIRD DR.
     MENTOR OH 44060

☐ URGENT   ☐ ASAP   ☐ NO REPLY

DATE
1/15/94
ATTENTION OF

TO:
     HARRY A. THOMPSON
     ROUTE 1 BOX 790
     WOLFE CITY TX 75496

SUBJECT

MESSAGE

DEAR HARRY:
     HERE IS YOUR MANUSCRIPT BACK. IT TELLS A HARROWING, GRIP-
STORY, THE BEST ACCOUNT OF KRIEGIE LIFE I'VE READ. A COPY IS
ON THE WAY TO WILL CAVANAGH WITH MY RECOMMENDATION FOR THE BOOK.
     I INTEND TO PUT A SECOND COPY IN A LOOSELEAF FOLDER WITH
THE WAR ROOM "KRIEGIE" DISPLAY. I HOPE YOU DON'T MIND.
     I'VE STARTED TO BUILD A DISPLAY OF ARTIFACTS USED BY 99TH
POWs. THINGS LIKE LISTS OF FOOD, A RED CROSS FORK AND SPOON,
A KRIEGIE DOGTAG, ETC. YOUR MANUSCRIPT WILL BE A GREAT ADDITION
TO IT. EVENTUALLY, IT WILL GO INTO THE 99TH ARCHIVES IN CARLISLE
BARRACKS UNDER YOUR NAME.
     THANKS AGAIN FOR YOUR CONSIDERATION AND HELP.

SIGNED

REPLY   SINCERELY,
                   Dick Byers
                   99TH IDA ARCHIVES CMTE.

SIGNED

NOTE:

I met Dick Byers in 1992 and asked him to read my
manuscript. His review was more than a review to me. It was
affirmation of my project to write this book. I include it here
because it seems to support the accuracy and validity of my
story.

Dick Byers died about three years ago. I regret that he
did not live to see this book.

THE RAID ON HAMMELBURG

"PATTON'S BIGGEST MISTAKE"?

What was Patton Thinking?

Should Patton Have Been Court Marshaled?

By

Karin K. Ramsay

Editor
for Harry A. Thompson,
POW in Camp Hammelburg during

Patton's Ill-Fated Raid

The telephone rang twice and both times I said no to what has become one of the most satisfying privileges of my life. "You have the wrong number", I told the caller, "I am only a small publisher focusing on encouraging people to write and preserve life stories as resources for family history. You need a larger publishing company."

Still, for some reason, he called a third time. Something in his tone caught my attention. "I am a WWII POW and I have written a book. I need a publisher and haven't found any willing to even read my manuscript." "Send it to me. I will read it. I will try to help you find a publisher."

Eighty-eight year-old Harry A. Thompson and his wife appeared the next morning. There, at my door, stood historical treasure: Harry and his wife with his manuscript supported by enough pictures, letters, papers, medals, dog tags, personal stories and documentation to excite anyone interested in history, especially WWII history.

Harry's original title for his book was *As I Remember, The Other Side of War*. Even though Harry told me almost immediately that Patton's son-in-law was also a POW in Hammelburg, and originally I thought of this book as Harry's story, the more I worked with him, the more I began to think of it as the story of General George S. Patton's raid on Hammelburg.

It didn't take me long to began to think of Harry's imprisonment in Hammelburg and what happened when Patton ordered his ill-fated raid as the focal point of Harry's life. Harry was imprisoned in Hammelburg Oflag XIII B, the same POW camp as Lt. Col. John Knight Waters, West Point graduate married to Beatrice Patton, daughter of General George S.

Patton. While Harry's courage when caught in situation after situation not of his own making inspired me, more and more I began to think about George S. Patton. I wondered what was Patton thinking to order a raid that had such terrible results for so many people? Why did Harry and "some historians call the raid Patton's biggest mistake"? I enlisted the help of my husband, Jack Ramsay who has a PhD. in historical research from the University of Edinburgh, Scotland and has several books on history in the bookstores, to help me organize my thoughts.

Here are the **rumors** and facts that have caused me to have questions; questions for which I will continue seeking to find reliable documented sources:

1. March 23, 1945 Patton met with other military commanders to decide who would be in charge of which Zones of Germany from the Rhine eastward. Someone informed Patton about the POW Camp at Hammelburg including the **rumor** that Patton's son-in-law, Lieutenant Colonel John WATERS, might be a prisoner in Hammelburg. Though the challenge was to move on to Berlin and win the war, Patton seemed to focus on the idea of a raid on Hammelburg to liberate the POWs, including his son-in-law.

2. **Rumor**: The next morning Patton sent his bodyguard, Major Al STILLER, to headquarters of Fourth Armor to instruct Commander Al HOGUE to launch a raid on Hammelburg. Commander Hogue had already received the same orders through command chain but felt the order was "ridiculous and dangerous". He relayed his concerns to his Commander, Manton S. EDDY, who agreed and Commanders Hogue and Eddy decided to refuse to follow Patton's orders to raid Hammelburg.

3. PATTON showed up, threatened insubordination, while admitting that there was a small possibility that his son-in-law might be a prisoner in that camp. **Rumor** says Lieutenant Colonel Creighton W. ABRAMS, Battalion Commander of Combat Command B of the 4th Armored Division suggested his whole Combat Command B be employed, a suggestion rejected by General Patton, insisting the mission required only a small task force. Abrams suggested the Commander of the 10th Armored Infantry Battalion, Lieutenant Colonel Harold Cohen head the Task Force. General Patton rejected Cohen but is **rumored** to have compromised by allowing COHEN to suggest the Task Force officer. Cohen chose S-3 officer of the 10th Armored Infantry Battalion, 24-year-old Captain Abraham J. BAUM. Though Hogue felt it was a "suicidal mission", he saw no way out and assigned Commander Abraham Baum to a Task Force to carry out a raid on Hammelburg.

4. March 26, 1945 Abraham Baum's Task force set out with not enough tanks, half-tracks or men to accomplish the task. **Rumor** has it that on the way they liberated 700 Russians at another POW Camp before they met a "fierce fight" at Hammelburg as Germans realized there was a breech in German lines.

5. March 27, 1945, German authorities are **rumored** to have notified Senior American Officer Col. Paul R. GOODE Oflag XIII B would be evacuated at 1600 hours, moving POWs further away from advancing American troops. At 1300 that afternoon, 3 hours ahead of the scheduled evacuation, American tanks appeared and suddenly the Germans changed plans and agreed to surrender the Hammelburg Camp. Three of Oflag XIII B staff officers* and one German officer were selected to carry the white flag of surrender to the American col-

umn. As they went through the gate, trying to negoti-
ate a truce, an SS private shot Col. John K. Waters,
seriously wounding him. (*WATERS could have been
part of the selected officers since, in 1944, Waters was
listed as "Executive Officer for Oflag 64", the Polish prison
from which he was transferred to Hammelburg. Col. Paul
R. Goode later arrived at Hammelburg and was made
Senior American Officer and Lt. Col. J. K. Waters is
listed as serving on staff at Oflag XIII B as "Welfare Officer" under Goode when Patton's raid occurred.)

6. Serbian doctors saved Patton's son-in-law's life. Serbians
with whom Harry Thompson and other American POWs
sometimes conversed occupied the adjacent compound
to Oflag XIII B. Twenty-seven Serbian doctors and medical officers were captured and had been in prison for
about four years and were successfully treating a variety of "kriegy" ailments with makeshift medicines and
poor equipment. Most seriously ill were treated in an
adjoining lazaret, which was a part of the Serbian lag
and contained 450 beds. Soon after the Americans arrived, the SMO of the Serbian compound assigned 60
beds for the exclusive use of Americans, and since "in-
valid" rations were issued there in addition to the other
advantages offered, the men who were admitted to the
Serbian lazaret had a better chance for recovery. After
the American lines had moved up, Waters was evacuated to a field hospital.

7. The number of POWs in Hammelburg, as well as equipment and men needed, were vastly underestimated. Fifteen hundred officer POWs were freed, though Baum's
Task Force had only enough vehicles to carry out 250
POWs, leaving his entire squadron and the POWs to
fend for themselves. The POWs had no weapons. All com-
munications with the Task Force were lost and they

found themselves surrounded by three German Divisions. On March 28, as the Task Force prepared to return to American lines with as many liberated POWs as they could carry, the Germans cut loose with everything they had. Capt. BAUM found a halftrack with a radio and is **rumored** to have tapped out his last message to the Fourth Armored Division Headquarters in Morse Code: "Task Force Baum surrounded, under heavy fire. Request air support." Both Task Force and remaining liberated officers took off into the woods. As few as one, no more than 15 men of the Task Force made it back to American lines. One report: "We trudged 11 or 12 miles back to Oflag and were exhausted when we got there." German guards who had taken off when tanks arrived returned and reoccupied the Oflag then ordered the POWs to prepare to leave on a march deep into German territory under the watchful eyes of fully armed and equipped German soldiers.

8. Word that "Patton sent almost 300 men to their doom for nothing" spread like wildfire throughout military. Patton blamed Omar Bradley, Commander Al Hogue, General Eisenhower, everyone except himself. It is **rumored** that BRADLEY was furious and wrote in his diary, "It was a story that began as a wild goose chase and ended in tragedy."

9. After the raid, as American lines advanced, PATTON visited his son-in-law and, upon seeing Lt. Col. WATERS, **rumor** says Patton cried and admitted he had been responsible for the raid. Patton's Main Force later liberated what remained of the Hammelburg camp. Most of the recaptured POWs, like Harry, had been taken on a forced walk of 241 miles deep into German territory. Later Patton freed a camp outside of Mooseburg and there found his bodyguard, Al STILLER, alive. Again it

is **rumored** Patton broke down, crying when he saw Stiller. (Both Harry and I find the thought of Patton twice crying a personality trait never before noticed.)

10. No one in the Army was willing to let media know the **rumor** that, because of Waters, Patton's Raid had happened. Still the Press heard and news broke in the American Press that "should have ended Patton's military career". On April 12, 1945 Fate intervened: President Roosevelt died. Those in a position to recommend Court Marshal for Patton became aware almost at the same time as President Roosevelt died. One reporter said, "someone could have committed numerous rapes in the street of New York and it wouldn't have shown up before Page Four!" The President's death temporarily saved Patton from disaster in the eyes of the American public.

11. It is **rumored** that PATTON, realizing media might not give up, assembled the SURVIVING MEMBERS OF BAUM'S TASK FORCE and classified the entire mission "Top Secret" after the fact in order that Press could not secure any more details.

12. Most curious to me is **what happened to some after the raid**. (Creighton ABRAMS, one of the men on those raids, became a General himself and in 1967, after the death of Patton, told the whole story of "the day Patton dismissed lives of nearly 300 men to try to rescue Lt. Col. Waters" and detailed how Patton "lied".) (Manton S. EDDY, **rumored** to have joined Commander Hogue in refusing to follow Patton's order to raid Hammelburg, was part of the 9th in Kasserine Pass in February 1943 during the initial German breakthrough. He was in command of the 9th until promoted to take charge of the XII corps in August 1944 to spearhead the advances of Lt. Gen. George S. Patton's Third Army as it crossed the

Rhine. He was relieved by Patton less than three weeks before the end of the war in Europe and was absent from all victory celebrations.) (Major Alexander C. STILLER, **rumored** to have been sent to headquarters of Fourth Armor to relay Patton's orders to raid Hammelburg, was somehow on the Task Force "to gain combat experience" though Captain Baum was put in charge. **Rumor** also has it that STILLER was captured and that Patton, when he freed Mooseburg, found bodyguard Al Stiller alive and again broke down and cried. If the **rumor** is true that Patton assembled the surviving members of Baum's Task Force and classified the entire mission "Top Secret" after the fact, STILLER would have been among those assembled.)

13. Lt. Col. John Knight WATERS, several years prior to his death, is **rumored** to have written a friend he made while a POW in Hammelburg that Gen. Patton, his father-in-law, did not know that he was a prisoner at Hammelburg when he sent the Task Force through front lines to liberate the American prisoners. Official reports indicate that American authorities did know Waters was a POW in Oflag 64 in Poland and did know that he and all POWs in Oflag 64 had been evacuated to Hammelburg.

14. Correspondents reported that Patton said he did not know until nine days after the Task Force reached Hammelburg that his son-in-law was among the prisoners. He produced his private diaries and said he attempted to liberate the prison camp because they were afraid that the retreating Germans might murder the American prisoners. Until I find it in a reliable document, I will consider it **rumor** that Gen. Patton later admitted: "I can say this, that throughout the campaign in Europe I know of no error I made except that of failing to send a combat command to take Hammelburg.

256

Otherwise, my operations were to me, strictly satisfactory."

It has been my privilege to assist Harry in collecting, combining his resources, adding Virginia's agonizing wait on the home front, and editing his wonderful manuscript. I will be forever grateful that Harry A. Thompson called a third time. I appreciate what he did with what he calls "My Little Bit" to preserve American freedom. He captures and preserves as a resource for generations to come a portion of history seldom told. I am fascinated with his unforgettable and ultimately uplifting story, <u>Patton's Ill-fated Raid</u>. Still … I find myself thinking about General Patton. Was the Raid on Hammelburg the "worst mistake of his military career", a mistake which "should have destroyed it", "should have ended in a court marshal"? What was he thinking? Was this his "biggest mistake"?

A court marshal for Patton at that time would have detracted from the one unique fact of WW II: a country completely united in the goal of winning a war. In all the **rumors** three threads are consistent: the results were tragic; the source for the idea always includes General Patton; and Patton's son-in-law, though wounded, was one of few POW's whose liberation was quickly accomplished. History will connect Patton with the ill-fated raid on Hammelburg. Still, General George S. Patton remains a great military man for which this country owes much. Harry and I welcome your research and comments.

-
Karin K. Ramsay, Editor for Harry's Book.

INDEX
Illustrations, Maps
and
Photographs

PATTON'S, ILL FATED RAID

INDEX

ILLUSTRATIONS, MAPS AND PHOTOGRAPHS

INDEX
EVENTS, PEOPLE, PLACES

INDEX

EVENTS, PEOPLE, PLACES

271

KILROY WAS HERE